Development NGOs and Languages

"Sensitivity to languages is central to any serious analysis of inequality between Global North and Global South. *Development NGOs and Languages* is a long overdue intervention in this area, exploring urgent questions of interpreting and translation in the work of international NGOs. Drawing on extensive geographical and institutional case studies, the book recasts development as an inherently multilingual operation. The result is essential reading for scholars and practitioners in this field."

—Charles Forsdick, *AHRC Theme Leadership Fellow, Translating Cultures*

"Humanitarian and developmental non-governmental organisations (NGOs) play a significant role in our complex and fragile world. They operate in diverse contexts which are often characterised by multilingualism. However, we know hardly anything about how NGOs communicate with local communities, and how they perceive the role of languages and cultural knowledge in their development programmes. This volume investigates development as a multilingual endeavour and focuses on the ways in which NGOs listen to the voices of those on the receiving end of aid, which can be listening through English or through translation. Empirical analyses of three UK-based international NGOs and case studies from Malawi, Kyrgyzstan and Peru, provide extensive insights into listening experiences and challenges faced. This highly absorbing and stimulating book is of interest both to scholars and practitioners (donors, NGOs) who can build on the valuable recommendations and thus ensure they deliver their missions of empowerment and social justice."

—Christina Schäffner, *Emeritus Professor of Translation Studies, University of Aston*

"*Development NGOs and Languages* makes us question fundamental assumptions about the nature of communication in relationships among local communities and the NGOs that serve them. So often couched in references to feedback and lost voices, Footitt, Crack and Tesseur critique extant approaches to development projects, and illuminate a novel way of seeing communication in development as a two-way process of dialogic exchange. They elucidate the complexity of the in-situ communicative experiences of local actors, and to demonstrate the ways in which multi-directional communication shapes and defines the listening space.

Filled with rich examples from different NGOs and different country settings, this book will make you think about the role of language and cultural understanding in development policy making and implementation."

—Julie Gilson, *Reader in Asian Studies, Department of Political Science and International Studies, University of Birmingham, United Kingdom*

Hilary Footitt · Angela M. Crack ·
Wine Tesseur

Development NGOs and Languages

Listening, Power and Inclusion

palgrave
macmillan

Hilary Footitt
Department of Languages and Cultures
University of Reading
Reading, Berkshire, UK

Angela M. Crack
School of Area Studies, History, Politics and Literature
University of Portsmouth
Portsmouth, Hampshire, UK

Wine Tesseur
School of Applied Language and Intercultural Studies
Dublin City University
Dublin, Ireland

ISBN 978-3-030-51778-6 ISBN 978-3-030-51776-2 (eBook)
https://doi.org/10.1007/978-3-030-51776-2

This Palgrave Macmillan imprint is published by the registered company Springer Nature Switzerland AG
The registered company address is: Gewerbestrasse 11, 6330 Cham, Switzerland

Acknowledgements

This volume is the result of a research project, *The Listening Zones of NGOs: languages and cultural knowledge in development programmes* (www.reading.ac.uk/listening-zones-ngos), funded by the Arts and Humanities Research Council (AHRC). We gratefully acknowledge their support, and that of the partner institutions in the project: the University of Reading, the University of Portsmouth and the International Training and Research Centre (INTRAC) in Oxford. Our colleagues in INTRAC, Vicky Brehm, Dr. Rachel Hayman and Sarah Lewis, were generous in sharing their experience and expertise with us. We were delighted to welcome Dr. Carmen Delgado Luchner from the University of Geneva as a Visiting Research Fellow during the course of the project. We would also like to thank our interpreter, Cholpon Akmatova, for her help in organising and conducting the research interviews in Kyrgyzstan.

Staff from Christian Aid, OxfamGB, Save the Children UK and Tearfund provided invaluable help, discussing the research and suggesting key contacts who informed our study. Our lively Advisory Board of academics and practitioners patiently offered guidance and support throughout, and we are grateful to Kate Bingley, Professor Tony Chafer, Linda Fitchett, Dr. Julie Gilson, Dr. Rachel Hayman, Helen Machin, Taitos Matafeni, Professor Barbara Moser-Mercer, Dr. Vanessa Pupavac and Professor Christina Schaeffner.

Above all, we are grateful to the many men and women, working in NGOs within and outside the UK, and to colleagues in Kyrgyzstan,

Malawi and Peru, who generously offered their insights; their voices and words echo throughout this volume. Without their contribution, it would have been impossible to begin to understand experiences in the Listening Zones of development, and we are profoundly grateful for their input to the research and to the final Report, available in six languages on the Listening Zones website:

- *Kulemekeza Anthu M'madera M'zitukuko zochita M'Maiko Ena: Kumvetsetsa Ziyankhulo ndi Chikhalidwe* (Chichewa).
- Respecting communities in International Development: languages and cultural understanding (English).
- *Le respect des communautés dans le cadre du développement international: langues et compréhension culturelle* (French).
- *Жамааттарга эл аралык өнүгүү контекстиндеги мамиле: тилдик жагдай жана маданиятты түшүнүү* (Kyrgyz).
- *Отношение к сообществам в контексте международного развития: языковая ситуация и понимание культуры* (Russian).
- *Respeto a las comunidades en el marco del desarrollo internacional: idiomas y comprensión cultural* (Spanish).

This project has been a collaborative enterprise in which themes and objectives have been discussed and developed by all participants, with individual members of the group taking responsibility for particular chapters. Hilary Footitt led on Chapters 1, 2, 8 and 10; Angela Crack on Chapters 3, 6 and 9; and Wine Tesseur on Chapters 4, 5 and 7.

We hope that this first book on the role of languages in development will contribute to a reimagining of development as a multilingual endeavour in which language is radically related to the vital issues of power and inclusion.

Prologue

Voices from the Listening Zones: Malawi, Kyrgyzstan and Peru

Malawi

Opereka chithandizo ochokera kunja amayamba kaye apangitsa msonkhano omwe amadziwitsa anthu za zolinga za ntchito ndi njira zomwe zigwiritsidwe ntchito, ukunso ndikomwe nkhani ya chiyankhulo imanenedwa. Za chiyankhulo ndi mbali yovuta. Nkhani ya chiyankhulo ndi yomwe imalepheretsa mabungwe omwe amafuna kutenga mbali mu ntchito yomwe ikuchitika.[1]

Umatha kupeza bungwe la m'dera lomwe lili ndi maganizo a anzeru. Ndiye umawamvetsera m'chiyankhulo chawo chomwe akugwiritsa ntchito pokuuza zomwe angapange kuti azitukule. Koma chifukwa choti sangathe kunena zomwe akufotokozazo m'Chingerezi, sangapatsidwe chithandizo cha ndalama. Anthu samapatsidwa mwai wa ndalama.[2]

[1] "International donors hold pre-programme meetings where they inform about the programme goals and approaches, where the language issue is also raised. It's a sensitive area. The issue of language is a barrier for organisations who want to participate in the programme."

[2] "You get a community-based organisation that has got brilliant ideas. And you listen to them in their language that they are using to tell you what they can do to move from

Yambani ndi mmene anthuwo amamvetsetsera. Ndili ndi chikhulupiriro kuti anthu ali kuzindikira kwa mmene zinthu zina zake zingathe kumvetsetsedwera mosavuta. Mawu omwe timavutika nawo, omwe amakhuzana ndi zolawula, mwina tikanakhala kuti tinaafunsa anthu a m'madera, za momwe akufunira kuti tiziauzira mosavuta, omwe ali ogwirizana ndi chikhalidwe, tikanatha kutenga amenewo ndikuwagwiritsa ntchito muzikalata zathu za ntchito ya chitukoko. Izi zimathandiza kuti tikapitanso kwa iwowo amazazilandira mosavuta.[3]

Kyrgyzstan

[Донорские организации], например, предъявляют такие же высокие требования к НПО-сектору, чтобы они с ними общались на английском. Я прекрасно владею местной средой, но я не могу этого сделать, потому что я не пройду их критерии, потому что там нужен английский… Поэтому мне кажется, что здесь есть какая-то нестыковка… между международными донорскими организациями и местными НПО.[4]

Бардык эл аралык баалоочулар же мониторинг кылуучулар… алардын бардыгы, албетте, англис тилин колдонушат. Жергиликтүү мониторинг кылуу топторунун отчетторду англис тилине которулат. Даяр болгон отчеттордун бардыгын эле которо беришпейт [орус же кыргыз тилине]. Ошондон улам болуп жаткан окуялар тууралуу кеңири маалымат алып, түшүнүүгө шарт жок болууда.[5]

A to B. But because they cannot present what they are saying in English, they cannot get any funding. The people never access grants."

[3] "Start from the people's own understanding. I believe that people have some kind of sense on how certain things can be easily understood. Terms that we had difficulties, that have related to taboo, maybe if we had asked the communities how they want that communicated to them easily, that is culturally fitting, we could take that and use it in our project document. That makes sure that when you go back to them, they'll accept it easily."

[4] "[Donors] for example, they want to hire an expert from an NGO sector, but they want this person to speak very good English… I have all the other skills that the donors want for a certain job, but because I don't speak English… I am not eligible for some of their jobs. And so, in this sense… there is a mismatch between international donors and local NGOs."

[5] "All international monitors and evaluators… their working language is only English. Reports of local monitoring groups are all translated into English. Not all final monitoring

Давайте возьмем права человека. То есть если для европейца эти слова… в эти слова они вкладывают определенный смысл, который взращивается со школы… то если мы переносим это слово, переводя его на русский или на киргизский для нашего населения, то для многих это будет вообще пустой звук. "Это где-то там, это у европейцев. Это европейские ценности." А если мы начнем говорить о сексуальных правах, о репродуктивных правах… Часто нам приходится для начала распаковать эти дефиниции, создать понимание для этого словосочетания, прежде чем начать диалог с человеком об этом.[6]

Peru

No hablamos inglés, entonces esa es una limitación, porque si uno habla inglés, va y va y tú le convences y le vendes tu proyecto, pero cuando no hablas inglés, esa es una limitante.[7]

el problema del idioma no es solamente un problema de la traducción o de una palabra a otra sino de cómo el significante es comprendido por cada agencia, cada agencia maneja su propio concepto… por supuesto confunde… todos los debates que hemos tenido sobre qué significa "output" para un donante.'[8]

No es un problema intercultural. No es un problema de si hablas o no hablas, es si entiendes el mundo desde el cual hablan ellos, y si ellos te

reports are translated [into Russian or Kyrgyz]. The wider public does not have access to them. We have very little understanding of what's going on there."

[6] "Let's take the simple phrase 'human rights.' So human rights for Europeans… they learned what human rights means from school, from early childhood… but the same two words in Russian and Kyrgyz, for a lot of people in the country, if you say human rights these are just two empty words for them. And normally… they think that, it's not here, it's somewhere else, and some people will say, 'ah, human rights, it's there! These are European values.' And let alone the concepts like sexual rights or reproductive rights… So, if you want to have a dialogue with someone about these concepts, then you have to unpack these words for this person. You need to explain exactly what is meant by that."

[7] "We don't speak English, and that's a limitation, because if you speak English, you can go and convince people, you can sell them your project, but when you can't speak English, it limits you."

[8] "The problem of language isn't just translating a word. It's how each individual agency understands it. Each agency has its own particular set of concepts… Of course, it gets confusing… you've got to learn each term, each word… all the discussions we've had on what exactly "output" means for a particular donor."

entienden el mundo desde el cual tú les estás hablando… no es… que lo científico es superior, sino son formas de saberes, de orígenes y construcciones distintas.[9]

[9] "It isn't an intercultural problem, it's not a problem of whether you understand the world from which they are speaking, and if they understand the world from which you're speaking… it's not that scientific knowledge is better, but that these are forms of knowledge, of origins and constructions which are very different."

Contents

List of Tables

CHAPTER 1

NGOs and Listening

Introduction

For decades now non-governmental organisations (NGOs) have faced a battery of criticism from development scholars for perceived failings in delivering their missions of empowerment and social justice (Bebbington, Hickey, & Mitlin, 2008; Ebrahim, 2003; Fowler, 2000; Long & Long, 1992; Mawdsley, Oakley, Porter, & Townsend, 2002; Mosse, 2005). NGOs stand accused of being unaccountable to their intended beneficiaries and (despite the corporate commitment to operational efficiency) being ineffective in delivering sustainable transformation (Andrews, 2014; Crack, 2013a, 2013b). It is widely held that NGO strategies and activities are distorted by donor priorities, often in ways that directly undermine their supposed mission and erode perceptions of their credibility in the target community (AbouAssi, 2013; Arts & Elbers, 2011; Bob, 2005; Chang, 2013; Dreher, Koch, Nunnenkamp, & Thiele, 2009; Morfit, 2011). Criticisms are varied but cluster around a central claim: that NGOs are not sufficiently appreciative of the realities of the lives of people that they aim to assist, nor adequately responsive to their needs and desires (Porter, Ralph-Bowman, & Wallace, 2013). These concerns are mirrored by the anxieties expressed by some NGO practitioners themselves about the extent to which power relationships on the ground may distort decisions about what 'counts' in practice as an expression of community views (Workshop Report, 2014).

H. Footitt et al., *Development NGOs and Languages*,
https://doi.org/10.1007/978-3-030-51776-2_1

This chapter looks at the ways in which the voices of local communities and the encounters between Northern NGOs and Southern groups are represented in development scholarship. Communication, it will argue, is a two-way process in which listening to the 'other' is a vital, but as yet largely unexplored, component. The chapter seeks to address this gap by drawing on research in fields outside Development Studies and International Relations—Listening Studies, Cultural Studies and Translation Studies—in order to propose a new theoretical framework, 'The Listening Zones of NGOs', as a structuring principle. By adopting the Listening Zones framework, the book aims to position languages and cultural awareness as key elements in addressing the alleged disregard for local communities on the part of NGOs. The research in this volume suggests that listening relationships that respect the foreign 'other' are intimately linked to positive project outcomes in development: 'No respect, no effect' (Krose, 2018).

'Voice' in Development Studies

Focusing on the lived realities of the communities NGOs seek to support, as they themselves choose to express these realities, mirrors a broader trajectory in development theory away from prioritising macroeconomic factors—debates around the balance between the market and the state—towards an emphasis on social capital which is understood as establishing norms of reciprocity and social solidarity in order to empower the poor so that they can act for themselves in processes of community-based local development (Harriss & de Renzio, 1997; Solow, 2000). As Bowles and Veltmeyer (2019) argue, whilst social capital has opened up a space for theoretical discussions which are not purely economic, it has also been accused of fostering a measure of political demobilisation, turning the rural poor away from the confrontational politics of social movements. Writers searching for alternative forms of development, the so-called 'Post-development' scholars, with their influential critique of development as colonisation (Escobar, 1997; Sachs, 1992), largely employ, as Gudynas (2019) suggests, a post-structuralist form of discourse analysis which assumes that social science has no especially privileged access to truth in development, that there are no agreed facts, but rather interpretations, and different ways of seeing and understanding. The lens of such development research tends to focus on the micro, on communities seeking to construct social and solidarity economies (Barkin, 2019), which, as illustrated by particular case studies (Albó, 2012; Farah & Vasapollo, 2011; Medina 2011), are clearly non-capitalist paradigms.

Faced with this search for alternative theoretical paradigms within the long-standing narrative of NGO failure, some development practitioners have moved to explore the potentialities of a qualitative approach, emphasising the need to examine relationships both within and between organisations, and to accept a priori the inequality of power intrinsic to the system. Eyben (2006) has claimed that aid workers have implicitly viewed society as a type of machine in which social change is both possible and predictable:

> The illusion of being in control leads to a neglect of relationships that would privilege different perspectives and offer new answers to managing the turbulent political environment of which donors are part, and contribute towards creating. (Eyben, 2006, p. 1)

She calls for a greater engagement with the relational processes that define boundaries and create meanings, accessed through a concentration on qualitative factors:

> ...experiences and concepts will often be shared through stories and anecdote, involving high levels of ambiguity as well as emotion. A relationship is a process, not a thing. It is characterised by conversations, assumptions and the power relations between the parties. (Eyben, 2006, p. 9)

This relational turn is in many ways a direct challenge to the logic of traditional NGO practice which tends to instrumentalise those communities which aid interventions aspire to support: "the project is a commodity, and thus those helped, the beneficiaries, become part of a commodity" (Krause, 2014, p. 4).

An emphasis on the relational implies both a context-sensitive approach to knowledges of local practice, and a more focused endeavour to hear the 'voices' of those on the receiving end of aid. For NGO practitioners, any active awareness of local contexts is necessarily situated within the framework of long-standing debates about the political and technical nature of 'knowledge' (Ferguson, 1994; Li, 2007), and of the relationships between so-called expert and indigenous knowledge (Chambers, 2008, 2014; Holland, 2013). As Hayman (2016) notes, promoting more context-sensitive praxis on the part of NGOs involves addressing the vexed methodological question of what actually counts as evidence for NGOs and their donors: material derived from an empirical social science apparatus favoured by the evidence-based policy movement in international development, or the "more fluid forms of knowledge" (p. 131) emerging from constructivist and interpretive traditions which give precedence to the participatory and the relational.

Goldstein (2013) argues that traditional framings of the local/global divide tend to be Euclidean in nature, producing an image of a static, linear universe in which other coordinates appear as intermediate points on the same trajectory. Within such a two-dimensional model, it can be difficult to discern the complexity of other social actors, whilst the language of space itself "implies magnitude and importance" (p. 112), and thus can easily represent concepts as travelling one way along a line from an advanced 'transnational' realm to a fixed, and largely ahistorical 'local'.

In this situation, the differences between a substantialist approach (prioritising entities, units and structures which are bounded and fixed) and a relational perspective (foregrounding process, fluidity and interaction) (Cornwall, Eyben, & Kabeer, 2008) are difficult to bridge. For example, the Evidence Principles toolkit devised by Bond (2013) to guide NGOs in assessing the quality of their evidence includes 'Voice and Inclusion' as one of its five key principles, balanced together with Appropriateness, Triangulation, Contribution and Transparency. The unspoken assumption is that a clear distance exists between international interveners and the local communities, that there is a barrier which might make it difficult to conceive of any relational mixing between them, any hybridity of the type which Boege and Rinck have discerned in instances of peacemaking practice: "the boundaries of 'the international' and 'the local' become porous and blurred in the context of the locale –there is nothing and nobody purely local (or international)" (Boege & Rinck, 2019, p. 219).

Beyond openness to local knowledges, actually hearing the voices of those on the receiving end of aid is represented within much practitioner reflection as deeply problematic. At the outset, voices from the foreign communities are expected to be difficult to access, so that NGOs find themselves engaged in searching for what is by definition elusive. Their pursuit is often described in the literature as being a process of 'capturing': "**capturing** subaltern voices" (Manyozo, 2017, p. 59), "Ensuring that the voices of poor people, particularly the most excluded and marginalised, are **captured**" (Bond, 2013). Even when these voices can be accessed, there is ongoing anxiety about their authenticity. Research methods specifically designed to "enable local people to share, enhance and analyze their knowledge of life and conditions" (Chambers, 1994, p. 953; see also PLA Notes, 1988), such as Participatory Rural Appraisal (later Participatory Learning and Action), give particular credence to the oral testimony derived from life story interviews and visual biographies, arguing that these should be seen as the genuine voice of people in low literacy societies. Slim and Thompson (1993), influenced by the oral history movement of the 1980s, suggested that oral testimony potentially brought the power of authenticity into development: "the raw accounting of experience has an authenticity and persuasiveness which it is hard to match" (p. 1). Authenticity in these terms is often explicitly linked to the gaining of political consciousness, the emancipation of those speaking, with the oppressed being organised in order to find their voices by a "liberating educator" who will "provide the subaltern with creative tools and skills, so that they may produce better and more politically conscious voices" (Manyozo, 2017, p. 77).

In practice, voice within development projects is often instrumentalised as 'feedback' within a project cycle, with the emphasis moving from the voices themselves, judged against standards of authenticity or/and political consciousness, to their functional role within wider processes of project effectiveness, particularly as these relate to issues of accountability. There is widespread agreement amongst practitioners, donors and academics that NGOs should strive to provide assurance that they are 'accountable' actors (Groves & Hinton, 2004; Jordan & van Tujl, 2007) within a nexus of multiple (and often conflicting) accountability relationships. These include 'upwards accountability' to governments and donors, 'internal accountability' to staff, 'peer accountability' to the wider sector, and what is termed 'downwards accountability' to affected communities and partners (Crack, 2013b; Edwards & Hulme, 1996; Ebrahim, 2003).

Achieving this downward accountability directs attention to what is sometimes termed "the exercise of voice" (INTRAC, 2016, p. 2), that is to say, the instruments that can elicit responses from the community concerned, and the methods that are most appropriate for doing so in different locales. For example the major DFID/INTRAC project on 'Beneficiary Feedback Mechanisms' (BFM) tested a range of contrasting feedback tools in six countries—Ethiopia, India, Pakistan, Somaliland, Tanzania and Zimbabwe. The results of low-cost methods (accessible mobile technology/SMS) for unsolicited feedback were contrasted with medium resource tools (like social science surveys) and high resource beneficiary-led approaches. In this situation, 'voice' is firmly positioned as part of the chronology of project delivery within a set of development relationships in which accountability effectiveness and "inclusion of the most marginalised" (INTRAC, 2016, p. 2) are synonymous with the mechanisms through which the voices are collected and the responses that they stimulate:

> A *beneficiary feedback mechanism* (BFM) is a context-appropriate mechanism which a) solicits and listens to, collates and analyses feedback, b) triggers a response/action at the required level in the organisation and/or refers feedback to other relevant stakeholders, c) communicates the response/action taken where relevant back to the original feedback provider and if appropriate, the wider beneficiary community. In this definition (a), (b) and (c) must all be present/true and a feedback mechanism is not functional if just one of them is present/true. (INTRAC, 2016, p. 8)

Spaces of Encounter

Whether voice is conflated with the feedback mechanisms of projects or is seen as elusive, or is treated as valid only in relation to criteria of authenticity and political consciousness, it is clearly in some senses a product of meetings between Northern interveners and Southern communities. The nature of these encounters on the ground has been explored by development anthropologists, ethnographers and postmodern geographers. Olivier de Sardan (1995), for example, adopting an actor-centred approach, has highlighted the interests, constraints and strategies of individual actors as key to an understanding of the dynamics of the development space, a site he views as a 'marketplace' or 'arena' (p. 581) within which actors fight for leadership positions (Coll, 2000, p. 102). In this representation, there is an inevitable gap (*décalage*) (Olivier de Sardan, 1995, p. 55) between the expectations associated with a project and the reality of its implementation.

Development ethnography has extended this notion of a space of brokerage by concentrating attention on the actors themselves; development brokers (Lewis & Mosse, 2006; Neubert, 1996) or *courtiers en développement* in the francophone literature (Bierschenk, Chauveau,

& Olivier de Sardan, 2000a; Droz, Steiner, & Weyer, 2010; Le Meur, 1996). Such brokers are located simultaneously as insiders and outsiders with roles and activities that are often blurred—they may, for example, simultaneously act as facilitators (Neubert, 2000, p. 243) and as gatekeepers (Bierschenk, Chauveau, & Olivier de Sardan, 2000b, p. 33). In case studies from across the world—including francophone Africa (Bako-Arifari, 2000; Blundo, 2000; Coll, 2000; Droz et al., 2010; Edja, 2000; Kossi, 2000), Vietnam (Salemink, 2006), Costa Rica (Luetchford, 2006), Nepal (Heaton Shrestha, 2006)—sites of development are portrayed ethnographically as networks of interactions and competing interests.

Research influenced by the 'spatial turn' in scholarship (Smirl, 2015, p. 8) on the other hand has directed attention away from these networks of brokerage in order to critique the ways in which the spaces of development themselves are contingent products of relationality, in a permanent state of construction and change. Following postmodern geographers like Massey (2006), such commentators have understood development as being located in an imaginary which is created physically by the lived experiences and built environments within the field, and imaginatively by the representations, practices and stories associated with its activities, what Lefebvre (1991, p. 39) termed 'perceived space', the space of everydayness, and 'lived space', as lived through its associated images and symbols. Smirl's study of 'Spaces of Aid' (2015), for example, pays equal attention to the memoirs of aid workers in the field and to the physical securitisation of their environments on the assumption that knowledge is necessarily embodied, existing in evolving geographies of embodiment. In these terms, agency is always manifested in matter. In such research, the notion of meetings, of negotiation and dialogic encounters in development, is largely replaced by a striking sense of separation. This is manifested in the physical and imaginative distances on the ground between international NGO (INGO) workers and local communities, marked out by the bunkers and protective fences, the securitisation of aid, that are the result of what Duffield (2014) has termed the "threat or actuality of pervasive violence (which) now affects all of us most of the time" (p. 257). For Smirl, the hotel, the headquarters compound, the white van and remote management of some aid practices produce not interchange and encounter, but rather a type of 'siege mentality':

> you don't speak the language, don't read the local press so are completely isolated from what is going on around you. This can mean that you have

> the impression that everyone is incredibly nice, or that everyone is out to get you. (Security Expert in Banda Aceh cited in Smirl, 2015, p. 99)

In this analysis, what Duffield (2019) describes as the 'computational turn' (p. 10), the steady penetration of digital technology in all its forms, may actually serve to increase rather than shorten distances between potential interlocutors:

> The textured histories, motivations and justifications of distant or now-hard-to-reach people, once familiar through face-to-face exchange or the ethnographic encounter, have been transformed for the convenience of mathematics into electronic data. (Duffield, 2019, p. 8)

In this space of development, increasing connectivity is seen as largely inseparable from cognitive and dialogic separation.

Dialogical Communication

On the whole, however, whether meetings are presumed to take place within complex networks of negotiation, or across distanced and separated spaces, writers have seldom paid much critical attention to the communicative nature of these encounters, contacts which inevitably involve a plurality of "voices, faces and languages" (Bickford, 1996, p. 129). Quarry and Ramíriz, examining communication practices in development, discern a variety of often competing myths about 'communication' typically held by those involved:

> (1) communication can be improvised any time; (2) communication is the same as medium; (3) communication units in agencies have a clear mandate; (4) communication is about sending messages; and (5) information will do the job. (Quarry & Ramíriz, 2009, p. 11)

Critiquing these beliefs, Hamelink (2002) argues for practitioners to replace these myths by an understanding of communication in development as being a two-way process of dialogic exchange:

> It should be the foremost priority on the development agenda to develop the capacity for social dialogue. To solve the world's most pressing problems, people do not need more volumes of information and knowledge – they need to acquire the capacity to talk to each other across boundaries

> of culture, religion and language.... The dialogue requires the capacity to listen, to be silent, to suspend judgment, to critically investigate one's own assumptions, to ask reflexive question and to be open to change. The dialogue has no short-term and certain outcome. (Hamelink, 2002, p. 8)

If communication in development is represented as dialogue rather than the unidirectional transmission of messages, the elusive search for voice, or the incorporation of project feedback, encounters between NGO workers and local communities are necessarily situated within in-between spaces, and these spaces will make considerable demands on all actors involved: "We reconstitute this in-between world through the joint effort to make sense, by creating auditory paths that allow the possibility of meaningful actions together" (Bickford, 1996, p. 173). For Dreher (2009), any bidirectional conception of listening will "not simply allow an other to speak, but rather foregrounds interaction, exchange and interdependence" (p. 450).

In this imagining, an assumed right to speak is extended into a 'right to be understood' with the sense of an obligation to listen to interlocutors who have been historically marginalised from public communication: "Without the inclusion of the subordinate claim of the right to be understood the right to communicate becomes too easily a unidirectional and egocentric democracy of Babel" (Husband, 1996, p. 210).

In the international world of development, a right to be understood inevitably transforms the dialogic process into what Dreher (2009, p. 448) describes as 'cosmopolitan listening'; transnational encounters in which a variety of languages are spoken. For Bickford, language is central to the power and control with which these meetings are conducted:

> a particular kind of listening can serve to break up linguistic conventions and create a public realm where a plurality of voices, faces and languages can be heard and seen and spoken. The goal here is not that each person will be heard in some sort of authentic pristine clarity, but that no person will have less control than anyone else, no one more liable to being distorted than any other. (Bickford, 1996, p. 129)

In development literature, this multilingualism of cosmopolitan listening is seldom directly addressed. For example, Lewis and Mosse's (2006) collection is entitled 'Brokers and Translators', but conceives of 'translation' not in an interlingual sense, but as a Latourian metaphor to describe "the mutual enrolment and the interlocking of interests that produces project realities" (p. 13), with projects understood as "a chain of translation" (Le Meur, 2006, p. 84). Some practitioners have engaged with the epistemological dilemmas inherent in cross-cultural research in development (Maclean, 2007), but with the unequal status of differently spoken knowledges (Powell, 2006) it has largely been through the work of sociolinguists that the multilingualism of these in-between spaces has been accorded a more central place. Thus, Robinson's early book on language use in rural Africa (1996) and his more recent co-written article on Cameroon, Morocco and Senegal (Robinson & Vũ, 2019), suggest that an informed recognition of the languages of local populations could contribute to more robust development outcomes. In his 2008 contribution, *The Sociolinguistics of Development in Africa*, Djité took as his paradigm the transfer of information and skills to the majority of the people in a multilingual environment, and their active participation in programmes that mattered to their everyday lives and well-being. Rather than focusing on the dialogic relations between intervening NGOs and local communities however, both Robinson and Djité are primarily interested in the links between African languages, literacy in the region, and broad national development goals:

> Language is an explicit contributing factor of development and needs to be taken into account in the formulation of innovative and visionary language policies in Africa for good education, health, economy and governance, all of which are conditional upon efficient communication. (Djité, 2008, p. 5)

The Listening Zones of NGOs

Introducing cosmopolitan listening into an analysis of communicative relationships between NGOs and local communities is far from easy. To begin with, the literature on listening maintains that listening as an object of research has long been the poor relation of 'voice'. Traditionally, a lack of voice, rather than a failure to listen, is represented as a key factor in the marginalisation of minorities (Husband, 2000), and in the social and political oppression of women (Butler, 1999; Weatherall, 2002). Communication itself tends to be unproblematically identified with Speech, so much so that Habermas (1991), for example, constructed his theory of communicative action on what he described as "the ideal speech situation" (pp. 196–203), rather than, as Macnamara (2018) points out, any "ideal listening situation" (p. 4).

Whilst listening has been theorised in the context of interpersonal relations, human resource management and therapeutic practice, it has received relatively little critical attention in the wider fields of institutional, governmental and political communication. Bickford (1996) emphasises the lack of research on listening in debates on contemporary democratic theory, noting that "this omission is particularly surprising given democratic theorists' emphasis on shared speech as a practice of citizenship" (p. 1). Purdy (2000) argues that the problem in extending an interest in listening to politico-institutional contexts lies in the traditional roots of listening research within a post-Enlightenment individualist 'psychology project' which follows the lead of cognitive science in viewing listening solely as an individual, rather than a community process. For Wolvin (2010), three major conceptualisations of listening have dominated the research that exists. They represent listening as physiological—how physiologically a message is received, as psychological—how we construct meaning out of a message, and as sociological—how we respond to a particular message in terms of our social and cultural conditioning.

Macnamara (2018, p. 3) compares these frameworks of individual listening with what she terms 'organisational listening', as undertaken by government agencies, institutions and NGOs. Listening in these settings is typically characterised by processes that are entirely different from those common to the personal one-to-one listening experience. Organisational listening is an overwhelmingly delegated exercise, undertaken through functions such as market research, public consultations, and feedback mechanisms, with an increasingly managerial and corporate commitment to forms and procedures. Listening in such contexts is mediated rather than direct and is usually asynchronous in that it seldom occurs dynamically in real time, but rather operates across both time and space.

Listening within the in-between spaces of NGOs and local communities in a dialogic relationship implies communication which is direct, and potentially uneasy. Rather than notions of a polite dialogue founded on liberal reciprocity (Coles, 1996), this listening is an inherently risky enterprise since it may well require the listeners to radically change their behaviour. In such uncomfortable communicative relationships, there is, as it were, no happy ending, no final erasure of distance. Cosmopolitan listening across cultures and languages does not signify any facile "romance of understanding", but rather an attentive engagement to those in-between spaces in which established hierarchies of language and voice can potentially be upset (Dreher, 2009, pp. 448 and 450).

Writers from Cultural Studies, with their particular interest in tracing "the human in the humanities" (Apter, 2006, p. 25) in the violent contexts of empire or colonialism, have framed these in-between spaces as relational multicultural encounters. In a key text in this scholarship, Pratt (2008) coined the term 'contact zones': "the space and time where subjects previously separated by geography and history are co-present, the point at which their trajectories now intersect" (p. 8). For Pratt, the use of 'contact zones' shifts attention towards the interactive and improvisational nature of the meetings:

> A "contact" perspective emphasizes how subjects get constituted in and by their relations to each other. It treats the relations between colonizers and colonized, or travellers and "travelees" not in terms of separateness, but in terms of co-presence, interaction, interlocking understandings and practices, and often within radically asymmetrical relations of power. (Pratt, 2008, p. 8)

'Contact zones' of international encounter are clearly spaces of language politics in the broadest sense. They are areas in which language communities meet, where governments and institutions have set an explicit or implicit agenda of language/translation policies, and where symbolic and cultural capital attaches to particular language practices (Bourdieu, 1986). Apter has called this a 'Translation Zone':

> In fastening on the term "zone" as a theoretical mainstay, the intention has been to imagine a broad intellectual topography that is neither the property of a single nation, nor an amorphous condition associated with postnationalism, but rather a zone of critical engagement that connects the "l" and the "n" of transLation and transNation. (Apter, 2006, p. 5)

The use of 'Zone' as a critical tool enables the relationality of encounters to be set within clearly delimited geographies that are not framed by the nation state or by ethnicities, and which can be conceived in both macro or micro contexts. Thus, studies of large multilingual empires (Baer, 2011; Wolf, 2011), as well as descriptions of the border areas of multilingual cities (Cronin, 2003), have employed 'Translation Zones' as a means of approaching what Simon (2013) calls "a relentless to-and-fro of language, …an acute consciousness of translational relationships, and …the kinds of polymorphous translation practices characteristic of multilingual milieus" (p. 181). In much of this research the emphasis is not on the negotiation of meanings between interlocutors, but rather on the fluid practices of relationality, with hybridisation, crossing points, mixing and what is called 'translanguaging' (using multiple languages simultaneously) as potentially key features.

In these Zones, language policies and translation practices are intimately related (Meylaerts, 2010) whether or not they are overtly expressed as such by the organisations concerned. Commentators from Translation Studies, drawing on Derrida's view (1996) that monolingual cultures always carry with them their mute twin, the multilingualism of the 'other', point to the silent but always ongoing process of translation beneath the surface, what Gentzler (2008, p. 10) terms a type of "hidden translation history", which necessarily plays a part in relationships formed. Marais's (2014, 2018) work on translation and complexity theory encourages researchers to look beyond traditional professional language mediators in the Listening Zones towards the broader contexts of informal economies where illiterate, semiliterate and partially educated people engage with regulatory environments that are mostly literate, written and formal.

Using the conceptualisation of a Listening Zone has clear advantages for a study which seeks to address listening relationships in international development. In the first place, it assumes from the outset that spaces of development are multivocal and multilingual, no matter what imaginative and physical checkpoints have traditionally been erected at 'monolingual borders' (Alcalay cited in Grossman, 2010, p. 55). Secondly, it prioritises the actual workings of communicative and auditory relationships on the ground rather than broad classifications of identity like nation state, ethnicity or North/South. Thirdly, it positions the co-creation of the listening space itself as the focus of study, rather than understanding listening as an incidental stage within a teleological development cycle in which project achievement, the establishment of consensus or the extent of understanding/misunderstanding are held as implicit criteria of success or failure. Finally, it assumes that these Listening Zones are potentially spaces of hybridity and learning, of ontological translation and cognitive porosity, spaces of mutuality, rather than of one-sided epistemic extraction: *"Si mulishaka kula zenu, basi muna weza to kumbuka siye benye tulitumaka muna pata hizo makuta"* ("Now that you've gotten your food [i.e. been paid for the research] couldn't you at least remember those of us who made that possible for you?") (Chiza Kashurha, 2019).

This volume asks a number of key questions about the Listening Zones of development:

- How have NGOs and donors arrived at the framings which characterise their listening today? What do their histories of listening in development tell us about how they understand listening?
- How do NGO workers in headquarters and in-country perform their listening, and what are the potential problems and uncertainties they experience?
- How does language mediation as part of vernacularisation operate on the ground in development programmes?
- What are the implications for those in the Listening Zones whose first languages are not the dominant ones in any development encounter? How do they perceive the relationships that are established with communities?

In macro terms, the relationality of Listening Zones has been constructed over time, formed by the particular listening histories of individual NGOs, by the stories that these organisations have traditionally told themselves about their relationships with communities in the development field. Chapter 2 compares the listening histories of three major UK-based INGOs, founded at different times in the twentieth century and with distinct listening traditions—Oxfam GB, Christian Aid, and Tearfund. The chapter argues that the presence of INGOs in a foreign country has to be read contrapuntally with their spaces of origin. It asks key questions about how an imaginary of the Zones is constructed around NGO perceptions of distance from/proximity to the foreign 'other' and explores the ways in which listening and learning in these multivocal sites have been historically enacted and supported.

Within the Listening Zones of development, there are several different actors—donor organisations, NGO workers at headquarters and in the countries concerned, language/cultural intermediaries, Southern NGOs (SNGOs) and the multitude of local communities affected by interventions. As listening subjects, these actors often have multiple positions, both listening and being listened to, and the succeeding chapters explore their separate roles in creating Listening Zones. Chapter 3 focuses on the UK Government as a major development donor. It examines the listening ideology of the Government from the mid-1960s until today, looking closely at the ways in which the nature of the 'international' in the spaces of development has been apprehended and framed, and the implications that this listening ideology has had for organisations seeking funding. Chapter 4 engages with the Listening Zones as created by UK-based development NGOs and examines the role of languages and cultural knowledge in the construction of cosmopolitan listening. The chapter records the voices of those who work for NGOs, both at headquarters and in the field, as they describe their listening experiences and explain how the foreignness of development impacts upon the relationships they form. Chapter 5 explores the place of language/cultural mediators as active listening conduits in development, examining the perceptions held by international NGOs and SNGOs of translators/interpreters, and the ways in which mediated and translated listening is understood both by the mediators themselves and by other development actors.

Whilst 'foreign' multivocal sites of development intervention are clearly numerous, the case studies in Chapters 6, 7 and 8—Malawi, Kyrgyzstan and Peru—have been chosen as Listening Zones that present key differences both in the status accorded to the English language (ranging from official language, to a rarely spoken language, to most widely taught foreign language) and in the duration and extent of UK-based INGO involvement (ongoing since 1964, beginning only in the 1990s, long standing but radically reduced over the past decade). Staff in these countries, speaking in English (Malawi), in Russian and Kyrgyz (in Kyrgyzstan, facilitated by an interpreter), and in Spanish (Peru), describe their listening relationships with anglophone donors and with speakers of other languages within their communities.

The Listening Zones of NGOs as conceived in this study are multivocal and multilingual spaces, constructed through the listening histories of NGOs, donor ideologies of listening, and the experiences and perceptions of INGO and SNGO workers, and language intermediaries. The foreignness of the Zones is a key factor in the communicative relationships between actors, whether this foreignness is overtly noticed or implicitly occluded. Chapter 9 explores the implications of the research for the ways in which International Relations and Development Studies traditionally constitute 'development', and suggests that the conceptual framework proposed in this volume and the ways in which different disciplines have worked together in the research alongside practitioners may offer fruitful opportunities for further work in the field. The experience of conducting cross-disciplinary research on the Listening Zones of Development equally presents challenges to the other contributing disciplines—Listening Studies, Cultural Studies and Translation Studies—and the chapter indicates some of the directions these challenges may take. Finally, Chapter 10 turns to the range of actors involved and draws on examples of innovative practice revealed in the case studies and the discussions to offer each group explicit recommendations on listening. It indicates some of the early donor/INGO reaction to the recommendations and suggests approaches through which this conversation on languages and cultural awareness can continue.

The questions addressed in this book involve the crossing of borders, moments of global connection in contact zones which bring together different actors in myriad types of encounter. The authors of this book have also found themselves engaged in the crossing of boundaries, firstly as academics working with development practitioners in a spirit of mutual critical enquiry; secondly, as researchers coming from different disciplinary backgrounds—the Arts and Humanities (Modern Languages and Intercultural Studies), Social Sciences (Politics and International Relations) and Translation Studies, itself traditionally a mixture of practitioner/academic reflection. Each of these disciplinary origins has its distinct ways of seeing and defining 'evidence', and a hinterland of customs and accepted practices around the articulation of the results. As such, writing this book has itself been a disciplinary 'contact zone', which we have negotiated by concentrating on agreed questions, reflecting together and at length on each chapter. The resulting volume tries to give a sense of the excitement of our discussion, not by stifling specific differences in writing voices, but rather by accepting the fact of difference, and working creatively with it in order to understand the nature of Listening Zones. Tsing has talked about the importance of recognising 'friction' in cross-disciplinary research, and accepting these interactions not as "truth or lies but as sticky engagements" (Tsing, 2005, pp. 4–6), with the ambitious objective of helping to define a newer field, rather than to fit easily into any existing ones from which we may have come.

References

AbouAssi, K. (2013). Hands in the pockets of mercurial donors NGO response to shifting funding priorities. *Nonprofit and Voluntary Sector Quarterly, 42*(3), 584–602.

Albó, A. (2012). *El Buen Vivir. Sumak kawsay. Una oportunidad para imaginar otros mundos*. Quito: Abya Yala.

Andrews, A. (2014). Downward accountability in unequal alliances: Explaining NGO responses to Zapatista demands. *World Development, 54,* 99–113.

Apter, E. (2006). *The translation zone: A new comparative literature.* Princeton: Princeton University Press.

Arts, B., & Elbers, W. (2011). Keeping body and soul together: Southern NGOs' strategic responses to donor constraints. *International Review of Administrative Sciences, 77*(4), 713–732.

Baer, B. J. (Ed.). (2011). *Literary translation in Eastern Europe and Russia.* Amsterdam and Philadelphia: John Benjamins.

Bako-Arifari, N. (2000). Dans les interstices de l'Etat: des courtiers en col blanc. Cadres ressortissants et développement local à Kandi (Nord-Bénin). In J. P. Chauveau, J. P. Olivier de Sardan, & T. Bierschenk (Eds.), *Courtiers en développement* (pp. 43–70). Paris: Karthala and APAD.

Barkin, D. (2019). Popular sustainable development, or ecological economics from below. In H. Veltmeyer & P. Bowles (Eds.), *The essential guide to critical development studies* (pp. 371–391). London and New York: Routledge.

Bebbington, A. J., Hickey, S., & Mitlin, D. C. (Eds.). (2008). *Can NGOs make a difference? The challenge of development alternatives.* London: Zed Books.

Bickford, S. (1996). *The dissonance of democracy.* Ithaca and London: Cornell University Press.

Bierschenk, T., Chauveau, J. P., & Olivier de Sardan, J. P. (Eds.). (2000a). *Courtiers en développement.* Paris: Karthala and APAD.

Bierschenk, T., Chauveau, J. P., & Olivier de Sardan, J. P. (2000b). Introduction. les courtiers entre développement et État. In J. P. Chauveau, J. P. Olivier de Sardan, & T. Bierschenk (Eds.), *Courtiers en développement* (pp. 5–42). Paris: Karthala and APAD.

Blundo, G. (2000). Elus locaux et courtiers en développement au Sénégal. Trajectoires politiques, modes de légitimation et stratégies d'alliance. In J. P. Chauveau, J. P. Olivier de Sardan, & T. Bierschenk (Eds.), *Courtiers en développement* (pp. 71–100). Paris: Karthala and APAD.

Bob, C. (2005). *The marketing of rebellion: Insurgents, media, and international activism.* Cambridge: Cambridge University Press.

Boege, V., & Rinck, P. (2019). The local/international interface in peacebuilding experiences from Bougainville and Sierra Leone. *International Peacekeeping, 26*(2), 216–239.

Bond. (2013). *Principles and checklist for assessing the quality of evidence.* Retrieved from: https://www.bond.org.uk/file/17815.

Bourdieu, P. (1986). The forms of capital. In J. G. Richardson (Ed.), *Handbook of theory of research for the sociology of education* (pp. 241–258). Westport, CT: Greenwood.

Bowles, P., & Veltmeyer, H. (2019). Critical development studies: An introduction. In H. Veltmeyer & P. Bowles (Eds.), *The essential guide to critical development studies* (p. 127). Oxford and New York: Routledge.
Butler, J. (1999). *Gender trouble: Feminism and the subversion of identity*. New York: Routledge.
Chambers, R. (1994). The origins and practices of participatory rural appraisal. *World Development, 22*(7), 953–969.
Chambers, R. (2008). *Revolutions in development inquiry*. London: Earthscan.
Chambers, R. (2014). Knowing in development: A radical agenda for the twenty-first century? *Forum for Development Studies, 41,* 525–538.
Chang, H. J. (2013). Hamlet without the Prince of Denmark: How development has disappeared from today's "development". In C. Rodger & D. Held (Eds.), *Global governance at risk* (pp. 129–148). Polity: Cambridge.
Chiza Kashurha, C. (2019, June 20). *"When will we get a report on your findings?": Reflections on researcher accountability from DRC.* Retrieved from: https://oxfamblogs.org/fp2p/when-will-we-get-a-report-on-your-findings-reflections-on-researcher-accountability-from-drc/.
Coles, R. (1996). Liberty, equality, receptive generosity: Neo-Nietzschean reflections on the ethics and politics of coalition. *American Political Science Review, 90*(2), 375–388.
Coll, J. (2000). Animateurs et coordinateurs. Les courtiers en développement de Malem-Hodar (Sénégal). In J. P. Chauveau, J. P. Olivier de Sardan, & T. Bierschenk (Eds.), *Courtiers en développement* (pp. 101–123). Paris: Karthala and APAD.
Cornwall, A., Eyben, R., & Kabeer, N. (2008). *Conceptualising empowerment and the implications for pro poor growth* (Paper for the DAC Poverty Network). Retrieved from: https://www.ids.ac.uk/files/dmfile/conceptualisingempowermentpaperforPOVNET.pdf.
Crack, A. M. (2013a). Language, listening and learning: Critically reflective accountability for INGOs. *International Review of Administrative Sciences, 79*(4), 809–828.
Crack, A. M. (2013b). INGO accountability deficits: The imperatives for further reform. *Globalizations, 10*(2), 293–308.
Cronin, M. (2003). *Translation and globalization*. London: Routledge.
Derrida, J. (1996). *Le Monolinguisme de l'autre: ou la prothèse d'origine*. Paris: Editions Galilée.
Djité, P. (2008). *The sociolinguistics of development in Africa*. Clevedon: Multilingual Matters.
Dreher, T. (2009). Listening across difference: Media and multiculturalism beyond the politics of voice. *Continuum: Journal of Media and Cultural Studies, 23*(4), 445–458.

Dreher, A., Koch, D. J., Nunnenkamp, P., & Thiele, R. (2009). Keeping a low profile: What determines the allocation of aid by non-governmental organizations? *World Development, 37*(5), 902–918.

Droz, Y., Steiner, B., & Weyer, F. (2010). Le courtier du virtuel: l'accès controversé aux informations médicales en ligne au Mali. *Sciences Sociales et Santé, 28*(4), 91–107.

Duffield, M. (2014). *The merging of development and security*. London: Zed Books.

Duffield, M. (2019). *Post-humanitarianism: Governing precarity in the digital world*. Cambridge: Polity.

Ebrahim, A. (2003). Accountability in practice: Mechanisms for NGOs'. *World Development, 31*(5), 813–829.

Edja, H. (2000). Médiateurs traditionnels à l'école du courtage en développement. Un exemple autour des projets du service allemand de développement (DED) à Kalalé au Nord-Bénin. In J. P. Chauveau, J. P. Olivier de Sardan, & T. Bierschenk (Eds.), *Courtiers en développement* (pp. 125–144). Paris: Karthala and APAD.

Edwards, M., & Hulme, D. (1996). *Beyond the magic bullet: NGO performance and accountability in the post-Cold War world*. Bloomfield: Kumarian Press.

Escobar, A. (1997). Unmasking development. In M. Rahema & V. Bawttree (Eds.), *The postdevelopment reader* (pp. 191–203). London: Zed Books.

Eyben, R. (Ed.). (2006). *Relationships for aid*. London: Earthscan.

Farah, I., & Vasapollo, L. (Eds.). (2011). *Vivir bien. Paradigma no capitalista?* La Paz: CIDES-UMSA.

Ferguson, J. (1994). *The anti-politics machine: Development, depoliticisation and bureaucratic power in Lesotho*. Minneapolis: University of Minnesota Press.

Fowler, A. (2000). NGO futures: Beyond aid: NGDO values and the fourth position. *Third World Quarterly, 21*(4), 589–603.

Gentzler, E. (2008). *Translation and identity in the Americas: New directions in translation history*. Abingdon: Routledge.

Goldstein, D. (2013). Whose vernacular? Translating human rights in local contexts. In M. Goodale (Ed.), *Human rights at the crossroads* (pp. 111–121). Oxford: Oxford University Press.

Grossman, E. (2010). *Why translation matters*. New Haven: Yale University Press.

Groves, L., & Hinton, R. (Eds.). (2004). *Inclusive aid: Changing power and relationships in international development*. London: Routledge.

Gudynas, E. (2019). Post-development and other critiques of the roots of development. In H. Veltmeyer & P. Bowles (Eds.), *The essential guide to critical development studies* (pp. 84–93). London and New York: Routledge.

Habermas, J. (1991). *The structural transformation of the public sphere* (T. Burger, Trans.). Cambridge: MIT Press.

Hamelink, C. (2002). Social development, information and knowledge: Whatever happened to communication? *Development, Journal of the Society for International Development, 45*(4), 5–9.

Harriss, J., & de Renzio, P. (1997). "Missing link" or analytically missing? The concept of social capital: An introductory bibliographic essay. *Journal of International Development, 9*(7), 919–937.

Hayman, R. (2016). NGOs and the evidence-based policy agenda. In L. Narayanaswamy, R. Hayman, S. King, & T. Kontinen (Eds.), *Negotiating knowledge: Evidence and experience in development NGOs* (pp. 129–145). Rugby: Practical Action Publishing.

Heaton Shrestha, C. (2006). "They can't mix like we can": Bracketing differences and the professionalization of NGOs in Nepal. In D. Lewis & D. Mosse (Eds.), *Development brokers and translators: The ethnography of aid and agencies* (pp. 195–216). Bloomfield: Kumarian Press.

Holland, J. (Ed.). (2013). *Who counts? The power of participatory statistics.* Rugby: Practical Action Publishing.

Husband, C. (1996). The right to be understood: Conceiving the multi-ethnic public sphere. *Innovation: The European Journal of Social Sciences, 9*(2), 205–215.

Husband, C. (2000). Media and the public sphere in multi-ethnic societies. In S. Cottle (Ed.), *Ethnic minorities and the media* (pp. 199–214). Buckingham: Open University Press.

INTRAC. (2016). *DFID Beneficiary Feedback Mechanisms (BFM) pilot: End-point review.* Synthesis Report. Retrieved from: https://www.intrac.org/resources/dfid-beneficiary-feedback-mechanisms-bfm-pilot-end-point-review-synthesis.

Jordan, L., & van Tujl, P. (Eds.). (2007). *NGO accountability: Politics, principles and innovations.* London: Earthscan.

Kossi, A. (2000). Dynamique associative, courtage en développement et stratégies d'insertion. L'association des ressortissants d'Enouli-Kodzo-Aza au Togo. In J. P. Chauveau, J. P. Olivier de Sardan, & T. Bierschenk (Eds.), *Courtiers en développement* (pp. 145–164). Paris: Karthala and APAD.

Krause, M. (2014). *The good project: Humanitarian relief NGOs and the fragmentation of reason.* Chicago: University of Chicago Press.

Krose, C. (2018, June 27). Unpublished paper presented at the Listening Zones Conference, Institute of Modern Languages Research. London: University of London.

Le Meur, P. Y. (1996). Les Courtiers Locaux du Développement. *Synthèse. Bulletin de L'APAD, 12,* 1–6.

Le Meur, P. Y. (2006). Governing land, translating rights: The rural land plan in Benin. In D. Lewis & D. Mosse (Eds.), *Development brokers and translators: The ethnography of aid and agencies* (pp. 75–99). Bloomfield: Kumarian Press.

Lefebvre, H. (1991). *The production of space* (D. Nicolson-Smith, Trans.). Oxford: Basil Blackwell.

Lewis, D., & Mosse, D. (Eds.). (2006). *Development brokers and translators: The ethnography of aid and agencies*. Bloomfield, CT: Kumarian Press.

Li, T. (2007). *The will to improve: Governmentality, development, and the practice of politics*. Durham: Duke University Press.

Long, A., & Long, N. (1992). *Battlefields of knowledge*. London: Longmans.

Luetchford, P. (2006). Brokering fair trade: Relations between coffee cooperatives and alternative trade organizations—A view from Costa Rica. In D. Lewis & D. Mosse (Eds.), *Development brokers and translators: The ethnography of aid and agencies* (pp. 127–148). Bloomfield: Kumarian Press.

Maclean, K. (2007). Translation in cross-cultural research: An example from Bolivia. *Development in Practice, 17*(6), 784–790.

Macnamara, J. (2018). Towards a theory and practice of organizational listening. *International Journal of Listening, 32*(1), 1–23.

Manyozo, L. (2017). *Communicating development with communities*. Abingdon and New York: Routledge.

Marais, K. (2014). *Translation theory and development studies: A complexity theory approach*. New York and Abingdon: Routledge.

Marais, K. (2018). Translation and development. In F. Fernández & J. Evans (Eds.), *The Routledge handbook of translation and politics* (pp. 95–109). London and New York: Routledge.

Massey, D. (2006). *For Space*. London: Sage.

Mawdsley, E., Oakley, P., Porter, G., & Townsend, J. (2002). *Knowledge, power and development agendas: NGOs North and South*. Oxford: INTRAC.

Medina, J. (2011). *Acerca del Suma Qamaña*. In I. Farah & L. Vasapollo (Eds.), *Vivir bien. Paradigma no capitalista?* (pp. 39–64). La Paz: CIDES-UMSA.

Meylaerts, R. (2010). Multilingualism and translation. In L. van Doorslaer & Y. Gambier (Eds.), *Handbook of translation studies* (Vol. 1, pp. 227–230). Amsterdam and Philadelphia: John Benjamins.

Morfit, N. S. (2011). "AIDS is money": How donor preferences reconfigure local realities. *World Development, 39*(1), 64–76.

Mosse, D. (2005). *Cultivating development: An ethnography of aid policy and practice*. London: Pluto.

Neubert, D. (1996). The role of local brokers in the development system: Experiences with "self-help projects" in East Africa. *Bulletin de L'APAD, 11*, 1–11.

Neubert, D. (2000). Le rôle des courtiers locaux dans le système du développement. Quelques expériences de "projets d'autopromotion" en Afrique de l'Est. In J. P. Chauveau, J. P. Olivier de Sardan, & T. Bierschenk (Eds.), *Courtiers en développement* (pp. 241–257). Paris: Karthala and APAD.

Olivier de Sardan, J. P. (1995). *Anthropologie et développement: essai en socio-anthropologie du changement social*. Paris: Karthala.

PLA Notes. (1988). *Participatory learning and action*. London: International Institute for Environment and Development.

Porter, F., Ralph-Bowman, M., & Wallace, T. (Eds.). (2013). *Aid, NGOs and the realities of women's lives: A perfect storm*. Oxford: Practical Action Publishing.

Powell, M. (2006). Whose knowledge? Whose reality? An overview of knowledge used in the development sector. *Development in Practice, 16*(6), 518–532.

Pratt, M. L. (2008). *Imperial eyes: Travel writing and transculturation*. Abingdon: Routledge.

Purdy, M. (2000). Listening, culture and structures of consciousness: Ways of studying listening. *International Journal of Listening, 14*(1), 47–68.

Quarry, W., & Ramírez, R. (2009). *Communication for another development: Listening before telling*. London and New York: Zed Books.

Robinson, C. (1996). *Language use in rural development: An African perspective*. Berlin and New York: Mouton de Gruyter.

Robinson, C., & Vũ, T. A. T. (2019). Literacy, languages and development in Africa: A policy perspective. *International Review of Education, 65*(3), 443–470.

Sachs, W. (Ed). (1992). *The development dictionary: A guide to knowledge and power*. London: Zed Books.

Salemink, O. (2006). Translating, interpreting, and practicing civil society in Vietnam: A tale of calculated misunderstandings. In D. Lewis & D. Mosse (Eds.), *Development brokers and translators: The ethnography of aid and agencies* (pp. 101–126). Bloomfield: Kumarian Press.

Simon, S. (2013). Translation zone. In D. L. Van & Y. Gambier (Eds.), *Handbook of translation studies* (Vol. 4, pp. 181–185). Amsterdam: John Benjamins.

Slim, H., & Thomson, P. (1993). *Listening for a change: Oral testimony and development*. London: Panos Publications.

Smirl, L. (2015). *Spaces of Aid: How cars, compounds and hotels shape humanitarianism*. London: Zed Books.

Solow, R. (2000). Notes on social capital and economic performance. In I. Serageldin & P. Dasgupta (Eds.), *Social capital: A multi-faceted perspective* (pp. 6–10). Washington, DC: World Bank.

Tsing, A. (2005). *Friction: An ethnography of global connection*. Princeton: Princeton University Press.

Weatherall, A. (2002). *Gender, language and discourse*. Hove: Routledge.

Wolf, M. (2011). *Die Vielsprachige Seele Kakaniens: Übersetzen und Dolmetschen in der Habsburgermonarchie 1848 bis 1918*. Wien: Bohlau.

Wolvin, A. (2010). *Listening and human communication in the 21st century*. Oxford: Blackwell.

Workshop Report. (2014, January 20). *Do NGOs need a languages policy?* (Workshop Report, University of Reading). Retrieved from: https://www.intrac.org/wpcms/wp-content/uploads/2016/09/DO-NGOs-Need-a-Languages-Policy_Workshop-Report.pdf.

CHAPTER 2

NGOs Constructing the Listening Zones

NGOs and History

The transnational spaces in which NGOs work, and their relationships with the foreign 'other', have been constructed over time. If, as Slim (1994) suggested, "historical reflection is seldom the first concern of relief workers" (p. 189), it nevertheless remains true that the values and identities that institutions espouse are in some measure a product of their past, operationalised today within contexts which are themselves framed by the historical beliefs and traditions of the communities concerned (Merli, Nunn, & Schipper, 2014). Concepts that are fundamental to the sector today, such as 'accountability', have roots in much earlier aid traditions that skewed 'accountability' towards donors rather than towards beneficiaries (Roddy, Strange, & Taithe, 2015). Thus, NGO activities on the ground at particular key moments create what Taithe (2016) calls "communities of practice" (p. 335). These facilitate the production of knowledge and, hence, future understandings of how we define key terms like 'development' and 'refugees'. Narratives of imagined humanitarian communities drawn from NGO experiences in the Cambodian border camps between 1979 and 1993, Taithe argues, gave rise to new paradigms like permanent emergency (see Duffield, 1997), and fostered a tendency to submerge deeply troubling epistemic distances between victims and helpers within discourses of trauma and genocide.

Of course, the NGO sector itself has its own institutional history, shaped by international events, financial constraints and organisational

H. Footitt et al., *Development NGOs and Languages*,
https://doi.org/10.1007/978-3-030-51776-2_2

change. Davies (2013), adopting a broad historical and geographical approach, discerns a cyclical process in transnational NGO activity, characterised by three major waves: the era up to 1914, the interwar years, and the period since the Second World War. Saunders (2009) points to five phases: nineteenth century to the 1950s, in which the focus was on humanitarian relief to war-afflicted countries; the 1950s–1960s, when attention moved to humanitarian crises in developing countries; the 1960s, with an emerging politicisation, amplified in the 1970s and 1980s; and finally, the mid-1990s onward, marked by high-profile mass mobilising coalitions. In more recent years, commentators have described a sector which has been responding over the past decade to "rapidly shifting, ambiguous and sometimes chaotic external environments" (Bond, 2015, p. 14), distinguished by pressures on spaces for advocacy, shifts in geopolitical power, changing models of finance, evolving technologies and erosion in public levels of trust. Duffield (2019) claims that there is a distinct NGO history bisected by the before and after of data connectivity and the remote sense-making tools associated with it.

These multiple histories of NGOs help us to reach a broader understanding of how key concepts are framed. They encourage us to engage critically with the origins of new paradigms and the successive movements of institutional change and direction. Relationships on the ground between interveners and communities are also themselves a product of history, of the practices and customs of encounter which have been established implicitly or explicitly over time, and of the stories institutions have traditionally told themselves about the ways in which they communicate with and listen to *their* foreign communities. As discussed in Chapter 1, Eyben's (2006) call for relationships to be at the centre of aid, and for organisations to learn through such relationships, focuses attention on the processes by which NGOs have listened to others, the assumptions they have made, and the ways in which the spaces of listening, their Listening Zones, have been constructed over time.

This chapter investigates the listening histories of three major post-1940 NGOs, each with rather different historical roots: OxfamGB which emerged in 1942 from a committee of concerned individuals, Christian Aid, which was created in 1943 from a coalition of British and Irish churches, and Tearfund, which was founded much later, in 1968, by a specific faith group in response to what it saw as lacunae in the approaches of other types of NGOs. The evidence for the study is drawn from the NGOs' own archives in the cases of Oxfam (the Bodleian Oxfam archive, 1943–2014) and Christian Aid (the SOAS Christian Aid archive, 1946–1990). Tearfund's archive is not yet available, but the agency has produced its own history (Hollow, 2008), which contains a wealth of primary material, and this is supplemented by interviews conducted with five former members of staff.

Historically, the Listening Zones of these organisations were as multivocal and multilingual as they are today; they were co-created by foreign interveners and local communities. The presence of INGOs in a foreign country has to be read contrapuntally with their spaces of origin (Blaney & Inayatullah, 2004; Said, 1995). The approach taken in this exploration of the histories of NGO Listening Zones applies insights derived from relational geography (Massey, 2006; Smirl, 2015). Space, in both physical and cognitive terms was crucial, the chapter will argue, in setting the parameters within which transnational exchanges in development activities were constructed. The relational geographies of these three NGOs, their transnational imaginaries, will be examined to provide answers to two main questions. Firstly, how did perceptions of the distance from/proximity to the foreign 'other' emerge over time in the NGO's imaginary? Secondly, how were the exchanges in transnational encounters between Northern anglophone INGOs and Southern communities, the listening to and learning from the 'other', enacted and supported over time? In a concluding section, the chapter underlines the relevance of these historical imaginaries to the ways in which NGOs today construct their Listening Zones.

OxfamGB

Defining the relational geographies of spaces of aid and development has always been difficult for NGOs like Oxfam. Over the years, the organisation has used a variety of metaphors to characterise itself–Oxfam was a "tapestry" made up of various threads (MS Oxfam, PRG, 2/3/8/27, 8.11.90) or an "amoeba" (Whitaker, 1983, p. 30). Nevertheless, a common theme in Oxfam's history has been the geographical mapping of a "frontline" (MSOxfam, PRG, 1/11/1, 23.9.92) with sites of meeting in which "field staff" (MSOxfam, PRG, 1/1/3, 23.10.73) made "contact with partners", "face-to-face" encounters with their foreign 'others' (MSOxfam, PRG, 2/3/8/31, 10.98). From the beginning, the notion of spending time and developing relationships on the ground was fundamental to Oxfam's self-perception of its working style, a willingness, "to invest an enormous amount of time in simply talking" (MSOxfam, PRG, 2/3/1/11, 24.11.97).

The group of concerned Oxford citizens who met in October 1942 to address the misery of war-torn Europe through a famine relief committee would be the basis of the future Oxfam, and would reflect in its historical development, as Black (1992) suggests, "major evolutions of twentieth century thinking" (p. 2). Oxfam initially operated in liberated Europe through intermediary aid organisations like the Friends Service Council or the British Red Cross. But by 1960 it had begun to recognise the need "for longer term help to certain of the agencies" (MSOxfam, PRG, 1/1/1, 20.6.60), although there was some discussion about the extent to which this support should be spread beyond Commonwealth countries which were thought to command more sympathy among the British public (MSOxfam, PRG, 1/1/2, 22.4.66). In the early 1960s, Oxfam gradually developed a different organisational model, managing projects on the ground within the countries concerned (Whitaker, 1983), and thus bringing NGO staff directly into the field. By 1967, it was employing ten Field Directors based outside the UK: four in Africa, two in West Asia, one in the Far East, two in Latin America and one in the Mediterranean/North Africa. These Oxfam workers were expected to build a rapport with groups in the locality, assess project applications and make recommendations to headquarters. Their recruitment profile stressed the need to have contextual knowledge of the regions, with foreign language competence identified as 'desirable' or 'important': "Knowledge of Arabic desirable or prior language ability" (Egypt); "knowledge of French important" (Kampuchea); "language facility (Somali/Arabic) desirable" (Somali) (MSOxfam, PRG, 1/13/1, 11.1.83). In the early conditions of service for overseas staff there was an assumption that the agency would contribute to language learning costs (MSOxfam, PRG, 1/13/2, 10.4.86), and as Oxfam expanded its staff in Oxford, it was expected that they too would have appropriate contextual experience: "They should have visited Latin America.... they must have good written and spoken Spanish and/or Portuguese" (MSOxfam, PRG, 2/2/1, 19.8.75).

By the mid-1970s, the agency accepted that there might be an issue with employing expatriates in these posts as opposed to local staff, but argued that the strength of the organisation lay precisely in this dialogue between Oxfam field representatives and communities in the developing countries, and that information sent back to Oxford might be "complicated when cultural and national differences also intervene" (MSOxfam, PRG, 1/12/1, 29.1.93). Intermediary mechanisms for bringing the voices of those outside the UK into discussions and policymaking in Oxfam headquarters historically took the form of paper trails from project applications to final field reports. In the early 1990s, it appeared, however, that the huge volume of reports and feedback from the field were, in practice, only rarely consulted by those at Headquarters: "The information arriving in Oxford in thousands of PASFs (Project Application Summary Forms) remains largely unused" (MSOxfam, PRG, 1/11/1.12.92). Gaining an overall institutional understanding of what Oxfam's field programmes were all about thus presented considerable problems, and by the 1990s the agency itself acknowledged a gap between "the overseas programme as understood by the field officers and the interpretation of the programme by the rest of Oxfam" (MSOxfam, PRG, 2/1/1, 1.93).

The growth and sheer geographical range of Oxfam's operations made the distance between headquarters and the field particularly difficult to manage. From the 1970s through to the early 1990s, the number of overseas Oxfam sites mushroomed. In 1991, there were over forty country and regional offices, and more than 3000 individual grants were processed in one year (MSOxfam, PRG, 2/1/1, 1.93). Given the incremental nature of this growth, there were inconsistencies between the various country offices: in Chile, a Programme Officer could be dealing with seventy-five projects, whilst in Ahmedabad, only two (MSOxfam, PRG, 1/13/7, 1991). In Latin America, Oxfam operated a regionalised structure, with a single office for six Andean countries, whilst in Africa there was a "plethora of small country offices" (MSOxfam, PRG, 2/1/1, 2.1989). These multiple and very different regional and project sites spilled over to an even broader area in the early 1990s when Oxfam came under pressure to work on the ground with other NGO networks, particularly those from the South, and to lead regional meetings on behalf of sister Oxfams (Oxfam Belgium, Oxfam Quebec, Oxfam America) that might not be represented there (MSOxfam, PRG, 1/12/1, 8.4.92; PRG, 1/13/7, 18.7.90).

In this situation, it was little wonder that those in the field complained about the pressures they were under in making meaningful contacts with communities. One reported in 1985 that he was supposed to visit two hundred projects twice a year as well as dealing with expanding administrative demands coming from Oxford (MSOxfam, PRG, 1/13/7, 22.4.85). And by 1998 there were increasing worries that distances, and the extraordinary growth in project activity were making "face-to-face opportunities" rare, with a concomitant "loss of personal relationships to solve problems… losing contact with partners" (MSOxfam, PRG, 2/3/8/31, 10.1998).

Attempts to bridge the gap between field and headquarters in the 1990s took the form of newly created intermediary management tiers—Regional Managers, or communications specialists—based in Oxford, and expected to facilitate a "two way process" (MSOxfam, PRG, 1/11/1, 6.4.93) of listening between the field and Oxfam's Headquarters and "represent the views and concerns of field staff within Oxfam debates" (MSOxfam, PRG, 1/11/1, 12.1992). Because of the variety of overseas arrangements, however, Regional Managers found that their actual relationships with Field Staff varied enormously, ranging from the Latin American case where the overseas office took the major initiative, leaving little room for the Regional Manager in Oxford, to the African experience where much smaller field offices permitted the Oxford-based manager to play a somewhat independent role. Without any discrete budgetary responsibility, these intermediaries found themselves sandwiched uncomfortably between the field and Oxford policymaking: "They felt 'at the neck of an hour glass'" (MSOxfam, PRG, 1/11/1, 17.3.93). So difficult was it to actually bring overseas stories into Oxfam's headquarters that the communications/campaigns unit in Oxford occasionally created their own fictitious frontline voices, using information gathered from various sources, in effect bypassing both regional desks and overseas specialists (MSOxfam, PRG, 1/11/1, 1.10.92). A growing imaginative gap thus opened out between the diversity and contextual differences across Oxfam's programmes of activity and the policymaking centre of the agency. With the voices of overseas communities largely positioned at the periphery of the organisational identity, there was "a gulf between policy makers and the reality of our work in the field, rhetoric and reality" (MSOxfam, PRG, 1/11/1, 14.12.92).

The extent to which these relational geographies fostered the passing and exchange of knowledge about the foreign 'other' and promoted institutional learning about the regions in which the NGO was operating was variable. In Latin America for example, as soon as Oxfam became active in the early 1970s staff reported back on what they judged to be important cultural issues: "The majority of Indians in the sierras speak Quechua or Aymara, yet with the exception of Peru… all have seen Spanish as the only language of the school system… schools are conducted in a foreign language"; "unless the Indians are taught in their own language and are helped to build up and preserve some tribal pride and cohesion there is no hope for them" (MSOxfam, PRG, 1/5/2, 11.1972–11.1973).

In broader terms, the distinctive alternative language of development spoken in Latin America and Brazil from the 1970s onwards came into the very centre of Oxfam's concerns, informing wider debates across the whole organisation. Oxfam's commitment in Latin America and Brazil at a time of considerable religious and social ferment, and the lively engagement of its Spanish and Portuguese-speaking representatives, brought a strikingly different foreign development lexicon right into the centre of Oxfam's institutional discussions and practices. During this period, Oxfam was said to be harmonising its thinking with progressive Brazilian and Latin American thinkers (MSOxfam, PRG, 1/5/2, 10.10.73), and vocabulary like '*concientización*' in Spanish or '*concientizacao*' in Portuguese were widely used in committees and reports. Senior Oxfam officers involved in Spanish-language debates on development regularly highlighted the importance of Spanish terms to describe the processes underway: '*cooperación popular*', '*informalización*' (of third world economies), '*organización de base*' (MSOxfam, PRG, 3/4/16, 1987–88). This foreign lexicon was then transferred to Oxfam's activities in other continents. For example, Field Directors in Asia were provided with helpful crib sheets: "In case you are as confused as some of us here have been by some of the ideas coming from Latin America, I am enclosing a copy of a brief and fairly succinct explanation of conscientization…" (MSOxfam, PRG, 2/2/1, 26.11.73).

By comparison, in dealings with anglophone ex-colonial African countries, this overt awareness of the cultural specificity of particular contexts of operation appeared much later in reports and policy discussions at headquarters. The agency's need to find conduits of aid that could be seen to be independent of both national governments and expatriate interference, however, encouraged a closer engagement with local ways of doing development. In Malawi for example, to avoid dealing with the repressive Hastings Banda government, Oxfam began to work with the University of Malawi Centre for Social Research, under the leadership of Louis Msukwa, "about the most knowledgeable Malawian there is in social development issues" (MSOxfam, PRG, 3/5/11, 11.12.84). Msukwa also provided Oxfam with its 1986 review of the country. His

Mulanje project, involving six Malawian researchers who stayed in villages for four months, specifically included a training programme to help local researchers explain the project to their communities in Chichewa. This initiative in effect employed local languages as a means of sharing development responsibility, "a process which enables people to take more control of their lives" (Trivedy, 1990, p. vii). In the wake of these changes, Malawian languages and concepts began to appear within Oxfam institutional documents in the 1990s. Future programme plans specifically noted the range of languages spoken by the majority of Malawians, as opposed to the small number of people who spoke English, and reports on Oxfam activity included quotations in Chichewa—"*Mutu umodzi susenza denga*" ("one head cannot carry a roof")—together with discussions of Malawian/Chichewa formulations of leadership (MSOxfam, PRG, 3/8/10, 26.11.96, 5.4.98).

Like other NGOs in the sector, the ways in which Oxfam staff framed their listening relationships on the ground were strongly influenced from the mid-1980s onwards by the key role of the government as donor, and concomitant expectations that agencies must be seen to be publicly responsible for taxpayers' money. This need for accountability contributed to a metadiscourse of evaluation and feedback, expressed in English, adding to the already burgeoning Anglo-dominated lexicon of aid and development (Cornwall & Eade, 2010). An examination of Oxfam's pioneering guidance for its Field Directors from 1985 onwards shows a tendency to try to standardise the ways in which Oxfam officers interacted with their local communities, using contemporary development lexis to express these relationships. Thus, the 1985 Field Directors' Handbook provided the previously autonomous Field Directors with clear directions on target audiences, and a checklist of questions in relation to each. The long section on 'Communication' defined the activity as "the interaction between those promoting change and the people with whom they work", and set out the function, channels and strategies of communication in ways seemingly uninflected by distinct contexts or cultures (Boyden & Prat, 1985). By 1995, the Handbook was offering reframings that critiqued previous participation shibboleths, and proposed to Oxfam personnel a new set of ethnographic tools derived from Participatory Rural Appraisal (PRA) to encourage more meaningful contact. The vocabulary (together with the corresponding acronyms)—Capacities and Vulnerabilities Analysis (CVA), Gender Framework Analysis (GFA), Environmental Impact Assessment (EIA), Logical Framework Analysis (LFA) and Cost-effectiveness Analysis (CEA)—equipped Oxfam workers with a structure implicitly assumed to be valid for any community or country. Diversity and particularity, the specific cultural contours of the regions and the multilingualism of the areas tended to recede (Oxfam Handbook, 1995).

Listening relationships between Oxfam and the field were increasingly enacted through the tools of accountability. Oxfam Evaluation Officers called for a systematised transfer of data; records of informal discussions, and details of meetings logged through diaries (MSOxfam, PRG, 1/13/7, 6.1991). By 1995, this had been reformulated into a number of listening indicators to measure participation: "How closely and how well programmes listen to those they are trying to support and thereby increase their 'porosity' to feedback? To what degree do programmes 'triangulate' information…?" (MSOxfam, PRG, 2/1/1, 1995–97). Although the expectation was that this higher standard of reporting would be positive in requiring a deeper understanding of the local situation, it inevitably framed the Oxfam/local community listening relationship as one which was both extractive and monolingual, with information required by the NGO named in English and taken out of the community for the purposes of evaluation (MSOxfam, PRG, 1/13/2, 1.1985). Whilst deriving its authority from Western models, the approach tended to be presented organisationally as objective and neutral, a kind of universal aid and development language, expressed in English, which at least some within Oxfam regarded with considerable suspicion (MSOxfam, PRG, 1/11/1, 27.11.92).

In this situation, the linguistic diversity of Oxfam's transcultural exchanges struggled to be heard in the organisation. Requests for project funding from local communities had traditionally arrived at Oxfam headquarters drafted in European languages. In 1973, the Overseas Director, calling it "such a simple matter that I hesitate to raise it", mentioned the case of one would-be applicant for funds who had not applied because he was unable to write in English. By 1991, however, it seemed that the institutional language of choice was still English (MSOxfam, PRG, 1/13/7, 6.1991). In 1986, when it embarked on an institutional programme of 'Knowledge of Oxfam' courses outside the UK, feedback suggested that more linguistic openness was needed across the whole organisation: "Inadequacies of English as the exclusive medium are often a barrier to effective communication" (MSOxfam, PRG, 1/13/3, 24.9.86). The dilemma faced by Oxfam was how it would be able to encourage narrative plurality within what was now a large global organisation: "We would expect each region to have its own flavour and distinctive configuration of programme/skills/size/spread/etc. However, it is essential to the success of Oxfam's Globalisation project… that the staff of every Region feel and behave primarily as part of a larger whole, as part of a global Oxfam, rather than primarily as part of a local Oxfam…" (MSOxfam, PRG, 2/1/1, 1999–2004). By this stage, overseas Oxfam staff were raising issues around "the multi-cultural nature of Oxfam and steps to make Oxfam a more multicultural organisation" (MSOxfam, PRG, 1/12/1, 23.3.93), and how in practice equitable cross-cultural working could be fostered (MSOxfam, PRG, 1/13/7, 6.8.90).

In 1990, the very process of consulting Oxfam staff throughout the world regarding the direction that a globalised and regionalised Oxfam should be taking revealed how difficult it was for the organisation to listen to voices that were not anglophone. To begin with, there was a major cultural problem in assuming that Western-derived concepts of strategic planning could be uncritically translated into a variety of different regional contexts. Consultative documents for Oxfam's Strategic Review were not accessible to many of those working with Oxfam worldwide. Whilst some papers were translated into French and Spanish, others were not, "many teams did not work in English, and this meant translating the draft plans into English, translating comments on the draft, re-drafting in the original language, working on the document, and then re-translating it". And given how complex much of the material was, ownership of the translation tended to rest with senior staff whose first language was English (MSOxfam, PRG, 1/13/7, 6.91). Whilst consultative staff workshops suggested that "Oxfam is a multilingual organisation with English as the primary language", there was no shared institutional idea of what this actually meant as regards language/translation (MSOxfam, PRG, 2/3/8/31, 10.98).

In general, the institutional approach to linguistic translation tended to be ad hoc. For example, in 1986 Oxfam considered adopting a policy to translate all its books into French and Spanish, with the potential addition of Portuguese and Arabic, but the cost was deemed prohibitive (MSOxfam, PRG, 1/13/3, 15.12.86). By the time the organisation was preparing for its major restructuring and regionalisation exercise ('Globalised and regionalised Oxfam') in the late 1990s, it was evident that there was still no formal translation policy, but rather a variety of practices funded by different budgets, translating documents mainly into French, Spanish, Portuguese, Arabic and English, with 'grey' publications for local/national use often translated into local or regional languages (MSOxfam, PRG, 2/3/8/31, 10.98). Given that corporate documents, books, journals, press statements and internal documents would now need to be shared across the whole global organisation, recognition grew in 1998 that some coherent language policy had to be developed: "It is clear…. that translation (including interpretation services) is a key Strategic Area for Oxfam's communications in a regionalised and globalized Oxfam" (MSOxfam, PRG, 2/3/8/31, 10.98).

Oxfam's transnational imaginary, as shaped by its history, was characterised by a spatial distancing of its overseas sites, and the framing of its relations with the foreign 'other' through an apparently neutral universal language of development, spoken in English. As it grew worldwide, Oxfam sought to perform the role of a multicultural institution, whilst at the same time retaining an implicit allegiance to monolingual practices:

> The issues of choosing which language to work in and coping with the lack of professional translators have dogged Oxfam for years. While it is a multicultural organisation, English is still the dominant medium, and many field staff are excluded from key debates because they lack proficiency in English. Oxfam has never been able to decide whether to use English and recruit and train staff in English, or whether to be multi-lingual and invest in translation resources, which would be costly. The problems and conflicts of language come up in every major exercise undertaken by the organisation, and yet the issue continues to be unresolved. (Burden & Wallace, 1994, p. 28)

Christian Aid

Unlike OxfamGB's origins in a committee of concerned individuals, Christian Aid drew its roots from institutions, major British and Irish church groups and organisations that had sought to alleviate suffering in liberated Europe. These bodies formed an ad hoc Christian Reconstruction in Europe agency in 1943 which merged with the British Council of Churches (BCC) Refugee Committee in 1949 to become a department of the BCC, later renamed the Inter-Church Aid Service. In 1952, Janet Lacey (1970), who had worked in the Youth Department of the

BCC, became the director of the organisation which would, in recognition of the success of its Christian Aid week in 1957, formally become Christian Aid in 1964. Whilst Oxfam moved quite rapidly from the use of intermediary organisations to a system of field offices, personnel on the ground and frontline activity, from its inception Christian Aid worked indirectly through a widely spread network of coalitions and partner groups. For Christian Aid, the concept of 'partnership', which marked its early origins, remained "not, for us, a matter of convenience but of principle" (Christian Aid, 2006, p. 3).

Constitutionally, Christian Aid operated as the overseas agency of the national British Council of Churches, working through the auspices of an international coalition based in Geneva, the World Council of Churches (WCC). Murray (1970) suggests that when the WCC decided in 1949 to extend its activity beyond Europe to other parts of the world, in particular those areas emerging from colonisation, the aid arm of the Council rapidly became its largest department, supported by a constellation of committees in individual countries across the world, of which Christian Aid was to be the UK component. The Christian Aid archivist, introducing the first deposited documents of the organisation, explained that, "Unlike other agencies, Christian Aid has no projects of its own or representatives overseas; it works entirely through local structures, mainly churches or voluntary organisations, or relies on a regional screening of projects by experts (cooperates with WCC)" (CA, Deposit Introduction, 9.1984-1.85).

Given that Christian Aid was the agency of the British Council of Churches, its early programmes extended particular help to foreign churches; in 1969, for example, thirty-six inter-church aid projects were being supported (CA, 2/D/3/4, 1969). Nevertheless, as the organisation increasingly drew its funds from a broader public, a distinction would be made between 'inter-church aid', aimed at strengthening minority churches, and other development projects:

> Work of development, rehabilitation and relief is financed with donations from all sources. But grants to church institutions for other purposes are made only from gifts of church people supporting Christian Aid's full range of commitments. (CA, 2/D/3/4, 1970s)

As the agency gained experience in the newly independent ex-British colonies, the need to overtly separate development aid from traditional missionary endeavour became even more evident. There was "a clear assumption that the old missionary days are gone, and only a limited number of expatriates should now be used" (CA, 2/A/1/5, 5.1973).

In the early years, although some project applications came to Christian Aid directly, most were received via "the worldwide network of churches and councils centred on the WCC" (CA, J/1, 1.1981, 1982). The process of decision-making on funding generally involved a discussion among WCC representatives, and then a dialogue between WCC officials and Christian Aid on the basis of a list of potentially suitable projects: "The size of our contribution will depend necessarily on the commitments that you obtain from other donor agencies" (CA, 2/A/1/8, 14.11.72). Assessing the feasibility of prospective programmes was normally the responsibility of the WCC: "Christian Aid has not the staff to perform its own feasibility studies so that projects through the WCC or the other agencies are usually accepted as feasible unless a review indicates obvious problem or inconsistencies" (CA, 2/D/13/6, 9.1972). When funding had been allocated, this arm's length managerial approach was largely continued: "once committed to a project Christian Aid exercises little further control over its progress. Reports are usually received direct from the project site and in some cases reports are also prepared by WCC staff" (CA, 2/D/13/6, 9.1972). The procedure, the agency suggested, was not unlike a simple money transfer operation, using the WCC as a channel for sending funding to selected projects (CA, 2/D/13/6, 9.1972).

This indirect operational model meant that programmes were seldom led on the ground or overseen by workers from the agency: "Christian Aid itself recruits people for work overseas only very rarely, as most of the projects with which we are associated find their personnel through organisations geared for this, i.e. Government, Missionary Societies, Volunteer Schemes" (CA, 2/D/14/9, 14.8.74). Whilst Christian Aid employees often had knowledge and experience of key areas, the existence of an international intermediary body like the WCC enabled the agency to administer a sizeable overseas programme with the minimum of staff, and without needing direct institutional contact with projects in the countries concerned. The role of local partner ecumenical coalitions was of primary importance.

It was recognised however that such a system necessarily favoured countries with effective Christian Councils, whilst those without ecumenical committees tended to be ignored. A review of Christian Aid in

1972 indeed argued that eight African countries had received no support at all from Christian Aid, whereas 66.5% of its funding had been disbursed to six relatively developed countries (in all probability ex-British colonies) (CA, 2/D/13/6, 9.1972). In addition, public criticism of WCC aid practices encouraged Christian Aid to recognise the increasing importance of a more direct engagement with the actual sites of development programmes rather than relying solely on information mediated by a third party:

> ...it is not enough to sit in London and only listen to the voices coming up to us through the official ecumenical channels. We must I feel go out and establish close relationships with the church groups that we work with in the Third World in order to enable us better to understand their priorities and problems. (CA, 2/D/28/2)

By 1974, with the growing pressures of accountability, and with local coalitions developing in confidence, Christian Aid began to review its managerial model:

> ... we will have to accept more responsibility for building up and maintaining relationships with partners in the third world... the doctrine to which Christian Aid has for a long time subscribed - "Christian Aid can have such a small overseas aid administration because we work through the ecumenical church structure... and rely on them to do most of the work for us" is no longer strictly true... we must have more capacity in our department. (CA, 2/D/28/2, 6.5.1974)

When the Sinclair Commission took evidence from key staff in the mid-1970s, there was a sense that more knowledge of overseas programmes was now needed, albeit mediated through partners: "a wide range of contacts worldwide to enable Christian Aid to be as aware as possible of the networks, relationships, problems and movements within the churches and ecumenical groups overseas" (CA, 2/D/28/2, 1973).

As well as its changing network of partner groups outside the UK, Christian Aid operated within a domestic nexus of church groups, representing itself to them as "the normal way by which Christians respond to the needs of their fellow Christians and those whom they serve" (CA, J/1, 3.1966). By 1975, however, "only a proportion of Christian Aid income came from a well-defined Christian source", a point emphasised by the relative sums of money derived from public appeals at Christmas and in Christian Aid week, as opposed to finance from denominational appeals and legacies (CA, 2/D/28/2, 12.2.75, 17.12.74). Nevertheless, liaising with church groups was key to the organisation, and took up considerable staff time; a Christian Aid week in the early 1970s might involve forming 2300 voluntary aid committees (CA, 2/D/13/6, 9.1972) with Area Secretaries arranging meetings and conferences to investigate "what Christians in Britain can do to help (people in the developing world) to control their destiny and master their own economic problems" (CA, 2/D/13/1, spring 1974). Listening to what the broad coalition of national church communities understood by development often placed Christian Aid in a difficult position, particularly in the late 1970s and 1980s because the WCC adopted a more radical funding policy and attracted press accusations of aligning itself with liberation movements in Latin America and South Africa. Christian Aid Week campaigners reported resistance to giving in many quarters on the grounds that "Christian Aid supports terrorists" (CA, 2/D/13/1, autumn 1974), and the organisation increasingly found itself being forced to check with the WCC on the exact nature of its aid; was money for the medical needs of Frelimo guerrillas, for example, actually freeing up other funds for war? (CA, 2/A/1/7, 14.06.74). In this context, listening to the coalition of church communities in the UK was represented as a matter of education for them, rather than for the agency:

> The constraints on Christian Aid policy are imposed by the answer to the question "What Christian partners do you choose to cooperate with in developing countries?" The more radical the partner, the greater the tension between what he sees as his priorities and what the conventional contributor in Britain intends. One of the justifications for Christian Aid's educational work is to narrow this gap. (CA, 2/D/28/2, 17.12.74)

Rather than Loy's (2015) representation of the agency's history as a linear move from faith, to secular development ideology, and then back to faith under the leadership of Dr Williams, it seems more accurate to picture Christian Aid historically as positioned within a complicated network of church congregations at home, and coalitions and partners overseas. The spatial mapping of Christian Aid created a highly complex imaginary in which the foreign 'other' on the ground would be apprehended at one remove through the medium of trusted groupings or partners.

Christian Aid, like Oxfam, was clearly subject to pressures and demands from the institutional and government donors with whom it began to deal, and the resulting quasi-universalist language of accountability adopted throughout large parts of the sector. The evidence of the archives, however, suggests that actors in Christian Aid also framed exchanges with their multiple sites of development within another discourse, a perceived explicit common language of the church. The extent to which this common language of church membership was seen as central to the transnational imaginary varied over the years. The organisation was a signatory for example to the Haslemere Declaration in March 1968, which called for a new discourse to interpret the evils of poverty within and outside the UK, and made no reference at all to the language of the church (CA, J/1), and Loy has argued that by the early twenty-first century:

> Christian Aid adopted the dominant secular discourse of development to the point that, when attending my staff induction in early 2009, I was told that the disassociation of Churches Together in Britain and Ireland from Christian Aid was "the best thing that has happened to us as an organisation". (Loy, 2015, p. 14)

Nevertheless, there is a constant theme in the agency's narrative that its vast network of partners across the world were:

> ... united to us not by shared experience in history for they have lived through quite different dramas and adventures than we have, and life looks vastly different to them from the way it presents itself to us. What unites us is this endless search for discipleship to Jesus Christ, how to serve our neighbour in the terms in which Jesus has disclosed. (CA, 2/D/5, 1973)

Historically, the organisation was imagined as a conduit through which churches in the UK would learn about Christian communities in the Third World. One approach to facilitating such transnational crossings was what some termed 'ecumenical travel', a way of bringing together churches in different cultural contexts. What was vital in this process was an acceptance of the discomfort of these intermediate cognitive spaces designed "to explore new ways of and new understandings of relationships between corporate bodies" (CA, 2/D/18/1, 10.1974). The model was that of being "in solidarity with each other even if we do not understand each other. The theologies in Latin America, Africa and Asia will probably not be after Western European taste... to learn from each other by patient probing and listening" (CA, 2/D/23, 1975). If there was a sense of the potentialities of exchanging religious experience, any productive interplay between theologies of the North and those of the South within Christian Aid discussions took some considerable time to materialise. Debates on religion and development were traditionally framed within parameters derived from the Global North (Christian Aid, 2010), and it was not until 2012 that the organisation looked overtly at the implications of other ways of thinking about development from the particular perspectives of theologians living in the Global South (Clifford, 2012).

By the 2000s, transnational exchanges between Christian Aid and communities in the South were, like those of Oxfam, increasingly expressed in the universalist language of monitoring and evaluation. The imaginative distance between London and the overseas field was still reflected at one remove through the presence of intermediary partners, but relational proximity was arguably diminishing. Staff working in the field claimed that the monitoring procedures they were being given "came from Christian Aid's auditors, not from programme staff, most of whom had hitherto eschewed them as unnecessary, given Christian Aid's relatively successful partnership tradition" (McGee, 2010, p. 643). In this situation, the local contexts of development would require "translating in Babel; brokering across an abyss" (McGee, 2010, p. 640) if they were to be shared across the institution.

Christian Aid's managerial tradition of indirect working through coalitions and partners, allied with its dual languages (accountability and an assumed common language of the church), doubtless contributed to the low salience accorded to the linguistic foreignness of the local contexts of development, as revealed in the archives. Initially, the organisation was seldom a direct employer of staff in the field. The WCC, rather than Christian Aid, generally established job descriptions for employees, and these often included a requirement for language and cultural understanding. For example, a call for a volunteer in Cusco specified that: "Should the volunteer already have Spanish, or show remarkable linguistic ability, s/he could learn Quechua – there are good courses in Cusco" (CA, 4/G/14/3, 17.9.80). The WCC itself had a formal language policy (English, French and German) and its own well-established language unit with translation and interpretation facilities (Dönch, 2008). In 1975, the WCC launched a highly professional two-week course in Lomé for African translators and interpreters with seventeen participants from Sierra Leone, Togo, Ghana, Nigeria, Cameroon, Zaïre, Kenya and Madagascar, as well as sponsors from Denmark, Germany, Nigeria and Madagascar.

Whilst the course itself concentrated on French/English interpretation, the tutors encouraged students to "find new ways of developing the use of African languages in their own countries because a language expresses the personality of a linguistic community" (CA, 2/A/1/3, 23.3-6.6.75).

Historically, Christian Aid's transnational imaginary appeared to have implicitly subcontracted the linguistic foreignness of its development spaces to others, either to intermediary coalitions like the WCC, or to partner s operating on the ground. The problematics of listening to the foreign 'other' were subsumed within a managerial model of partnership, and an institutional policy which was largely monolingual, albeit with some recognition of the need for inclusivity. As suggested by a contemporary Christian Aid staff member:

> ... it is about being networked into local societies. It is having staff who by virtue of being mainly local nationals in the country where they work have the ability to have, to engage directly with the people we seek to help so we reduce the number of layers that are in between us and the communities we seek to serve.... and I think it's therefore so important that when we work on internal conversation, and particularly clarifying concepts and developing strategy, that we do so in, although it's primarily in English, that we do so in such a way that is not sort of widening the divide but invites people in and invites people to contribute. (Interview CA5, manager, 26.5.17)

Tearfund

In 1968, some twenty years after the formation of Christian Aid and Oxfam, a new organisation, Tearfund, was launched. Whereas the older agencies had been born in response to the misery of war, and then moved their activities into the area of development, Tearfund entered the aid sector with the express aim of filling what they perceived to be a gap left in the field of development by agencies like Oxfam and Christian Aid: "Many Christians were convinced that money given should not be lost in world systems, governments, the World Council of Churches and the like. Other agencies such as Oxfam and Save the Children did good work but were not Christian" (Macaulay, cited in Hollow, 2008, p. 18). Tearfund's origins were thus explicitly faith-based, rooted in the long-running debate in evangelical circles about the priority Christians should give to social concerns, as opposed to spiritual needs. The NGO's immediate forerunner, the Evangelical Alliance's Refugee Fund, had been established as a way in which "gifts from churches and individuals may be distributed to evangelical agencies in different parts of the world that are engaged in caring for the material and spiritual needs of refugees" (Alliance Executive Council, 1.1960, cited in Hollow, 2008, p. 19). In 1968, the Fund adopted the name 'Tearfund' and, with the support of high-profile Christians like Cliff Richards, began to extend its remit to a broader range of projects with mailed-out appeals to churches in the UK seeking financial support. By 1973, eighty percent of its aid was allocated to long-term programmes.

Whilst the now extensive literature on the role of faith in development (Clarke, 2013; Clarke & Jennings, 2008; Clarke, Ware, & Ware, 2016; Rakodi, 2012) has largely concentrated on the links between an explicit faith base and processes of development, it has not concerned itself, as this chapter will do, with the transnational imaginary of such an organisation, i.e. Tearfund's perceptions of distance from/proximity to the overseas field, and the ways in which the institution's transnational exchanges were enacted and supported.

The early decision-making processes of the agency showed the central role played in Tearfund's history by missionary societies and the personal contacts these had already established in particular countries. For example, the first people who were directly funded by the organisation to work overseas perceived themselves to be operating not through Tearfund but through the South American Missionary Society (SAMS): "My connection at that time was very much with SAMS. I viewed the Tearfund connection more as support to bolster the responsibility I had taken with SAMS…" (McKerney, cited in Hollow, 2008, p. 90). In 1973, eighty percent of Tearfund's resources were still being channelled through missionary societies: "The very early days were undoubtedly more missionary-oriented because we really did not have access to the indigenous churches" (Macaulay, cited in Hollow, 2008, p. 86). Whilst Tearfund initially drew on the previous relationships formed by missionaries, the agency gradually began to designate local churches as its operative bodies overseas: "Projects must… be related to the life of the church, and not merely facilitate the activities of individual missionaries" (Tearfund letter to Missionary Societies, cited in Hollow, 2008, p. 92). Tearfund's own perception of its history places the local church, and relations with it, as a constant at the centre of the agency's transnational imaginary:

> We believe that the local church is best placed to deliver this kind of development: it is embedded in the local community, trusted, respected, influential, with an incredibly long reach and members motivated to see lives transformed. This means the drive for tackling poverty is locally owned and its momentum is sustainable. (Tearfund, 2019, p. 8)

As it increasingly professionalised its activities, Tearfund sought to provide new conduits for the voices of local churches to be heard in its own central decision-making procedures. It appointed regional advisers who were national Christians rather than UK expatriates (Hollow, 2008, p. 98) and established a Partner Panel to feed directly into its strategy-making: "The idea was to give our partners a voice in the way we ran the whole organisation, to recognise them as key stakeholders and to hear their perspective, because it was often different from our own perspective but really important" (Balfour, 2005, cited in Hollow, 2008, p. 101).

From the mid-1970s onwards, the approach of working directly with indigenous church organisations stimulated the growth of development sections within local churches, an innovation which revealed in some cases—the Kale Heywet church in Ethiopia (Dalelo, 2003), for example—the unresolved tensions that could arise in evangelical circles between the demands of spiritual work and those of social action. To meet these challenges, Freeman (2018) suggests, Tearfund increasingly moved to embrace a conceptualisation of development understood as transformation within an integral holistic mission. Crucially, the methodology associated with this would be centred on micro-relationships in the overseas regions, relying on the local church itself as the main agent of transformation. By the early 2000s, Tearfund's modus operandi envisaged a process of discussion and training sessions within the particular local church, leading outwards to the community, and then on to the formulation of shared plans to change lives.

Cognitively, these mission working methods were rooted in an imaginary that owed much to the foreign 'other', influenced as it was by the writings of Latin American evangelical theologians like the Ecuadorian René Padilla. Padilla, who would indeed become Tearfund's International President in 1998, had reflected at length on a philosophy of evangelism and social activism which could respond to the challenges of Liberation Theology (Kirkpatrick, 2016). Encounters with the 'other' in this imaginary were cognitively situated in the evangelical notion of 'servant leadership', with its emphasis on listening and learning (Ouedraogo, cited in Hollow, 2008, p. 98).

The stress on relationality within a very local church community was reflected in conscious attempts to recognise the multilingual diversity of development activities, and to provide specific support in enacting these exchanges. Whether the impetus for such initiatives was more clearly related to Tearfund's missionary origins, to its 'servant-hearted' vision, or to a methodology that prioritised the micro is unclear, but the organisation was said by some of its key workers to have always demonstrated "a great respect for other local languages" (Interview, ex-member of staff 3, 14.7.17). From the late 1980s, Tearfund produced a range of publications specifically designed to disseminate information to local communities in an accessible form through informative newsletters (*Footsteps*), toolkits (*Roots*) and guides (*Pillars*), all of which would be available in local languages.

Much of the inspiration for these language support activities came from the research of one particular staff member, Isabel Carter (1999a), who had concluded, on the basis of fieldwork in Uganda and Ghana, that there was "an enormous, largely unmet hunger for relevant agricultural information", and that locally generated 'more widely appropriate materials in local languages' could be shared, and have potentially wide effects (Carter, 1999b, pp. 115–116). From an original print run of 1000 in 1986, the newsletter *Footsteps* grew to around 50,000 copies, produced in seven languages (Hollow, 2008, p. 108). In 2010, the magazine had a back-catalogue of ninety-seven editions and had been translated into French, Spanish, Portuguese, Hindi, Bangla and Burmese, as well as several local languages. The objective was to enable readers to make practical use of the advice contained in each issue—how to build a bicycle trailer, digging pit latrines—within formal and informal training sessions in their own local contexts. A survey of *Footsteps* readership between 2012 and 2014 noted that "Footsteps is unique not primarily because of its content but because of its target audience. There is a lot of information being disseminated by the development sector but participants often commented on how *Footsteps* spoke to them in their context" (*Footsteps*, 2015, p. 5).

Underpinning this support for transnational exchanges was a conception of interlingual translation itself as a form of self-empowerment. Workshops were set up in the regions to translate some of Tearfund's key publications, the aim being to translate together, with and alongside people in the communities, rather than seeking to translate for them:

> The "Pillars" process doesn't use translators.... The plan was always that... people should translate themselves, and you had three levels of check, well, four levels of check in some ways, built in. You'd have, people would always work in twos and threes, in a workshop, that was always the first thing. Then their work would always be checked with another small group. Then at the workshop you'd pull out who were obviously the better people, the more skilled in the writing and use of language who would become a little editorial committee, so they would check the final draft. And then there would always be an outside person who would double-check it. So you had all those levels to check what was being done. (Interview, ex-member of staff 3, 14.7.17)

Unlike OxfamGB and Christian Aid where the place of translation was either marginal or totally occluded, Tearfund situated the interlingual exchange of information as itself being a means of empowerment:

> The sort of passion and the empowerment that people would feel when their little, tiny ignored language was taken seriously and they were able to translate it, you know, was so empowering to people. I mean that's not the international languages... Some of the first languages that we translated, people could not believe that it was possible for them to a) to do translation themselves, which was what "Pillars" was all about, and b) that this could be actually made available... (Interview, ex-member of staff 3, 14.7.17)

The 'Pillars' experience with its series of funded workshops encouraged participants to work independently, selecting their own materials and working in groups to translate together without input from professional outsiders (Carter & Carter, n.d.). Development in these terms was a process of vernacularisation rooted in interlingual translation.

Whilst this understanding of translation as part of community empowerment was unusual in the sector—Tearfund's Learning Zone (Tearfund, n.d.) is also remarkable today, hosting material in eight languages—it would be fair to say that the story the agency itself tells about its past has tended to position this linguistic support of transnational exchanges at the periphery of its main historical journey. Indeed, only four pages of Hollow's (2008) 216-page history of Tearfund is devoted to the *Footsteps* project (pp. 107–110), and staff most closely involved with the original initiative clearly felt that it had been a struggle to mainstream the work within the institution:

> We were never at the core of what Tearfund did, and yet the impact of the publication, which was so well supported and lots of stuff was contributed by the staff and by partners, the impact of that was such that it was kind of drawn into Tearfund but it was never at the heart of the planning I suppose, and I think that was always a bit of a frustration, really. (Interview, ex-member of staff 3, 14.7.17)

Conclusions

In the histories of these NGOs, there are clear phases which they shared in common with each other, as well as with other agencies in the sector: the evolution from aid-directed work to a greater engagement with development activities; the professionalisation of NGO activity, linked to the responses to donor requirements for greater accountability in programmes; and the recent problematics of organising globally. What has also emerged, however, is the distinct histories of their transnational relationships, the ways in which they gradually developed perspectives on the foreign 'other', and the 'power, politics and learning' (Lewis, 2009, p. 43) that these listening histories imply.

The imaginative distance between the NGO headquarters and the communities with whom the agency worked has varied over time. In an organisation like OxfamGB, close face-to-face listening was initially conducted by staff on the ground who fed back their experiences, framed by the context of the specific cultures concerned. Gradually, however, with the organisation's incremental growth, it was seen as more difficult to sustain close listening relationships and ensure that the voices of those in the communities were able to be heard in Oxford, and thus influence policy discussions and institutional change. In Christian Aid, the agency's history, rooted in partnerships and coalitions, tended to construct a vicarious listening relationship where interchange between the INGO and the local communities was indirect and mediated by others. In Tearfund, the organisation's close historic links to missionary societies and local churches constructed a set of more atomised local Listening Zones, intimately linked to the transformation methodology adopted by the agency.

The extent to which learning from the overseas field was perceived as valuable by the Northern NGO and permeated its thinking was variable too. In the cases of OxfamGB and Tearfund, it was clear that Latin American development movements associated with Liberation Theology or its evangelical counterparts were directly responsible for key changes to practice. On the other hand, the historic colonial closeness of Britain to parts of Africa seemed to delay understanding of the distinctly different contributions that these countries might make to development thinking. Enacting and managing transnational exchanges implied adopting discourses that would support mutual listening. In each of the NGOs, the lexicon of monitoring and evaluation became a frequent conveyer of listening practices, with the power implications intrinsic in these asymmetrical relationships seldom being questioned.

In Christian Aid and Tearfund, the salience of an additional language of encounter, that of the common church or faith, on occasions served as a supplementary vehicle for listening. In Oxfam GB, the diverse linguistic foreignness of the sites in which the NGO operated was overlain by the apparently universalist language of development accountability. The agency perceived itself as global and strove to reconcile the variety of cultures with which it was engaged within a unified institutional vision. The process of creating this vision, however, did not involve any lengthy critique of the monolingualism of the organisation, nor any review of its implications for Oxfam's language/translation policy. Christian Aid positioned transnational exchanges within its partnership model, effectively ceding direct responsibility for listening to intermediary groups within what remained a largely monolingual organisation. Of these three NGOs, only Tearfund, with its localist focus, showed an explicit awareness of the languages of the regions in which it was working, committed itself to translating information widely, and used the process of translation itself as a means of local empowerment.

These histories raise vital issues about the ways in which NGOs construct their Listening Zones today. Firstly, there is the role of spatial imaginings which historically have produced close or distant relationships between the NGO as an institution and its communities of practice. Secondly, there are the perceptions of the cultural diversities of context, and the various languages of listening employed by an NGO—the universalist lexicon of development speak, an assumed common language of church or faith, or the English language itself—which have served to flatten out and homogenise diversity, thereby affecting any listening relationship. Thirdly, there is the extent of institutional awareness of the foreignness in development sites which is reflected in the languages spoken on the ground. These mediate the voices of the communities, which historically have been ignored, left for others to deal with, or creatively embedded in the process of empowerment. The Listening Zones of development today are formed by temporality, by the practices of the past, and by the institutional stories that actors have told about themselves: "history shapes *how* we think, not just what we think. And how we think has profound implications for the way in which we behave" (Davey & Scriven, 2015, p. 117).

References

Black, M. (1992). *A cause for our times. Oxfam: The first 50 years.* Oxford: Oxfam.

Blaney, D. L., & Inayatullah, N. (2004). *International relations and the problem of difference.* New York: Routledge.

Bond. (2015). *Tomorrow's World. How might megatrends in development affect the future roles of UK-based INGOs?* London: Bond.

Boyden J., & Prat, B. (1985). *The field directors' handbook: An Oxfam manual for development workers.* Oxford: for Oxfam by OUP.

Burden T., & Wallace, T. (1994). *Strategic planning review* (Oxfam Research Paper 10). Oxford: Oxfam.

CA, Christian Aid (SOAS, University of London)-

Deposit Introduction, P. M. Housego (archivist), September 1984–January 1985.

2/A/1/3 Africa: Education, WCC, 1975.

2/A/1/5 Africa: Urban industrial mission 1971–73.

2/A/1/7 WCC reports/policy 1974–81.

2/A/1/8 Africa Desk WCC 1971–74.

2/D/3/4 Christian Aid Board Projects Sub Committee 1970.

2/D/5 National staff consultation 1974.

2/D/13/1 British Council of Churches meetings 1974.

2/D/13/6 Review of Management of Christian Aid 1972–1973, 1972–74.

2/D/14/9 Liberation movements 1974.

2/D/18/1 Staff correspondence: overseas aid administration 1974.

2/D/23 Overseas Aid Department, 1975.

2/D/28/2 Working papers 1974–75; draft Sinclair Report.

4/G/14/3 Peru 1980–85.

J/1 Annual Reports and publications 1960–84.

Carter, I. (1999a). *Factors influencing agricultural information flow within farmer groups in Uganda and Ghana* (Unpublished Ph.D. thesis). University of Leeds, Leeds.

Carter, I. (1999b). *Locally generated printed materials in agriculture: Experience from Uganda and Ghana* (Educational Research Paper No. 31). London: DFID.
Carter, I., & Carter, M. (n.d.). *Pillars workbook.* Retrieved from: https://learn.tearfund.org/~/media/files/tilz/publications/pillars/english/pillars/pillars/_workbook_eng.pdf?la=en.
Christian Aid. (2006). *Turning hope into action: A vision of a world free from poverty: 2005–2010 Strategic framework.* London: Christian Aid.
Christian Aid. (2010). *Theology and international development.* London: Christian Aid.
Clarke, G., & Jennings, M. (Eds.). (2008). *Development, civil Society & faith-based organisations: Bridging the sacred and the secular.* Basingstoke: Palgrave Macmillan.
Clarke, M. (2013). Good works and God's work: A case study of churches and community development in Vanuatu. *Asia Pacific Viewpoint, 54*(3), 340–351.
Clarke, M., Ware, A., & Ware, V. A. (2016). Domains of faith impact: How "faith" is perceived to shape faith-based international development organisations. *Development in Practice, 26*(3), 321–333.
Clifford, P. (2012). *Theology from the Global South. Perspectives on Christian Aid's work.* Retrieved from: https://www.christianaid.org.uk/sites/default/files/2017-08/theology-global-south-perspectives-christian-aid-work-april-2012.pdf.
Cornwall, A., & Eade, D. (2010). *Deconstructing development discourse: Buzzwords and fuzzwords.* Rugby: Practical Action Publishing with OxfamGB.
Dalelo, A. (2003). *The church and socio-economic transformation: The impacts of the community development services of the Ethiopian Kale Heywet Church.* Addis Ababa: Ethiopian Kale Heywet Church.
Davey, E., & Scriven, K. (2015). Humanitarian aid in the archives: Introduction. *Disasters, 39*(S2), S113–S128.
Davies, T. (2013). *NGOs: A new history of transnational civil society.* London: Hurst.
Dönch, R. (2008). The language policy of the WCC. *Ecumenical Review, 60*(4), 394–403.
Duffield, M. (1997). NGO relief in war zones: Towards an analysis of the new aid paradigm. *Third World Quarterly, 18*(3), 527–542.
Duffield, M. (2019). *Post-humanitarianism: Governing precarity in the digital world.* Cambridge: Polity Press.
Eyben, R. (2006). *Relationships for aid.* London: Earthscan.
Footsteps. (2015). *Readership survey 2012–2014.* Teddington: Tearfund.
Freeman, D. (2018). From "Christians doing development" to " doing Christian development": The changing role of religion in the international work of Tearfund. *Development in Practice, 28*(2), 280–291.

Hollow, M. (2008). *A future and a hope: The story of Tearfund, and why God wants the church to change the world*. Oxford: Monarch Books.

Kirkpatrick, D. (2016). C. René Padilla and the origins of integral mission in post war Latin America. *Journal of Ecclesiastical History, 67*(2), 351–371.

Lacey, J. (1970). *A cup of water: The story of Christian Aid*. London: Hodder & Stoughton.

Lewis, D. (2009). International development and the "perpetual present": Anthropological approaches to the re-historicization of policy. *European Journal of Development Research, 21*(1), 32–46.

Loy, C. (2015). *Resurrection beyond the secular: Pursuing a theological paradigm of international development* (Unpublished Ph.D. Thesis). King's College, London.

Massey, D. (2006). *For space*. London: Sage.

McGee, R. (2010). An international NGO representative in Columbia: Reflections from practice. *Development in Practice, 20*(6), 636–648.

Merli, C., Nunn, P., & Schipper, L. (2014). How religion and beliefs influence perceptions of and attitudes towards risk. *World disasters report: Focus on culture and risk* (pp. 37–63). Geneva: International Federation of Red Cross and Red Crescent Societies.

MSOxfam. *PRG*. Oxford: Bodleian.

1/1/1 to 3 Minutes of Grants sub-committee, later Overseas Aid Committee 1955–1974.

1/3/1 to 23 Minutes of the Africa Field committee 1963–1992.

1/5/1 to 14 Minutes of the Latin America and Caribbean Field Committee 1966–1992.

1/11/1 to 3 Minutes of the Africa Management Team 1991–1996.

1/12/1 Minutes of the Overseas Committee, 1.1991–6.93.

1/13/1 to 18 Minutes of the Area Co-ordinators and Senior Management Team 1981–2004.

2/1/1 to 6 Papers relating to planning and reporting 1985–2005.

2/2/1 to 7 Policy statements and related papers 1964–2007.

2/3/1/1 to 17 Correspondence of the Overseas Aid Director and the Overseas, later International, Division Director.

2/3/8/27 Internal correspondence and papers of the Overseas Division Director: management of programmes.

2/3/8/31 Internal correspondence and papers of the International Director and his/her deputies: regionalisation.

3/4/1 to 26 Country annual reports 1969–(2007).

3/5/1 to 32 Tour Reports 1956–2003.

3/8/1 to 15 Strategic Plans 1985–2004.

7/3/1 to 31 Correspondence 1943–2005.

Murray, G. (1970). Joint service as an instrument of renewal. In H. Fey (Ed.), *The ecumenical advance: A history of the ecumenical movement. Volume 2, 1948–1968*. Geneva: The World Council of Churches.

Oxfam Handbook. (1995). *Handbook of development and relief* (Vol. 1). Oxford: Oxfam.

Rakodi, C. (2012). Religion and development: subjecting religious perceptions and organisations to scrutiny. *Development in Practice, 22*(5–6), 621–633.

Roddy, S., Strange, J. M., & Taithe, B. (2015). Humanitarian accountability, bureaucracy, and self-regulation: The view from the archive. *Disasters, 39*(S2), S188–S203.

Said, E. (1995). *Orientalism*. London: Penguin.

Saunders, C. (2009). British humanitarian, aid and development NGOs, 1949–present. In J. McKay, M. Hilton, & N. Crowson (Eds.), *NGOs in contemporary Britain: Non-state actors in society and politics since 1945* (pp. 38–58). Basingstoke: Palgrave Macmillan.

Slim, H. (1994). Editorial. *Disasters, 18*(3), 189–191.

Smirl, L. (2015). *Spaces of aid. How cars, compounds and hotels shape humanitarianism*. London: Zed Books.

Taithe, B. (2016). The cradle of the new humanitarian system? International work and European volunteers at the Cambodian border camps, 1979–1993. *Contemporary European History, 25*(2), 335–358.

Tearfund (n.d.). *Sharing Tearfund's learning and resources across the world*. Retrieved from: learn.tearfund.org.

Tearfund. (2019). *50 years of faith in action*. Teddington: Tearfund.

Trivedy, R. (1990). *Action research in Southern Malawi* (Oxfam Research Paper 1). Oxford: Oxfam.

Whitaker, B. (1983). *A bridge of people: A personal view of Oxfam's first forty years*. London: Heinemann.

CHAPTER 3

Donor Listening

Introduction

This chapter analyses how language shapes the way in which a major donor engages with the Listening Zones of development. It uses the UK government as an example of a donor, and particularly focuses on the various bodies that have administered UK development aid. It considers how language has been positioned in the way that government conceives of the purpose, the delivery and the effect of aid. It traces how the history of UK development aid has been shaped by (dis)engagement with languages, from the mid-1960s to the present day. It is based on interviews with officials from the Department of International Development (DFID), and analysis of the archives of DFID's predecessors: the Ministry of Overseas Development (ODM) and the Overseas Development Administration (ODA), as well as the Foreign and Commonwealth Office (FCO). The chapter interprets the data through the lens of constructivist institutionalism, to understand the deep-rooted ideational dynamics that guide and frame development policy in relation to language. It argues that local languages have generally not received sustained attention from government ministers and civil servants involved in aid administration. Neither have matters of translation and interpretation. Policymakers and officials have engaged with the Listening Zones of development with the explicit or implicit assumption that local languages have little relevance in achieving development goals.

H. Footitt et al., *Development NGOs and Languages*,
https://doi.org/10.1007/978-3-030-51776-2_3

Insofar as language has been a focal point in aid, it has been in connection with a long-term commitment to promote English language teaching (ELT), mainly during the ODM/ODA years. Support for ELT during these years was underpinned by consensus amongst the political elite that the promotion of English was advantageous for developing countries and the UK. Discussions about ELT were framed by a language ideology about the unique characteristics of English, which was reinforced by American-influenced political, economic, technological and cultural global trends. There was broad agreement that the best way to maximise the effect of limited resources was to target aid strategically, such as funding teacher training and curriculum development. Britain was thought to have a comparative advantage in this regard. There was a shared view about the nature of Britain's national interests in a postcolonial age (as least as far as ELT was concerned), particularly concerning the need to project 'soft power' over the Commonwealth. Notions of moral duty were commonly attached to practices of aid giving, and Britain was thought to be well positioned to improve the lives of the poorest by increasing access to ELT. Such perceptions were reinforced by appeals from developing countries for funding for ELT initiatives. These assumptions became entrenched over time and formed the cognitive template through which the political elite perceived the benefits of providing aid for ELT. It was deeply embedded and so was resistant to change. In other words, policy was ideationally path dependent.

Powerful actors at strategic points in time can disrupt dominant ideational frameworks. This occurred when DFID was established, headed by Clare Short, the first Secretary of State for International Development. Short, who played a vital role in shaping the priorities and practices of the new Department, ended support for ELT. She was sceptical about its effectiveness in reducing poverty, and she disliked its colonial connotations. Funding for ELT was later restored, but it was more restricted than had it been during the ODM/ODA years. ELT has therefore diminished in importance for DFID, but what persists is a generalised neglectful attitude towards local languages.

The legacy of the historical disregard for local languages is manifest in DFID's policy papers and guidelines; they do not tend to contain explicit and detailed consideration of language, despite the emphasis on beneficiary feedback in recent years. DFID participants admit that they generally assume that NGOs have sufficient language capacity to conduct their role satisfactorily, even though NGOs are generally not asked direct questions by DFID in this regard. There appears to be little systematic, in-depth reflection within DFID about the role of language in the relationship between communities and their delivery partners. Such disengagement with local languages may seem curious given that the organisation operates in environments with high linguistic diversity. Interpreted through the lens of constructivist institutionalism, this 'blind spot' can be explained in terms of an ideational and historical context where local languages have not been regarded as pertinent to the pursuit of Britain's international development goals.

The perceptions of development policymakers and officials towards local languages has received little analysis elsewhere, particularly in terms of the historical context. This chapter is a departure from the traditional approach to language policy research, whereby language policy texts are analysed to uncover national discourses. In contrast, drawing on literature from Politics and International Relations, the chapter examines official documents pertaining to development aid to uncover the government's attitudes towards languages and its position on ELT. It contributes to historical research on language policy that examines how elites shape policy discourses (Tollefson, 2015, p. 142), and builds on research about the construction of Anglocentric narratives that legitimise the promotion of English in the Global South, based on perceptions of multilingualism as a deficiency that causes social and economic 'backwardness' (Wiley, 2006, pp. 140–143). This chapter demonstrates how constructivist institutionalism can offer language studies an explicit vocabulary to theorise the path-shaping power of ideas.

It is split into three main sections. The first section considers the value of constructivist institutionalism to the analysis of the shaping of language and development policies. The second addresses the archival research, which spans the period that ODM/ODA was in existence. The third section examines the interviews and document analysis pertaining to DFID.

The Value of a Constructivist Institutionalist Approach

This article is informed by ideational approaches to political analysis, which reject the notion that social reality is constituted by material conditions. Rather, the political and social world is constructed by the ideas of the actors who inhabit it, and the intersubjective understandings that they share with others. Focusing on ideas enables the analyst to interrogate the role of actors in reproducing discourses that shape political decisions and establish policy trajectories. It also permits a deeper understanding of how ideas are embedded in the design and development of institutions. Constructivist institutionalism is a distinct strand of this broad theoretical tradition.

Institutions can be broadly defined as "formal or informal procedures, routines, norms and conventions embedded in the organizational structure of the polity or political economy" (Hall & Taylor, 1996, p. 938). Constructivist institutionalism emerged from critiques of different branches of 'new institutionalism' (Bell, 2011; Hay, 2006, 2010, 2016). The latter is commonly defined with reference to Hall and Taylor's (1996) categories of historical institutionalism, rational choice institutionalism and sociological institutionalism. Constructivist (see also discursive) institutionalism is distinguished by its preoccupation with the role that ideas play in shaping institutions and processes (Schmidt, 2008). Constructivist scholars criticised new institutionalism for an excessive focus on institutions at the expense of individual actors, which produced a structuralist account that downplayed the salience of agency in shaping political outcomes. Moreover, they argued that new institutionalist scholarship tended to avoid in-depth examination of how the perceptions, preferences and motivations of actors are shaped, and how this then informs policy (Ross, 2013). Constructivists maintain that actors are not analytically substitutable, and that their interests cannot be deduced from their institutional context (Hay, 2010, p. 68).

For example, rational choice scholars assume that states are motivated by self-interest, which is understood to be 'necessary' or 'inevitable' given external conditions. In the context of the present study, it could be assumed that Britain's attempts to push its advantage in ELT are 'inevitable' responses to a 'self-help' international system where states are compelled to compete to enhance their power and influence. The problem with this position is that it implicitly assumes that interests are fixed and exogenously given. As Hay (2016) argues, rationalist accounts "are typically part of an analytical rather than a genuine ontology in that they are chosen less for their ontological credibility than for the analytic convenience they afford" (p. 529). Rationalism obscures how political processes are *authored* and elides the role of the agents that produce and reproduce ideas that become institutionalised. To return to the words of Hay, "this is to deny agency, contingency and, in the process, the very politics which constructivism seeks to identify and interrogate" (2016, p. 529). In contrast, constructivists contend that social and political realities are constructed by actors that develop intersubjective understandings about the world, and develop practices based on these understandings. They focus on how perceptions of interests are generated and rendered actionable (Wendt, 1999, pp. 113–135): interests are not taken for granted, but instead are the *explanandum*. By placing ideas at centre stage, constructivism enables us to understand institutions as comprised of a complex blend of intersubjective understandings that shape institutional development and guide policy pathways (Blyth, 2002).

A particularly valuable contribution of constructivist institutionalism is the notion of 'ideational path-dependence', which describes how institutions are forged by a set of ideas that become so deeply embedded that they exert an independent path-dependent effect (Cox, 2004). Such ideas become the cognitive template through which decision-makers and other key actors understand their identities, conceive of their interests, and undertake strategic actions (Hay, 2010, p. 69). Language ideology is defined as "sets of beliefs about language articulated by users as a rationalization or justification of perceived language structure and use" (Silverstein, 1979, p. 193). Incorporating the concept of language ideology in a constructivist institutionalist framework provides a powerful lens for interpreting how language and development policies are shaped. For example, it will be seen in the ODM/ODA/FCO archival analysis that the policy discussions were framed by a metanarrative of English as synonymous with modernisation and development (Pennycook, 2014). English was associated with economic and political development and scientific and technological progress, and it was thought to have the potential to unite culturally diverse territories and foster regional and international stability. The inexorable global spread of English, associated with the growth in the hegemonic influence of the USA, seemingly gave credence to Anglocentric language ideology (Wright, 2016, pp. 155–178). I argue that the cognitive template of policymakers was fundamentally shaped by an Anglocentric language ideology, along with ideas about national interest, moral duty and the strategic targeting of aid.

UK Development Aid and the Promotion of English: Insights from the Archives of DFID's Predecessors

This section of the chapter is primarily based upon analysis of material from ODM, ODA and the FCO from 1964 onwards, retrieved from records available at The National Archives, Kew, London. It begins with an outline of the main features of the administration of UK development aid over this period. It then turns to examine the strategic targeting of aid and how notions of instrumentalism and altruism shaped debates and decision-making on aid.

The history of ODM/ODA is partly characterised by organisational turbulence. Wilson's Labour government of 1964 established a separate Ministry, with its own Minister, to administer aid. Titled the Ministry of Overseas Development (ODM), it assumed the responsibilities of several government departments relating to overseas assistance, including the former Department of Technical Cooperation. It was purposely established as a separate entity from the Foreign and Commonwealth Office (FCO) to ensure that foreign policy considerations did not dominate aid policy (Hewitt, 1978). The first White Paper of the new Ministry in 1965 stated that the primary objective of ODM was to raise living standards in developing countries, with particular focus on the Commonwealth and Dependent Territories.

When the Conservatives were returned to office in 1970, the Ministry was retitled the Overseas Development Administration (ODA) and subsumed into the FCO, signalling the government's intent that foreign policy priorities should dictate the disbursement of aid. Despite the reorganisation, "the policies, practices and staff largely remained intact" (Barder, 2005, p. 7), and when the Labour Party was elected in 1974 the decision was reversed, with a separate Ministry being established once more (reverting to the title ODM). The Ministry's second White Paper in 1975 stated that a higher proportion of British aid would concentrate on helping the poorest people in the poorest countries, with an emphasis on rural development. There was also a reassertion of the UK's responsibilities towards its dependencies. These principles underpinned the stated mission of UK aid until the establishment of DFID (Ireton, 2013, p. 43). In addition, Wilson introduced an Aid and Trade Provision that linked aid to non-concessionary export credits tied to the procurement of British goods and services (Barder, 2005, p. 9).

The Ministry's status changed again under the Conservative government of 1979, where it was downgraded to a department of the FCO under its previous title of ODA, and the aid budget was slashed as part of a wide programme of public expenditure reform. A review of aid policy was conducted in 1981, which concluded that greater emphasis should be given to political, industrial and commercial objectives, whilst remaining focused on the Commonwealth. In fact, as the Aid and Trade Provision illustrates, instrumental motivations had always driven aid policy to some degree. However, even during the Thatcher years, altruistic rhetoric about the UK's responsibilities to less developed countries accompanied the focus on the national interest. As will be seen, these dual foreign policy aims shaped discussions and decisions about the promotion of English through development aid in profound ways.

Strategic Targeting of Development Aid for ELT

Over the decades, policy discussions about the funding of ELT have been consistently framed by assertions of the need to target aid 'strategically'. It is possible to trace the emergence of these ideas at an elite level by examining the development of the British Council, which has always been central to the promotion and support of ELT overseas. A key event in the British Council's history was the publication of the Drogheda Report (1954), which recommended that it should be reformed "to be more in line with the Government's political, strategic and commercial needs" (cited in Ireton, 2013, p. 151). The Report urged greater efforts to support the spread of English/ELT in developing countries, especially in the Commonwealth, for fear that it "might be supplanted as a lingua franca, either by regional languages such as Hindi and Arabic, or by some other European languages" (cited in Dua, 1996, p. 579). The notion that the British Council and ELT could be useful tools in the promotion of the national interest was therefore well established before the creation of ODM/ODA.

ELT was an early priority for ODM. Policymakers claimed that there was a "well-nigh insatiable demand in the developing Commonwealth for the teaching of English" soon after the Ministry was first established (ODM Parliamentary Undersecretary of State, cited in Taylor, 1965). ODM argued that a strategic way to address this demand was through providing capacity building, expertise and infrastructure, especially in Commonwealth countries. 'Unprecedented' funding, of which the British Council was a major beneficiary, was channelled into ELT in the 1960s (Smith, 2016), and by the mid-60s, ODM had undertaken to provide more than one-third of the British Council's grant-in-aid. One of the outcomes was the British Council's scheme Aid for Commonwealth English (ACE), which was designed to produce ELT specialists who could provide expert advice to Commonwealth countries, as well as the associated scheme for Aid for British for Commonwealth Science Teaching (ACTS).

The British Council was also tasked with administering ODM funds in the expansion and improvement of ELT educational facilities in developing countries. This included the development of regional ELT centres that trained local teachers and provided guidance on "modern techniques in language teaching" (British Council and Ministry of Overseas Development Working Party, 1966). It also assumed responsibility for teaching posts in non-Commonwealth countries and the Indian subcontinent, providing training opportunities in the UK and services for international students, amongst a plethora of other activities with relevance to ELT. ODM had responsibility for recruiting teachers for developing Commonwealth countries (mainly under the Overseas Services Aid Scheme), and around three hundred such teachers were appointed through the Ministry within the first two years of its establishment. Other forms of ODM assistance in the teaching and learning of English included the financing of the Centre for Educational Teaching Overseas, Commonwealth Teacher Training bursaries and student scholarships. In short, the broad policy approach to ELT was to concentrate on capacity building, materials and infrastructure.

Echoing ODM assessments, ODA argued that aid for ELT needed to be deployed strategically through the provision of capacity building and expertise. For example, the English as a Foreign Language (EFL) Scheme was launched in 1972, alongside existing means of support to provide specialist ELT advisers in key posts in non-Commonwealth countries. It was designed to "operate at senior levels and in areas where the multiplier effect of aid is greatest—e.g. teacher training, the development of materials and syllabuses, and inspectorial and advisory services" (Overseas Development Administration and British Council, 1971). This reinforced the practice of disbursing ELT-related aid strategically.

The second incarnation of ODM was guided in its funding decisions by strategic considerations, and ELT was no exception. To quote from correspondence from the office of Reg Prentice (Secretary of State for

Overseas Development 1975–1976) with regard to ELT: "To exert the maximum leverage, we try to concentrate our aid at a fairly advanced level" (Douglas, 1975). ODM maintained the focus on the provision of expertise and capacity building, most particularly in Commonwealth countries. The teaching of English in the host countries created a cadre of trained personnel who had a great stake in the perpetuation and penetration of English, increasing the body of support for the continuation of aid (Dua, 1996, p. 581).

Likewise, the second incarnation of ODA perceived development aid to be facing a major challenge: "an enormous and unquenchable demand for the English language" (Iredale, 1986). It claimed that "there is no aid-worthy country that does not need and want some form of ELT support" (Macmillan, 1982). Appeals from recipient countries for aid reinforced the embedded language ideology that held that English was inseparable from political and economic progress. It was argued that it was impossible to meet an infinite demand, and so ELT needed to be deployed strategically. ODA funded the Key English Language Teaching (KELT) programme, which provided over 150 experts in various countries, who were seen to "form an integral part of our aid projects, frequently contributing their skills to other elements of the aid programme" (Iredale, 1986). KELT was primarily targeted towards curriculum development and teacher training to ensure that the aid had a long-term impact. This included universities and institutes of public administration as well as schools.

The archive shows that numerous senior diplomats and civil servants supported the ODM/ODA approach, arguing that ELT initiatives provided an excellent return on investment. For instance, an account of a conference in Nairobi reveals that "one of the points made most forcibly by a number of Heads of Mission… was the importance of English language teaching as an instrument of British influence and the great benefits which could accrue to us in non-anglophone countries in Africa for minimum outlay" (Robson, 1981). It was argued that ELT provided an opportunity to cultivate loyalty amongst the political and business elite who were more likely to access English tuition (Sharp, 1981).

The political context to development aid underwent a notable shift under the Conservative period of rule that began in 1979. The Thatcher administration sought to 'roll back the state' and implemented severe cuts to the British Council's grant-in-aid. Aid was projectised and expected to deliver cost-effective and measurable results within a limited timeframe.

It ordered that ELT should compete for funding with other areas of development aid on a geographical basis, which was a departure from ODM's (proclaimed) focus on the rural poor. The importance of aid for ELT continued to be "recognised at the highest level in ODA" (Iredale, 1986), but it was henceforth largely targeted to projects with an occupational purpose or as part of a national education system where English was the medium of instruction (Iredale, 1997, p. 127). Nonetheless, it was arguably easier for ELT than it was for some other areas of aid activity to make the case that the UK had a competitive advantage relative to other donors, and to show measurable results within the life of a project cycle. Thus, ELT could demonstrate its 'value for money' in ways that were aligned with the embedded ideological views regarding the commercial advantages of English language competence.

Moreover, ODA perceived an additional benefit to ELT: increased language competence would positively reinforce other forms of assistance. An ODA review of ELT development aid in 1984 argued that "English is an indispensable tool for all development work, enabling Third World countries to interpret offers of aid from national and international agencies" (Macmillan, 1982). Similar assertions had been made by ODM during its first incarnation: "it may be necessary to teach English to enable a developing country to obtain maximum benefit from some other form of British aid" (ODM, 1967). Likewise, a report produced during ODM's existence in 1974–1979 stated:

> Competency in English is also becoming increasingly necessary for a developing country's economy to enable it to interpret offers of aid from English-speaking donor countries, produce development plans, take part in negotiations for aid, obtain and maintain the appropriate capital items and make full use of offers of technical expertise. (British Council, 1973)

In line with the prevailing language ideology, English was associated with national autonomy and competence in government. Policy had long been framed by claims of an inexhaustible demand for ELT, and successive governments aimed to maximise influence with limited resources by boosting national capacity, providing expertise, investing in learning materials and assisting with curriculum development. The Thatcher government had political reasons to claim the language of 'value for money' as their own, but actually both ODM and ODA had consistently been concerned with the cost-effectiveness of ELT. Ideas about strategic prioritisation therefore became deeply embedded over decades. They formed part of the cognitive template of policymakers alongside notions of instrumentalism and altruism, to which we now turn.

Notions of Instrumentalism and Altruism

Discussions about the rationale for funding ELT initiatives reflected a broad bipartisan consensus about the purpose of development aid, which is that it should serve a mixture of instrumental and altruistic goals (although the Conservative Party tended to emphasise the former, and the Labour Party—rhetorically, at least—stressed the latter). The 1965 White Paper that accompanied the creation of ODM stated that the government expected the country's long-term interests to be served by aid policy. However, it also underlined Britain's moral obligation to assist countries struggling to make their way out of poverty (ODM, 1965). This was the first formal expression of the blend of self-interest and moral duty that would characterise British development aid over the decades that followed (Burnell, 1991). A parliamentary speech by Labour MP Roderick MacFarquhar illustrates the interplay of these dual concerns, which was a common feature of debates on ELT policy: "...because it is advantageous to us and because we helped to make English a world language we have an interest and, indeed, a duty to help ensure that it is...spoken everywhere in intelligible forms" (MacFarquhar, 1977).

The 'intense cultivation of ELT' by ODM/ODA was largely spurred by anxiety about preserving British influence after decolonisation (Phillipson, 1992, p. 113). Both Labour and Conservative governments were concerned with promoting intra-Commonwealth communication. The British government, at a meeting of Commonwealth Prime Ministers, produced a memorandum that stated: "For those having no single indigenous tongue [English] provides an important internal bond and for all it is the most useful medium of international communications in politics, in commerce and, above all, in education and science..." (Commonwealth Secretariat, 1968). In line with Anglocentric ideological views, English was portrayed as an international lingua franca shorn of historical and cultural meaning that provided an advantageous replacement for local languages.

The spread of English was thought to promote stability and prosperity, and so financing ELT was understood as a moral obligation as well as a politically astute move (British Council, 1973). Perceived moral duties were strongly expressed: "language is of central and crucial importance in development… it would be criminally neglectful to withhold the means of fostering and encouraging it" (Macmillan, 1982). Local languages were at best regarded as an irrelevance to development; at worst a potential hindrance. For example, it was noted in an ODM briefing paper that:

> [African] indigenous languages are ill-adapted to the requirements of modern technological society. Indeed, it is only through possession of a European language that their administrators, businessmen, engineers and technicians can gain access to the knowledge needed for further development and improved living standards. (Smith, 1968)

For the newly independent African countries, European languages such as English "probably indeed provides the only medium through which an advance can be made from tribal separation to national self-consciousness" (Smith, 1968). The legacy of colonialism in shaping policy was conspicuous; ideas about the superiority of Western models of development rested on narratives of the 'deficiencies' of 'non-Western' states in the Global South.

The FCO and overseas diplomats appealed to the same blend of duty-based and self-interested reasoning when corresponding with ODM/ODA about proposals for ELT initiatives. A good example includes an official from the Embassy in the Congo, who wrote to the newly established ODM to appeal for support of a proposal to build an English language centre: "This is one of the few things which the British are especially equipped to do in the Congo and which, in my opinion, we ought to do in our own interest and also in the wider interest of African unity" (Millard, 1964). It was argued that there would be long-term economic benefits for the UK: "We have a real interest in seeing that these future managers start right with a bias towards British goods and British methods" (Millard, 1964). Moreover, it was said that the UK had a geopolitical interest in funding ELT in the Congo, given that there was intelligence that the Russian Embassy was planning to make inroads in language education: "…we understand that they had plans to teach the Congolese English and get across their message that way" (Millard, 1964).

ELT was also framed as a security issue by the FCO and ODA. Senior figures pressed for increased expenditure on ELT to ward off Soviet influence and reach the political and economic elite. For example, the Cultural

Relations Department strongly supported a project to establish an English Language Centre at the University of Sana'a in Yemen: "…not least because many of those who study there are likely to be the YAR's future leaders… If we do not provide the service, there is every likelihood that the Yemenis will turn to others, particularly the Soviet Union, for training in numerous key areas of Yemeni development" (Macrae, 1982). The then Minister for Europe, Douglas Hurd, wrote to Neil Marten, the Minister for Overseas Development, to strongly endorse the FCO's stance: "There are powerful political reasons for our whole-hearted involvement in this project. Our aid programme is a very important element in our strategy to stem Soviet influence, and [ELT] is the core of our aid" (Hurd, 1982). Considerations of realpolitik eclipsed the altruistic narrative in policy debates regarding geopolitically sensitive areas.

In sum, this section of the chapter has demonstrated that features of UK development aid regarding languages remained relatively consistent from the establishment of ODM until the creation of DFID. Language generally did not feature in policy discussions about aid, apart from how aid could be used to promote the spread of English. Policy had long been framed by claims that there was an inexhaustible demand for ELT in the developing world, and a deeply held conviction that English was the language of economic, political and scientific progress. Both Labour and Conservative governments agreed on the need to strategically target aid for ELT. Official and unofficial documentation reveals that debate and decisions regarding aid for ELT were shaped by perceptions of the national interest, particularly in terms of maintaining influence in Commonwealth territories. Also important in this regard were perceptions of Britain's moral obligations to boost the life opportunities of the world's poor. The altruistic narrative only worked by tapping into a language ideology that presented English as an unproblematic good. The archival research did not uncover extended reflection on the potential for local languages to contribute to development, much less the benefits for donor countries of speaking the languages of recipient countries. Quite the contrary: aid for ELT was occasionally justified by claims that it would help recipient countries to understand the donor better. Local languages were implicitly or explicitly framed as an obstacle to development goals.

Listening to the Voices? Perceptions at DFID on the Role of Languages in Development

This section presents an exploratory analysis of how officials at DFID perceive that NGOs listen to communities and engage with local languages. It is largely based on confidential interviews with nine senior DFID officials in 2017: four men and five women. They included individuals with significant leadership, management and advisory responsibilities. They were targeted because of their senior positions, as it was thought likely that their views would have an impact on DFID decision-making and policy implementation. Their job titles cannot be revealed without breaching their anonymity. The participants spoke in a private capacity, and not as representatives of DFID, and it should be borne in mind that the sample size is small, so the findings may not represent wider sentiment within DFID. The interview data was supplemented by document analysis, drawing on information from DFID's website. The dataset included corporate reports, official guidance, policy papers, transparency data, consultation reports, impact assessments, research and analysis, from 1997 onwards. Before analysing the data, however, we first outline the main features in the administration of UK development aid, 1997–present.

ODA's fortunes took a radical turn when it was made into a separate Department for International Development (DFID) following the election of the Labour Party in 1997, presided over by Clare Short in the newly created Cabinet post of Secretary of State for International Development.

Constructivist institutionalists argue that powerful actors at strategic points in time can disrupt dominant ideational frameworks and have a decisive role in shaping policy pathways. This occurred when Short, who played a crucial role in shaping the priorities and practices of the new Department, ended support for ELT in 1997 (Coleman, 2017, p. 453). Short was critical of the colonial undertones of ELT initiatives, and the lack of convincing evidence that ELT contributed to poverty reduction. In recent years, limited funding from the international development budget has been revived for the British Council to provide training and expert advice in ELT. Recipient countries have included those associated with the Commonwealth and British colonial history, such as Bangladesh (Erling, 2017). In addition, the Peacekeeping English Project has provided thirty-eight conflict-affected countries with expertise on curriculum design, teaching methodology and assessment for ELT aimed at the military, police and other security forces (British Council, n.d.). These exceptions underline the persistence of the notion that ELT-related aid should be disbursed strategically.

Despite these exceptions, ELT no longer enjoys the same high profile in the overseas assistance portfolio. Significant in this regard was the Conference on Language in Education in Africa, held in South Sudan in 2012, attended by a range of intergovernmental organisations and NGOs. DFID countersigned a Statement of Principles at the Conference in support of a mother tongue-based (MTB) multilingual education approach (Coleman, 2017, p. 456). The British Council signed the same document, and thereafter announced a policy change to withdraw support for English medium education at lower levels of schooling, in favour of an MTB approach. The policy change reflected growing acceptance by development experts of substantial pedagogic research in a variety of linguistic contexts that consistently demonstrated that MTB education was the most effective at achieving learning outcomes across the curriculum (UNESCO, 2012). The policy pathway that has guided long-term support for ELT-related aid has therefore been severely disrupted.

DFID was established during a shift in international development discourse towards a so-called 'people-centred' approach to aid, in which it was claimed that participation and partnership are crucial in achieving development outcomes (Cornwall & Eade, 2010). DFID followed the example of other major donors in channelling increasing amounts of funding through NGOs. There was an emerging consensus in the donor community that NGOs had a closer connection to communities than government agencies, and so were likely to spend aid more effectively (Edwards & Hulme, 1995).

A core commitment of DFID is "listening and responding to the voices of those left furthest behind", in alignment with the UN Sustainable Development Goals (DFID, 2019a), and DFID claims that it aims to empower the poorest by enabling beneficiary feedback through organisations that they fund to implement projects. But DFID has faced intense pressure to root out corruption and waste in the organisations that it funds and demonstrate the cost-effectiveness and impact of aid. In response, different governments have enacted measures to enhance the transparency and scrutiny of aid spending, including the introduction of the International Development (Reporting and Transparency) Act 2006, and the establishment of the Independent Commission for

Aid Impact. In addition, DFID has introduced tougher requirements for NGOs in receipt of their funds to evidence impact and to demonstrate that monitoring and evaluation (M&E) processes are rigorous. They are also increasingly making use of 'payment by results', whereby organisations that apply for funding only receive payment when they can demonstrate that they have met their targets. DFID claims that this approach is designed to "bring more people out of poverty for good and ensure that we are getting the greatest value for money on behalf of the British taxpayer" (DFID, 2014a). Moreover, DFID claims that payment by results can strengthen practices and mechanisms of beneficiary feedback, particularly where payment is determined by the ratings that beneficiaries give to aid providers (DFID, 2014a).

Payment by results and the broader evidence agenda has been roundly criticised for curtailing the voice of people and communities by those who favour more participatory forms of development (Ahmad, 2011; Eyben, Guijt, Roche, & Shutt, 2015; Valters & Whitty, 2017). As discussed in Chapter 1, such critics argue DFID perceives the purpose of listening to communities as a means of monitoring organisations that implement projects. They argue that this instrumental approach is problematic since it fails to realise the radical potential of listening, which should be to shift the power balance in favour of communities and to prompt development practitioners to engage in critical self-reflection. However, the literature provides few interview-based insights into how officials at donor organisations perceive the role of listening to their institutional mission. In order to explore these issues further, participants were asked a series of questions on the themes of listening, language and culture.

Perceptions of Listening Relationships Between DFID-Funded NGOs and Communities

Participants were asked to describe how DFID uses the concept of listening, and they responded that it was used in terms of beneficiary feedback, M&E processes and needs assessment. Acquiring feedback from aid recipients was said to be "fundamentally… part of good development" (DFID official 9). Three participants who had long careers in DFID described an evolution in listening activity during the department's existence. When DFID implemented projects in its early years, there were relatively more opportunities to listen directly to communities through participatory methods. DFID's shift in focus to budgetary support resulted in listening "more to people in the centre: technocrats and politicians" (DFID official 6). DFID's concentration on project support involves listening to communities vicariously through M&E exercises. This is an interesting parallel to the move towards vicarious listening by NGOs noted in Chapter 1. Participants noted that now that DFID is not active at the implementing end of the aid chain, it mainly accesses the voices of 'beneficiaries' through reports provided by NGOs and consultants. There are opportunities for DFID personnel to interact at a grassroots level: "…the most direct opportunity for [DFID] to have the most direct conversation with someone from a country that you're working in would be in the context of a field visit" (DFID official 7). However, the weight of expectations for listening to communities lies with the NGOs and their partners. Listening is seen as an important part of data collection for identifying needs and impact on the ground (DFID official 3). In return for DFID funds, NGOs are expected to be responsible for acquiring 'beneficiary feedback' and reporting the results to DFID. Participants identified DFID's guidelines for stakeholder consultations as an example of best practice for NGOs in listening for the purpose of evidence-based planning and project evaluation. Listening is therefore a delegated activity and the connection that NGOs supposedly have with communities is seen as their main benefit: it's "part of the selling point of NGOs, right?" (DFID official 6).

Participants were asked about the extent to which they reflected on the quality of listening that takes place between NGOs and communities, particularly in terms of whether NGOs have appropriate language skills. The responses revealed a common assumption that NGOs have the capacity to listen to communities: "The whole concept of beneficiary feedback would be based on the ability to actually understand the feedback from the beneficiaries so a coherent level of appropriate and different language knowledge would be something that would be assumed" (DFID official 3); "We sort of assume that the NGOs have taken care of it" (DFID official 1); "It's an assumption rather than something that we check" (DFID official 2). Moreover, these assumptions also extend to the belief that NGOs usually perform well at listening: "We generally feel that NGOs are good on this" (DFID official 4); "NGOs tend to be good at this stuff" (DFID official 6). Participants commonly agreed that NGOs are generally not asked specific questions regarding the language capacity of the organisation. Rather, their ability to communicate with the people they work with is taken for granted. A participant who was involved in assessing NGO applications for a major funding call explained that DFID's central focus at the selection stage was on the credibility of the deliverable outcomes that were promised:

> ...it was more about 'what are you achieving and how will you achieve this?' rather than the methods they used to get their information... I guess the assumption is that people are listening and talking to the communities – if it's going to work that's what they have to do... (DFID official 9)

Only two participants, distinguished between different types of NGOs in their answers, and four others acknowledged the lack of systematic reflection within DFID on the quality of listening by NGOs: "it's pretty amateurish and ad hoc" (DFID official 2). One participant mused on the policy implications of neglecting to attend to these issues: "We should ask some questions, really, because some NGOs do it better than others" (DFID official 1).

The document analysis paralleled the interview findings. In recent years, DFID has promoted the notion of 'embedding evaluation' into all of their funding activities. The principle of stakeholder involvement has been a key component of policy documents and guidelines. DFID's guidance for implementing organisations stipulates that it is necessary to evidence that programmes have been designed to incorporate engagement with stakeholders. However, such guidance typically does not explicitly mention the need to consider language appropriate to the local context and issues concerning the use of language intermediaries (DFID, 2013a, 2015b, 2018a). Evaluation reports on DFID-funded initiatives have periodically acknowledged that stakeholder involvement has been poor, but there is little in-depth reflection on the role that language issues may have played in these outcomes (DFID, 2013b, 2014b, 2015a). A notable exception is the report that was published by DFID's Safeguarding Unit (2018) following the Oxfam sexual exploitation scandal in Haiti. This report acknowledged that the "plethora of national and ethnic languages in many international aid settings often prevents aid workers from communicating directly with communities", which can undermine reporting of sexual violence (DFID Safeguarding Unit, 2018, p. 15). It recommended that safeguarding mechanisms be put in place that accommodate those who do not speak the main language, which could be a sign that there is a rising awareness of linguistic issues in the Department. It is notable, however, that listening is still implicitly framed as unidirectional (aid worker to communities) rather than bidirectional.

Perceptions of the Role of Language and Cultural Knowledge in Development Work

Participants were asked to describe DFID's expectations regarding the recruitment of language intermediaries by NGOs. It was said that it is sometimes the case that the terms of reference for a project team will include language competence if they are to undertake fieldwork. DFID may also pose questions to NGOs about language competence if they are working in a region of high ethnic tension. However, the majority of the participants did not appear to have given deep thought to issues of language mediation, and had little to say on the matter. Again, it is seemingly assumed that interpreters and translators perform their role adequately where needed: "my assumption is that... the international NGO community have the right staffing in terms of language" (DFID official 7).

Participants were asked to comment on the extent to which DFID reflected on the role of cultural knowledge in listening. Responses were more detailed and emphatic. All the participants used personal anecdotes from their past experience of development work to stress the importance of cultural awareness to communicate with local people:

> So certainly a lot of the Westerners, even if you speak the language, are not going to be able to express or hear what people want to say because it's much more nuanced than just being able to speak the language... The whole power relation thing of it and the cultural understanding... (DFID official 4)

Participants particularly noted the importance of having an awareness of gendered power relations, in line with DFID's long-standing focus on the rights of women and girls. This includes the need to be mindful of the space within which communication takes place, and how some spaces may effectively silence marginalised people. For example, women in highly patriarchal societies may not be able to speak freely in public spaces. They may also be effectively silenced in the private sphere by the intimidating presence of powerful figures such as husbands and mothers-in-law. Participants insisted that it was crucial to understand the complexities of the local context in development work, including considerations of ethnicity, caste, clan, disability and socio-economic factors. The document analysis reinforced the interview findings. References to 'voice', 'inclusion', 'listening' and 'culture' are plentiful, but especially prevalent in DFID's policy and guidance materials on gender-based issues. DFID gender mainstreaming guidance stipulates that consultations should aim for maximal inclusivity, and that measures on inclusion should be incorporated into M&E frameworks. The guidance also advises on the need to be aware of gendered spaces. However, the role of languages and language intermediaries in a gender-sensitive communication strategy is relatively unexplored (DFID, 2013c, 2018b).

One participant expressed concern that the funding success of some NGOs may reflect their ability to write a professional proposal that meets institutional expectations, rather than their actual capacity to listen to communities. DFID's grant conditions presume that applicants are fluent enough in English to abide by corporate requirements (DFID, 2018c, 2019b). This may be true of large Northern-based INGOs but will rarely be the case for grassroots organisations that speak and work in languages other than English. The latter are significantly disadvantaged in funding competitions, especially given that those on the shortlisting panel may have an inherent bias towards applicants that speak English:

> I don't think this is on purpose but just subconsciously – some who speaks your language, you're automatically drawn towards and this could disadvantage others who don't speak your language who might even be in far more need for support and partnership… So what happens is that normally NGOs come to these local communities and always speak on their behalf and submit proposals on their behalf and get the majority of funding to that community through them… an NGO like Oxfam or Save the Children or whomever, that becomes a proxy representative of that community whether that community likes it or not. (DFID official 5)

Participants were asked to reflect upon issues that impede listening relationships in development work. They expressed sympathy for the diverse challenges facing NGOs that want to increase their language capacity. They acknowledged that NGOs grapple with significant pressures imposed by small project cycles:

> And there is such a rush – especially for donor-driven projects – there is such a rush to report back within timeframes, sometimes rather difficult timeframes I admit… and most crucial bit of the translation actually gets completely lost in the urgency to transcribe it into English. (DFID official 8)

As Bornstein, Chapman, and Wallace (2007) have also observed, the strictures of the project cycle exacerbate the difficulties that NGOs face in building a relationship of trust with the community. The participants noted the ideal project-planning scenario should involve an extended period of needs assessment where NGOs establish a strong relationship with the community. However, they acknowledged that this is difficult for NGOs to achieve in reality given the pressure to chase after funds and abide by restrictive logframe requirements.

Resource issues also come into play. One participant pointed out that it would not be 'realistic' to expect international staff to be trained in the local languages in the context of high staff turnover and restricted budgets: "I don't think we would fund NGOs for [language acquisition] either" (DFID official 2). Three participants remarked that the evidence agenda and the results-based framework discourages NGOs from improving aspects of their performance that cannot be easily measured or shown to contribute to intended outcomes. It was argued that DFID's risk-averse approach and preoccupation with 'cost-effectiveness' distracts from the importance of listening: "I think that the problem is that listening – building knowledge and understanding over communities – is hard to quantify. It's difficult to demonstrate that listening contributes to value for money" (DFID official 1). For one participant, the interview raised problematic issues that do not just pertain to DFID but to international development donors more generally:

> And I think a challenge for us as a sector is the way we fund organisations. The fact that we often need, you know, to behave with a certain level of professionalism that maybe we can't expect from the local organisations and also the cycle of funding, the fact that it's shorter and it doesn't lend itself to being able to support these more grassrootsy [sic] organisations… in that way you would want to if you were really trying to understand the local context. (DFID official 9)

To summarise a key finding from this section of the chapter, there is a default assumption within DFID that NGOs are generally 'good' at listening to communities, and that they have the requisite language competence to conduct their work. NGOs that receive DFID funds are not asked routine questions about their use of interpretation/translation and language intermediaries. Indeed, the words 'assume' and 'assumption' appeared frequently in the transcripts: they occurred in every interview in relation to NGOs, listening and language competence. The document analysis reflected this institutional complacency, since there was a general lack of extended commentary, guidance or reflection on language. Participants were more assertive in discussing the importance of cultural awareness in development work, particularly regarding the need for sensitivity to gendered power relations, which correlates with the extensive DFID literature in this area. Participants remarked on the intense funding-related pressures that affect NGOs and acknowledged that these could affect the capacity of organisations to build relationships of trust with communities. It was also noted that differences in English competency could magnify the power inequalities between large INGOs and local SNGOs.

Conclusion

This chapter explored how language shapes the way in which a major donor engages with the Listening Zones of development, using the UK government as a case study. The overarching theme is the consistently low profile of local languages over decades of debates and decisions regarding British aid. The first section of the chapter explored the archives of DFID's predecessors, and found that local languages were seen as inferior and detrimental to the aim of development aid: which was to bring societies into the 'modern world' and to promote British influence. English language teaching was promoted through the strategic targeting of aid. A deeply embedded language ideology held that English was associated with prosperity, stability and modernisation. Discussions and decisions about ELT-related aid were shaped by perceptions of how it could contribute to both the national interest and Britain's obligations to the world's poor.

Aid for ELT has significantly declined since DFID's establishment, partly because of the overwhelming evidence of the superiority of MTB education. Nonetheless, the second section of the chapter reveals persistent and generalised disengagement with local languages within DFID. This is particularly striking given DFID's insistence on the importance of 'beneficiary' feedback. NGOs distribute DFID funds and are expected to listen to the communities that receive aid in return. Listening would seem to be minimally dependent upon implementing organisations and local people and communities being able to communicate, ideally in the local language. Yet it appears that there is little interrogation or reflection on the part of DFID officials as to whether NGOs have the language capacity to listen and communicate. Whilst issues pertaining to culture are foregrounded in DFID policy (particularly gender), languages are largely invisible. DFID is principally concerned with 'value for money' and has stringent reporting requirements. The participants acknowledged that local organisations might be significantly disadvantaged by these priorities and procedures, even though they may have the linguistic and cultural resources that large INGOs lack. DFID's general disregard for linguistic issues should be understood in terms of a historical-ideational context where local languages have not been deemed relevant to the attainment of the UK's development goals by policymakers and officials.

The chapter reveals an insular and exclusionary Listening Zone where discussions about development policy issues take place between elite actors. The archives of DFID's predecessors do not indicate that there were sustained efforts to listen to communities affected by development aid, even through intermediaries. DFID claims to value 'beneficiary' feedback but does not listen to communities directly. DFID's 'listening' to communities is also unidirectional and largely takes place vicariously, through NGOs and other delivery organisations. This parallels the move that INGOs have taken towards vicarious listening through their local partners, as discussed in Chapter 1. For both DFID and INGOs, 'listening' to communities increasingly occurs at one or more remove. The Listening Zone between NGOs and DFID is shaped by institutional complacency on DFID's part about NGO capacity to deliver development projects without explicitly articulated language policies and/or explicitly funded language support. As will be seen in the case study chapters, this complacency is misplaced.

References

Ahmad, T. (2011). *The 'right' results: Making sure the results agenda remains committed to poverty reduction*. Oxford: Oxfam.

Barder, O. (2005). *Reforming development assistance: Lessons from the UK experience*. Retrieved from: https://www.cgdev.org/publication/reforming-development-assistance-lessons-uk-experience-working-paper-70.

Bell, S. (2011). Do we really need a new 'constructivist institutionalism' to explain institutional change? *British Journal of Political Science, 41*(4), 883–906.

Blyth, M. (2002). *Great transformations: Economic ideas and institutional change in the twentieth century*. Cambridge: Cambridge University Press.

Bornstein, L., Chapman, J., & Wallace, T. (2007). *The aid chain: Coercion and commitment in development NGOs*. Rugby: Practical Action Publishing.

British Council. (n.d.). *Peacekeeping English Project*. Retrieved from: https://www.britishcouncil.org/partner/track-record/peacekeeping-english-project.

British Council. (1973). *The background to British Government-Financed ELT work in developing countries* (OD17/696). English language teaching, Working Party Report (first revised version British Council final). The National Archives, Kew. London.

British Council and Ministry of Overseas Development Working Party. (1966, February 1). *Ministry of Overseas Development brief for meeting* (OD17/320). The teaching of English as a second language—Policy. The National Archives, Kew. London.

Burnell, P. J. (1991). Introduction to Britain's overseas aid since 1979: Between idealism and self-interest. In A. Bose & P. J. Burnell (Eds.), *Britain's overseas aid since 1979: Between idealism and self-interest* (pp. 1–31). Manchester: Manchester University Press.

Coleman, H. (2017). Milestones in language planning and development aid. *Current Issues in Language Planning, 18*(4), 442–468.

Commonwealth Secretariat. (1968, November 21). *Meeting of Commonwealth Prime Ministers, January 1969*. Memorandum by the British Government (FCO 68/156). Commonwealth initiatives: English in the Commonwealth. The National Archives, Kew. London.

Cornwall, A., & Eade, D. (Eds.). (2010). *Deconstructing development discourse: Buzzwords and fuzzwords*. Rugby: Practical Action Publishing.

Cox, R. H. (2004). The path-dependency of an idea: Why Scandinavian welfare states remain distinct. *Social Policy and Administration, 38*(2), 204–219.

DFID. (2013a). *Additional guidance for GPAF initiatives focused on empowerment and accountability*. Retrieved from: https://assets.publishing.service.gov.uk/government/uploads/system/uploads/attachment_data/file/261855/Additional-Guidance-GPAF-Initiatives-Empowerment-Accountability-nov13.pdf.

DFID. (2013b). *International Development Evaluation Policy*. Retrieved from: https://www.gov.uk/government/uploads/system/uploads/attachment_data/file/204119/DFID-Evaluation-Policy-2013.pdf.

DFID. (2013c). *Gender and the Global Poverty Action Fund*. Retrieved from: https://assets.publishing.service.gov.uk/government/uploads/system/uploads/attachment_data/file/207456/GPAF-Gender-Guidelines-june13.pdf.

DFID. (2014a). *Payment by Results Strategy: Sharpening incentives to perform*. Retrieved from: https://www.gov.uk/government/publications/dfids-strategy-for-payment-by-results-sharpening-incentives-to-perform/payment-by-results-strategy-sharpening-incentives-to-perform.

DFID. (2014b, February). *Rapid Review of Embedding Evaluation for UK Department for International Development*. Retrieved from: https://www.gov.uk/government/uploads/system/uploads/attachment_data/file/292208/Embedding-Evaluation-Review.pdf.

DFID. (2015a, June 18). *DFID's evaluation framework for payment by results*. Retrieved from: https://www.gov.uk/government/uploads/system/uploads/attachment_data/file/436051/Evaluation-Framework-Payment-by-Results3.pdf.

DFID. (2015b). *Smart rules: Better programme delivery*. Retrieved from: https://www.gov.uk/government/uploads/system/uploads/attachment_data/file/472771/Smart_Rules_1November_to_31_March_2016.pdf.

DFID. (2018a, September). *Guidelines for NGOs applying for CHASE humanitarian response funding*. Retrieved from: https://assets.publishing.service.gov.uk/government/uploads/system/uploads/attachment_data/file/741972/Guidelines-Humanitarian-Response-Funding-Sept18.pdf.

DFID. (2018b, March). *DFID Strategic vision for gender equality. A call to action for her potential, our future*. Retrieved from: https://assets.publishing.service.gov.uk/government/uploads/system/uploads/attachment_data/file/708116/Strategic-vision-gender-equality1.pdf.

DFID. (2018c, October). *Programme expenditure: Eligible cost guidance for accountable grant arrangements*. Retrieved from: https://assets.publishing.service.gov.uk/government/uploads/system/uploads/attachment_data/file/755867/Eligible-Cost-Guidance.pdf.

DFID. (2019a). *Leaving no one behind: Our promise*. Retrieved from: https://www.gov.uk/government/publications/leaving-no-one-behind-our-promise/leaving-no-one-behind-our-promise.

DFID. (2019b, April 1). *Smart rules: Better programme delivery*. Retrieved from: https://assets.publishing.service.gov.uk/government/uploads/system/uploads/attachment_data/file/791174/Smart-Rules-External-Apr19.pdf.

DFID Safeguarding Unit. (2018, October). *Sexual exploitation, abuse and harassment (SEAH) in the international aid sector: Victim and survivor voices. Main findings from a DFID-led listening exercise*. Retrieved from: https://assets.publishing.service.gov.uk/government/uploads/system/uploads/attachment_data/file/749741/Listening-Exercise1.pdf.

Douglas, A. J. A. (1975, August 20). *Letter to Luce and MacFarquhar* (OD 17/691). English language teaching policy. The National Archives, Kew. London.

Dua, H. R. (1996). The spread of English in India: Politics of language conflict and language power. In A. Rubal-Lopez, A. W. Conrad, & J. A. Fishman (Eds.), *Post-imperial English: Status change in former British and American colonies, 1940–1990* (pp. 557–588). New York: Mouton de Gruyter.

Edwards, M., & Hulme, D. (Eds.). (1995). *NGO performance and accountability in the post-Cold War world: Beyond the magic bullet*. London: Earthscan.

Erling, E. J. (2017). Language planning, English language education and development aid in Bangladesh. *Current Issues in Language Planning, 18*(4), 388–406.

Eyben, R., Guijt, I., Roche, C., & Shutt, C. (Eds.). (2015). *The politics of evidence and results in international development: Playing the game to change the rules?* Rugby: Practical Action Publishing.

Hall, P. A., & Taylor, R. C. (1996). Political science and the three new institutionalisms. *Political Studies, 44*(5), 936–957.

Hay, C. (2006). Constructivist Institutionalism. In B. A. Rockman, R. H. Rhodes, & S. A. Binder (Eds.), *The Oxford handbook of political institutions* (pp. 56–74). Oxford: Oxford University Press.

Hay, C. (2010). Ideas and the construction of interests. In R. Beland & R. H. Cox (Eds.), *Ideas and politics in social science research* (pp. 65–82). Oxford: Oxford University Press.

Hay, C. (2016). Good in a crisis: The ontological institutionalism of social constructivism. *New Political Economy, 21*(6), 520–535.

Hewitt, A. (1978). British Aid: Policy and practice. *ODI Review, 2,* 55–66.

Hurd, D. (1982, June 25). *Letter to Rt Hon Neil Marten MP* (FCO 8/4871). English language projects in YAR. The National Archives, Kew. London.

Iredale, R. (1986, October 17). *Report on Britain's support for the learning of English* (OD 52/88). English language teaching—Policy. The National Archives, Kew. London.

Iredale, R. (1997). The English language as aid. In C. Beaumont & G. Abbott (Eds.), *The development of ELT: The Dunford seminars, 1978–1993* (pp. 126–127). Hemel Hempstead: Prentice Hall.

Ireton, B. (2013). *Britain's international development policies: A history of DFID and overseas aid*. Basingstoke: Palgrave.

MacFarquhar, R. (1977, July 28). *Debate on English language teaching overseas* (OD 52/35). English language teaching policy. The National Archives, Kew. London.

Macmillan, M. (1982, October 18). *ODA evaluation of the Key English Language Teaching (KELT) scheme* (OD 52/81). Evaluation of the KELT Scheme. The National Archives, Kew. London.

Macrae, J. E. C. (1982, 24 June). *Letter to underwood* (FCO 8/4871). English language projects in YAR. The National Archives, Kew. London.

Millard, G. E. (1964, 24 July). *Letter from British Embassy in Leopoldville* (FO 371/176735). Overseas Refugees Charities. The National Archives, Kew. London.

ODM. (1965). *Overseas Development: The work of the new ministry.* Ministry of Overseas Development. London: HMSO.

ODM. (1967). Teaching of English as a second language general (OD 17/442). Ministry of Overseas Development. The National Archives, Kew. London.

Overseas Development Administration and British Council. (1971, October). *The setting up of an English as a Foreign Language scheme* (OD17/673). English as Foreign Language. The National Archives, Kew. London.

Pennycook, A. (2014). *The cultural politics of English as an international language.* London: Routledge.

Phillipson, R. (1992). ELT: The native speaker's burden? *ELT Journal, 46*(1), 199–212.

Robson, J. A. (1981, March 17). *Letter to Luce from Robson of East Africa Department* (FCO 106/372). English language teaching in Burundi. The National Archives, Kew. London.

Ross, F. (2013). Bringing political identity into discursive and ideational analysis: Welfare reform in Britain and the United States. *British Politics, 8*(1), 51–78.

Schmidt, V. A. (2008). Discursive institutionalism: The explanatory power of ideas and discourse. *Annual Review of Political Science, 11,* 303–326.

Sharp, D. J. (1981, February 25). *Letter to Sharland* (FCO 106/372). English language teaching in Burundi. The National Archives, Kew. London.

Silverstein, M. (1979). Language structure and linguistic ideology. In C. L. Hofbauer, P. Clyne, & W. F. Hanks (Eds.), *The elements: A parasession on linguistic units and levels* (pp. 193–247). Chicago: Chicago Linguistic Society.

Smith, D. M. (1968). *English language teaching in Francophone countries* (FCO 25/781). English language training centre. The National Archives, Kew. London.

Smith, R. C. (2016). *ELT and the British Council, 1934–2014: Research notes.* Retrieved from: http://www2.warwick.ac.uk/fac/soc/al/research/collections/elt_archive/research_projects/britishcouncil/.

Taylor. (1965, May 28). *Letter from the Parliamentary Under-Secretary of State to the Minister of Overseas Development* (OD17/320). The teaching of English as a second language—Policy. The National Archives, Kew. London.

Tollefson, J. W. (2015). Historical-structural analysis. In D. C. Johnson & F. M. Hult (Eds.), *Research methods in language policy and planning: A practical guide.* Chichester: Wiley.

UNESCO. (2012). *Why language matters for the millennium development goals.* Bangkok: UNESCO.

Valters, C., & Whitty, B. (2017). *The politics of the results agenda in DFID: 1997–2017*. London: Overseas Development Institute.
Wendt, A. (1999). *Social theory of international politics*. Cambridge: Cambridge University Press.
Wiley, T. G. (2006). The lessons of historical investigation: Implications for the study of language policy and planning. In T. Ricento (Ed.), *An introduction to language policy: Theory and method* (pp. 135–152). Oxford: Blackwell.
Wright, S. (2016). *Language policy and language planning: From nationalism to globalisation*. Basingstoke: Palgrave.

CHAPTER 4

The Listening Zones of UK-Based Development NGOs

Introduction

While Chapters 2 and 3 provided insights into the listening histories of NGOs and of the UK government, here we examine the listening practices of INGO staff based in UK headquarters and in-country today. Following the theoretical framework described in Chapter 1, this chapter examines listening as a relational process (Eyben, 2006), and examines how the assumptions, geographical locations and language of development actors influence these processes of listening as a two-way dialogue in development programmes.

The chapter is structured around NGO workers' responses as they emerged during interviews: it starts by exploring listening as an institutional, mechanistic process that is largely organised in English, and then moves on to describe listening as an informal phenomenon that takes place in the in-between places, where listening is not regulated by paperwork and institutional requirements. The chapter explores the concept of the Listening Zone in all of its complexity, in which listening can take on various shapes and guises. Through its analysis of interviewees' responses, the chapter illustrates the relevance of conceptualising the Listening Zones as a space of coexistence, hybridity and mixing, in which the important role of language to power and control in transnational encounters is recognised.

The interviews drawn on in this chapter were conducted with thirty NGO practitioners who at the time of interviewing were working

H. Footitt et al., *Development NGOs and Languages*,
https://doi.org/10.1007/978-3-030-51776-2_4

(twenty-four interviewees) or had worked (six) for Christian Aid (eight), OxfamGB (five), Save the Children UK (nine) or Tearfund (eight). Interviewees were based either in UK international headquarters (nineteen interviewees), or overseas (eleven) and held a range of posts, including country managers, programme coordinators, specialist advisors and communication and translation managers. Interviewing took place between January and June 2016 either in person or over Skype. Interviews were semi-structured and lasted forty-five minutes on average. The audio recordings of interviews were transcribed and coded in order to identify recurring themes. Interviews were held in English, as all interviewees used English as part of their job in the INGO they worked for. Nevertheless, the choice for English may inadvertently have affected power relationships between interviewer and interviewed (Bigelow & Warriner, 2019), particularly for those interviewees based overseas whose first language was not English. A longer discussion on our language choices as researchers is included in Chapter 9.

In interviews, we asked NGO workers questions on what listening meant for them, and in what context the concept of listening was used in their organisations. In addition, we asked if and how attention was paid in the organisation to the role of language and cultural knowledge during listening efforts. As will become clear throughout the chapter, many of the themes identified in Chapter 2 as constitutive of NGOs' listening histories re-emerge in the responses that NGO workers shared: the meta-discourse of evaluation and accountability; the role of geographical location (headquarters or in-country) in shaping relationships; the challenges involved with translating the seemingly universalist lexicon of development while ensuring cultural sensitivity and diversity; and the largely unchallenged predominance of English. Whilst Chapter 2 has explored how these features have historically emerged as part of NGOs' listening ideologies, this chapter interrogates how NGO workers in headquarters and in-country as key actors in the Listening Zones perform their listening activities today, and what potential problems and uncertainties they experience. Furthermore, the chapter challenges some of the assumptions of DFID officials about NGOs' ability to listen (multilingually), as described in Chapter 3, by presenting the listening perceptions of NGO workers themselves. The chapter thus contributes to the Listening Zones framing by providing a platform for these key actors, who find themselves structurally placed between international donors and local communities.

Institutional Listening

In the first instance, when interviewees were asked how the concept of listening was used in their organisations, they generally referred to NGO institutionalised mechanisms and procedures of listening. Responses were set in an institutional discourse of accountability to 'beneficiaries'. In some cases (NGO 1, manager, UK; NGO 26, desk/advisory officer, Africa; NGO 27, manager, UK), these institutional narratives were embedded in broader frameworks of international agreements across the NGO sector:

> I think at the moment in the aid world generally, in the humanitarian world in particular perhaps, there's an increased focus on, it's called a bunch of things: communicating with communities, accountability to affected communications, community engagement and accountability depending on the organisation you're in. (NGO 11, desk/advisory officer, UK)

Answers within the framework of accountability described listening as a mechanistic process, built-in throughout the development project cycle. Those interviewees who were high-level managers or experts in Monitoring and Evaluation (M&E) processes provided lengthy descriptions of how listening was achieved:

> when it comes to beneficiaries, we would want to listen to them in different ways as part of the needs assessment process. We would want to talk to them, find out what their needs are in that particular locality, ask them to prioritise the assistance that they're looking for and we would do that at the beginning of a project, like while a project is being designed, we would want to keep that discussion going during the implementation of a project so we can hear back from them, then we would want to continue listening towards the end or after the end of the project so we can understand their views on how they think a project went. So, we'd probably call the listening in the first stage needs assessment or baseline survey. We'd probably call the ongoing listening, we'd probably call that monitoring or beneficiary accountability. And then the final listening we would be, we would call that review or evaluation to learning. (NGO 24, manager, UK)

Characteristic of these answers was the high level of development lexis: 'needs assessments', done through 'baseline surveys', monitoring through 'community consultations' (NGO 14, desk/advisory officer, Asia; NGO 15, manager, Africa), setting up 'complaints and feedback mechanisms' which could be achieved through 'suggestion boxes' and 'one-to-one interviews' (NGO 15, manager, Africa). This type of lexis, it could be argued, is not only specific to the sector, but also demonstrates a grounding in Western scientific research methods: the need to 'cross reference things', ensuring there was 'triangulation of methods' (NGO 1, manager, UK), and describing the process of listening as one of 'getting the voices of affected people' (NGO 26, desk/advisory officer, UK) and 'collect[ing] field level information' (NGO 18, manager, Africa). From these discussions, 'listening' appeared as a process that should lead to learning and to institutional change, comprising a number of different mechanisms that would allow NGOs to demonstrate and to ensure their accountability to beneficiaries:

> It's not about saying that we will be listening, no, you have to do it in practice, to put it into... to incorporate it into your approaches, it has to be in the design itself. (NGO 15, manager, Africa)

Whilst initial responses to 'what is listening?' often started with confident and clearly structured narratives on accountability mechanisms built into the project cycle, as interviews went on, responses became more complex and interviewees tended to express uncertainty about the success of institutionalised forms of listening. The picture that gradually emerged of NGOs' Listening Zones was one of extreme complexity, which encompassed many more processes than those established as intrinsic to accountability. The Listening Zone was a space populated by multiple actors, in which listening relationships were heterogeneous and could vary from project to project. A project might involve "direct work with communities, with children, with youth, with men and women, with local government structures and with local civil society organisations, but also with central authorities and donors and other international actors" (NGO 13, manager, Africa). Within this web of relationships, there were various issues that had an impact on who NGO staff would listen to, when listening would take place, in what format, language and so on. Interviewees discussed a variety of issues that they perceived as potential obstacles to successful listening, including the power of the donor, the size of the NGO, the geographical distance between INGO headquarters and their in-country programmes, and the predominance of English.

Working in a web of relationships, NGOs were in theory required to listen to all parties involved in development programmes. But interviewees indicated that in practice, there were different types of listening, depending on the actor that was being listened to: "In terms of the type of listening, I think the intensity, you know, there are audiences that we actively listen to and that actively listen to us. And there are audiences that we just hear as opposed to listen" (NGO 17, communications, Africa). Those most 'actively' listened to were identified as the actors with the most financial or political power, particularly international donors (NGO 17, communications, Africa). International donors typically require NGOs to submit progress and evaluative reports and to collect specific data, often quantitative, in order to demonstrate project success and value for money (see Chapter 3). Interviewees indicated that donor demands could heavily influence the ways in which NGOs engaged in listening to communities: they could influence the questions that NGOs were asking, the specific moments at which they would make time and space to listen to people, the format in which they were doing so and so on. Listening to local communities was done through focus groups, community meetings or one-on-one interviews, during which NGO staff aimed to collect answers to questions that had been predesigned by a team of international experts in the shape of surveys and questionnaires, either on paper or digitally on tablets (NGO 23, manager, UK). This highly mediated type of listening was geared towards taking stock of project progress and mapping the NGOs' internal learning, but it did not always allow for discussions that fell outside the remit of predesigned listening. Interviewees argued that listening efforts left little space for personal engagement and could eventually overlook the very people that NGOs set out to help.

> A lot of the time in NGO, we are - we're focused on the artefacts, you know, anecdotes toward these data about people statistics or the trends and things like that. Whereas, we forget that at the end of the day, it's about bringing people out of poverty. (NGO 3, manager, Asia)

Donors' pressure on INGOs to demonstrate successful project outcomes and to turn projects around in a relatively short timeframe meant that at its worst, listening could take the shape of a tick-box exercise, organised just for the sake of it, but from which no action would result:

> I think in theory at least there's quite a lot of emphasis placed on listening and the quality of listening, so actually hearing what somebody is trying to tell you rather than just leaving a gap for somebody to talk. But whether that's how it works in practice I think is a different question. (NGO 11, desk/advisory officer, UK)

Although having listening mechanisms in place had advantages in terms of collecting data in a structured and organised way, which would be comparable across different settings, staff recognised that the process might be too restrictive:

> The point of listening, it's to engage, ask questions and see what people are saying. Or just… maybe it's not… once we design the questions we're asking, we are already honing it to a specific area, so maybe it's more about being open to just 'Okay, what do you want to say to us?' rather than us asking specific things and listening to what they're saying. (NGO 10, desk/advisory officer, UK)

Whilst staff based in headquarters who only briefly visit in-country programmes could find the guidance of predetermined questions useful, it might not assist them in understanding the local realities of people. The physical distance from in-country programmes and local communities was something that various interviewees based in headquarters struggled with. They talked about the feeling of not "being there", which was "a real handicap in my work" (NGO 21, manager, UK); of being placed at "one level removed" with "things happening beyond our remit" (NGO 20, communications, UK). In addition, staff in headquarters tended to work on a portfolio that included a wide range of countries, meaning that it was difficult "to have someone linked to a country" (NGO 10, desk/advisory officer, UK). In-country staff, from their end, also identified issues related to the geographical distance that separated them from their international colleagues and donors. Some expressed the view that a country's language, history and geographical location affected the way in which colleagues in headquarters engaged with in-country programmes. Participants from countries in which English did not have an official status felt that linguistic and cultural differences placed them in a disadvantaged position. A staff member based in Latin America pondered:

> I think that sometimes there is a limitation especially when the colleagues from headquarters they don't speak Spanish or they don't have interest in

> this language or in this context. So, sometimes there are tensions about that. Because probably, for some colleagues it's easier to communicate better with the African or maybe the Asian partners or staff instead of the Latin American because the language, the context and the history is different. (NGO 4, manager, Latin America)

Similar comments emerged from NGO staff based in French-speaking African countries (NGO 2, manager, Africa). A factor that further complicated the feeling of distance, and in some cases, disengagement, was the size of the INGO. The larger an organisation was, the more complex its internal procedures were perceived to be. For in-country staff, this could mean that there was less time to spend with communities.

> The very fact that [our organisation is an X] billion a year organisation… Growing, wanting to grow, seeing that growth will bring resources, that will bring capabilities, that will bring influence across a more wide geographic spectrum, and, thematically, very, very complex areas means that we have created complexity… probably the bulk of our time is spent on our own internal processes and requirements. (NGO 13, manager, Africa)

In the eyes of this interviewee, the abundance of internal processes ultimately led to less priority being placed on consultation with community members. This seemed in itself paradoxical since the majority of such processes had been put in place precisely to ensure that INGOs were accountable to the communities with whom they were working.

Listening Through English

Interviewees' responses indicated that institutional listening mechanisms were not sufficient to ensure that local communities and partners could participate in shaping development projects. One of the shortcomings of institutional listening that interviewees identified was that listening mechanisms largely ignored the role of language. More specifically, interviewees commented at length on the challenges they faced with using development discourse transnationally, as this discourse was considered to be linked to anglophone and Western understandings and frameworks of development (Cornwall & Eade, 2010). These issues were described as operating at two levels: firstly, the seemingly unquestioned use of English by international NGOs and donors, and secondly, the abundance of development jargon. Interviewees, particularly those based in-country, spoke at length about the predominance of English in reporting contexts, and problematised the fact that in-country staff were asked to report on their activities in English. For example, one in-country participant related:

> …we do a lot of case studies or success story productions in the communication unit here, and most of them come from the field offices at the grass-root level, that's where the stories happen… One impairment is they are required to write the success stories in English, which I'm trying to change right now, I don't think that's a fair requirement, I don't think it's also the right way to go because, like I said, the proficiency of English falls down as you go lower in command within [our organisation], but they're still required to submit stories in English, and it's a very difficult situation right now because these are people, English is their third language or fourth language and it's sort of an unfair requirement. (NGO 17, communications, Africa)

Interviewees recognised that the common requirement for reporting in English implied that those with English language skills were being advantaged in recruitment processes (cf. Roth, 2018):

> There is probably a threshold capability in English language, both verbal and written, that sometimes means, erm, people who perform very well in those kinds of assessment may not actually have the disposition, may not have the skills, may not have the confidence to be engaging as effectively in their interaction with [beneficiaries] as we would wish. (NGO 13, manager, Africa)

While in-country staff were expected to be at least bilingual with a high level of fluency in English, language skills were not an essential requirement for international staff, but rather "a desirable" (NGO 11, desk/advisory officer, UK), "preferred, but in the absence of that… we wouldn't insist on it" (NGO 24, manager, UK). The dominant position of English often created a sense of nervousness or embarrassment with native English-speaking interviewees, who tended to be aware of their privileged position. Those who had limited foreign language knowledge spoke self-consciously about their lack of language skills: "My French is very ropey" (NGO 25, desk/advisory officer, UK); "I speak a little bit of Portuguese but that's it… I have terrible language skills" (NGO

10, desk/advisory officer, UK). Some explained what held them back from learning, which was often a mix of other priorities, especially when deployed to humanitarian crisis situations:

> There were new challenges, internal challenges that needed to be addressed urgently. Those, uh, dominated my attention, my energies, and I did not prioritise taking the time to learn Kiswahili. So it is, uh, very much to my disadvantage, very much to my, erm… well, it doesn't reflect well on me as a development practitioner, for sure. (NGO 13, manager, Africa)

> [Portuguese] is not the most useful language for work anyway. But it would be good. But then again, the countries that I work in, I mean it would be like… learning local Zambian languages or Tajik or Bengali. (NGO 10, desk/advisory officer, UK)

Language learning was described as something INGOs were not overtly supporting, neither for in-country staff nor those at headquarters. Money might perhaps be found on a case-by-case basis, but there was no organised institutional support:

> *Participant*: "But on a longer term, employing people on a longer-term basis to go and work in our international development programme, erm, I would really expect people to try to learn the language of the country, erm… But you know if you…"
> *Interviewer*: "What would you expect [your NGO] to pay? I mean language is quite expensive."
> *Participant*: "Well you see this is the point, this is why I say I'm ashamed to say I don't think we really invested in this."
> (NGO 27, manager, UK)

Instead, headquarters staff collaborating with in-country colleagues from a distance or during country visits would do so largely in English. At headquarters level, the generally accepted attitude was that "we are an international organisation, English is the language. Therefore, publications are in English. Full stop" (NGO 6, communications, UK). Nevertheless, there was a feeling that this attitude had started to be challenged, particularly as a consequence of organisations having decentralised over the years (NGO 6, communications, UK; NGO 24, manager, UK). Some headquarters staff were acutely aware of the linguistic burden placed on in-country colleagues, and they highlighted the steps that they were taking within their teams to allow in-country colleagues to use their national languages: Spanish, French, Arabic and Portuguese (NGO 24, manager, UK). Such steps involved, for example, inviting in-country colleagues to submit documents in other languages in their programme, and using Google Translate in the first instance to understand the gist of non-English documents. After a first scan, a professional translation was sometimes commissioned. This way of working was a strategy to become more sensitive to people's linguistic backgrounds:

> We're a little bit embarrassed to be so Anglo-centric; we would like to be more grassroots... basically we are sensitive to the need to let people communicate in their own language where possible. (NGO 24, manager, UK)

It is important to note here that these multilingual strategies were not encouraged through institutional policies or guidelines but were initiated by individuals. In sharing their feelings of shame, and relating the strategies chosen to address the predominance of English, it became clear that the interviewees were conscious of the clash between organisational values of inclusion, participation and 'listening' and the largely monolingual working practices of headquarters.

On their part, in-country participants, expressed frustration at the lack of recognition from their organisation's headquarters about the linguistic burden they carried, providing oral and written translation between INGO headquarters staff and international donors, and local communities and/or partner organisations, though this was not officially part of their job descriptions. In-country staff spoke of the challenges involved in acting as language mediators and the requirement to write in English, and the lack of support from headquarters to address these challenges. For example, when asked about potential assistance from headquarters in checking the English language in reports written in their office, a participant based in a French-speaking environment said:

> Actually, we are on our own to be frank. I mean, this is something that is challenging because we fear that we forgot that there are no English-speaking countries. We struggle more to give the required quality to our report compared to those who are from English-speaking countries. But it is taking me too much time when it comes to produce my annual report. (NGO 2, manager, Africa)

In addition to the lack of support in checking and improving the quality of English in reporting, INGO headquarters were also not perceived to be openly and actively acknowledging the English language learning needs that their in-country staff might have:

> I have been struggling over these few years about giving my staff the opportunity to go and seek other countries, English speaking countries to be – they are performance staff. They are challenging their English language so this comes out to be very very difficult because of resource limitation. (NGO 2, manager, Africa)

The need for English at the in-country level had effects further down the development chain as well, for example, when recruiting suitable in-country partner organisations for consultations:

> …for example, if [the INGO], say, we need a partner to participate in advisory group or working group, but we need that the people speak English. And then that is difficult because people need a lot of experiences, but they don't speak English. And then, we can't say these people – or propose these people to participate in this working group for example. I think it's something that they need to review and revisit that the way in which [the INGO] would involve partners in this – and approve because I think it's really important that [the INGO] listen directly to partner. (NGO 4, manager, Latin America)

Making the ability to speak English a requirement for participation implied that a pre-selection of who is listened to already takes place before the meeting: those who speak English are often male and from elite backgrounds, with access to education. This practice stands in stark contrast to INGO claims that their programmes set out to be inclusive of those considered most vulnerable, in particular women and girls.

Even when participants in consultation meetings spoke English, communication problems could emerge, particularly because of the widespread use of anglophone buzzwords in development settings. Many words that were central to INGO projects were considered as lacking in conceptual clarity, which could lead to misunderstandings: "Just speaking between native English speakers using some of these terms, people all mean different things" (NGO 7, manager, UK). Interviewees acknowledged that there was often an assumption that people understood such terms in the same way. Particularly when working in English only, the idea that key concepts might actually mean different things for people working in other linguistic and cultural environments was not one that came naturally. One interviewee arrived at this realisation during the interviewing process. This participant talked about the amount of jargon used in their INGO, suggesting that it had taken months to master this language when they had first joined the organisation. When asked if the meaning of these concepts was discussed and negotiated with in-country colleagues, who worked in different cultural and linguistic contexts, they replied:

> I don't know. I mean not explicitly, when I've visited, I think we've… well I've had the perception that we've understood each other, maybe we haven't! …Because I've never been in country and struggled when talking about something that we use in [this NGO], like language, never struggled to… they use the same terminology it seems… in the country offices all of the people I've worked with speak English. (NGO 10, desk officer/advisory, UK)

The absence of this type of discussion could potentially result in misunderstandings, yet there were no institutional guidelines that encouraged negotiating and agreeing on definitions of common terms. Some interviewees resorted to informal ways of listening to address conceptual confusion, going beyond the project mechanisms of institutional listening that largely ignored language.

Informal Listening

As interviewees described perceived shortcomings in institutionalised listening, responses emerged that highlighted the need for a variety of listening strategies including "looking at formal and informal spaces, making sure that we're using verbal and written, kind of both information, giving an information, receiving, those kinds of things from an inclusivity perspective" (NGO 1, manager, UK), at the same time articulating the feeling that there was currently "a gap in our accountability practice" (NGO 1, manager, UK). Answers that identified a type of listening that was not connected to managerial notions of accountability emphasised values of trust, the commitment to help others, to stand by people, and demonstrate respect for their ways of working and being. Typically, these responses emphasised the need to engage in a dialogue with local communities, and the importance of making time to engage in these types of conversations:

> Listening for me is about taking time to invest in relationships. It's about setting time aside to learn from others. It's about making a concerted effort to exchange information and do something with that information. It's about valuing people as well, because if you're listening you are valuing what they're saying. Especially if you then... if that is then translated into action, you're not just listening but you're actively listening, you do something with what you're hearing, that's even better. (NGO 30, manager, UK)

Such listening demanded courage. For in-country staff and partners who would have designed the projects they were running, it could be particularly challenging to open up to criticism and consider other ways of conducting a particular project during monitoring and evaluation (NGO 17, communications, Africa). Partners could be reluctant to listen to local communities: "It's a lot of hard work, and partners would recognise it's hard work and some of that's about this cultural issue of, you know, making sure that you're listening to everybody in the community" (NGO 7, manager, UK). For headquarters staff, there was a particular challenge in aiming to listen outside one's own frameworks, one's own language and one's own worldview:

> We say that's what we do [listening], but it's quite easy to stay in traditional mode, that we're – you know, a developed – coming from a developed country and we are offering something to other people... And so I think the real challenge in listening, if you like, is to make – is to try and think that you're not doing it through that lens and I am not sure that we always succeed in – you know, with that. (NGO 7, manager, UK)

Being open to listening to what the 'other' had to say was described as a risky enterprise that could potentially harm working relationships. It seemed that what was needed to be able to truly listen was a close working relationship between NGO staff and in-country partners, in which both parties would feel comfortable enough to ask difficult questions. The need for relationships of trust particularly emerged when interviewees discussed their uncertainty regarding the possibility of not having fully understood what local partners had written in English project applications and reports. For example, one interviewee described their tenacious approach in questioning the meaning of some of the terminology used by in-country partners, more specifically the concept of 'safe spaces':

> *Participant*: "…we don't know if what they mean by that is a space that – so a safe space could apply to women survivors of gender-based violence. That kind of terminology is used often…"
> *Interviewer*: "Yes."
> *Participant*: "…in dealing with those, that kind of programming, creating a safe space for women to be able to talk about their problems. In the context of the [local civil war], what does a safe space mean?"
> *Interviewer*: "Yes."
> *Participant*: "Does that mean somewhere that you might not be bombed?"
> *Interviewer*: "Yes."
> *Participant*: "That you're creating people, you're helping people have a place where they might be able to come to or that it might have some electricity and water that their home doesn't have. And okay, we will be, hopefully have a conversation over Skype or something and we will establish what that meant."
> (NGO 7, manager, UK)

Such a conversation would take place in Arabic, with, in this case, UK-based staff making an effort to speak in a language that was not their own in order to understand what the English term 'safe spaces' meant for in-country partners. In this interviewee's response, there was a great awareness of the lack of conceptual clarity in English humanitarian jargon, and the challenges involved in initiating conversations about the meaning of certain terms, as this implied admitting not understanding, and risking offending the other party involved, who may think "you're suggesting that… they are not literate in English" (NGO 7, manager, UK).

This example shows the concern of staff in headquarters regarding how to raise such issues in a sensitive way, and it shows their commitment to creating successful working relationships with their partners in which good communication— potentially in the language of the other— is central. However, such commitment to interrogate the meaning of concepts multilingually was not always present and was highly dependent on the agency of individual actors. Another example on reporting quality again shows that the practices that ensure successful communication often depended on personal agency and initiative. This interviewee was trying to improve the quality of reporting and shared that many of the reports they had read came across as very dry:

> But when you speak to people, then you get the detail that you want. And so, I asked them 'What if you wrote your report in Arabic and then we can translate it after?' we tried that, and that worked much better. The quality of the reporting was much better, and I think it extends further than just reporting, but in general in documentation I think there's an assumption that everyone is able to communicate well in English, when clearly that's not the case. But that's the expectation, maybe. (NGO 14, manager, Asia)

Other participants also acknowledged that writing in another language was challenging and resulted in low-quality reporting: "The report were fairly badly written... but then how surprising is that when they're writing in a second language that they're not confident in speaking anyway?" (NGO 24, manager, UK). But action to address this issue was not widespread. Rather, there seemed to be an acceptance that writing in English was the institutional norm, or perhaps, as one interviewee reflected, the problem was that monolingual English speakers did not consider the amount of effort it takes to write in a foreign language (NGO 14, manager, Asia):

> And so, we get annoyed and frustrated at people who submit reports but, you know, they could probably write circles around you if they wrote in their native tongue. So, yeah, I think it's... it's something we need to work on, I think, as an organisation, how to better tap into extremely intelligent people who maybe don't have the confidence or the right tools to be able to write in the way that we want them to be able to write and think. (NGO 14, manager, Asia)

What became evident here, again, was the gap in institutional practice and guidelines to encourage reflection on the challenges involved in working and writing in another language. This lack of institutional interest generally leaves NGO workers to comprehend and then tackle the issue on a purely personal basis. In other words, these linguistic issues are dealt with through personal agency in the absence of institutional priority.

Listening Through Translation

A similar absence on guidelines was noted for another recurring type of language practice, namely working with interpreters and translators. Despite the transnational scope of NGOs' work, interviewees reported that their organisations did not tend to have policies in place that dealt with translation and interpreting. When language and/or translation policies did exist, these tended to be geared towards translating information targeted at external audiences, such as the media, private and public donors and the general public in the context of fundraising and branding campaigns. Consequently, the languages these policies covered were limited to a handful of widely spoken, mostly colonial languages, including English, French and Spanish, and to a lesser extent Portuguese and Arabic. Ensuring successful communication between INGO staff and local communities was considered as a process that could naturally be handled by in-country staff who were assumed to have both the local cultural understanding and necessary language skills. Development programmes generally imply a long-term commitment for INGOs to work in a specific country, and it was therefore assumed that the necessary expertise to operate in a certain context would have been established over the years (NGO 13, manager, Africa).

Relying on in-country staff to provide interpreting services during meetings with local communities was common, although language mediation did not tend to be part of their job description (NGO 11, desk/advisory officer, UK; see also, Chapter 5). In-country participants generally spoke with confidence about providing these oral services, which stood in stark contrast to how they described their experiences when writing reports in English. For example, an interviewee who indicated that writing in English was extremely difficult expressed the following when asked who provided language mediation during meetings with UK colleagues:

> ...actually, when it comes to [orally] translating, you find for instance that within our team... There are those who are bilingual for instance. Me, I can translate. There are others who can translate from French to English and vice versa... We make sure that we maintain this kind of atmosphere that there is always someone who can translate in both languages. (NGO 2, manager, Africa)

This is not to say translation and interpreting were considered as unproblematic, but rather that local staff had arrived at ways of dealing with these issues:

> The challenge is then when you are, we are on the field. The poor communities at the village level. ...Ideally, we, if for instance there are young men

> who have finished their studies, that didn't find a job up in the, in the capital city or in the big town… so we recruit local to do the role of translators. Because, they understand better all the jargon of the communities. So, they can do a very good translation which is very helpful for us. (NGO 2, manager, Africa)

Particularly for those based in African countries, oral multilingual working practices were considered part of everyday life: "Obvious we get somebody to [orally] translate for us… it's a well-informed issue, it's not a surprise" (NGO 15, manager, Africa).

Whilst staff from headquarters were generally at ease with relying on their in-country colleagues to provide interpreting during their visits, suspicion arose when these services were provided by externally recruited interpreters. There was a concern that colleagues visiting in-country programmes were:

> bringing back interpretations of what people are saying rather than actually what the people are saying… I want to hear it from them. So, in the process of briefing or seeking out interpreters, we said we need word for word. We don't want the interpreter to interpret what they think the person said. (NGO 6, communications, UK)

Headquarters staff working with interpreters described a variety of strategies to deduce whether the interpreting provided was accurate. This included looking at body language, observing people's response: "if there's complete silence and people like looking at each other, like I have no idea what you're talking about, and then we have to like try and reframe the questions" (NGO 10, desk officer/advisory, UK); or comparing the length of the original phrasing to that of the oral translation (NGO 12, manager, Africa). Many participants who relied on interpreting spoke with uncertainty about the success of working with local partners and communities through translation:

> Obviously, I've run workshops with partners and also gone to the field and met all of our project participants and I don't know how they've received what I've said because I can't understand. (NGO 10, desk/advisory officer, UK)

Language was frequently described as a barrier by staff from headquarters, particularly during data collection in communities. Some participants described careful strategies that had been put in place to deal with the need to translate questionnaires into local languages in a way that was culturally relevant and understandable by organising workshops, for example, or providing training beforehand for local staff and enumerators who would be collecting the data (NGO 23, manager, UK). One interviewee explained how they had rolled out a questionnaire, which involved a process of translation back and forth between English and Portuguese during the design stage and a six-day training course for enumerators to explain the purposes of the research with the aim of "making sure they understood how it was supposed to be delivered" (NGO 10, desk/advisory officer, UK). But the participant also pointed out that, because there was no way to check the translation into local languages by enumerators while they were collecting the data, "that work could all be wasted if we are then doing it in a local language and they're asking something completely different" (NGO 10, desk/advisory officer, UK).

Whilst there were occasional checks from team managers who would sit in on interviews, this was only for a fraction of the surveys that were conducted, meaning that "there's probably things that fall through the gaps" (NGO 10, desk/advisory officer, UK). There was even less institutional reflection on the translation processes that occurred from local languages into English, i.e., the translation of participants' responses into the language (and format) typically used to deliver reports to headquarters. If any policies or mechanisms were in place to control the quality of translation, these were focused on translation from English into local languages. The interview data thus demonstrate that the few mechanisms that were in place were concerned with transferring information from the INGO in English into local languages to local communities, but not with what local communities were sharing in their own languages and how this was transferred into English.

Conclusion

Through an analysis of NGO workers' responses to questions on how they listen to the local communities they work with, this chapter has interrogated the listening practices of staff, both in-country and at UK headquarters, of four INGOs. The chapter followed the structure of participant responses, beginning with a discussion of the characteristics of institutionalised listening, which tended to be defined in terms of accountability, including accountability to local communities (downwards accountability) and donors (upwards accountability) (Crack, 2013; Ebrahim, 2003; Edwards & Hulme, 1996). Institutional listening was embedded in anglophone, quasi-universalist frames of data collection through focus groups, one-on-one interviews and suggestion boxes. These responses echoed widespread processes in the NGO sector of 'capturing voices' for the purposes of monitoring and evaluation (see Chapter 1; Bond, 2013; INTRAC, 2016; Manyozo, 2017), but the participants questioned the potential success and usefulness of a type of listening that was mechanistic and predefined according to Western notions of development. The way in which the idea of accountability was transformed into practice was generally felt to be too restrictive, leaving insufficient space for real dialogue and action. There was a perceived disconnection between the expectations of such institutionalised forms of listening and the possibilities to do so effectively with the limited resources available and within strict time constraints.

Moreover, institutionalised listening was considered as being largely organised through English and as favouring those actors in development contexts who were able to speak English and 'development speak' fluently (Cornwall & Eade, 2010). Participants considered the low status that was accorded to language by NGOs to be a key issue. They related that language needs and challenges were not systematically discussed in the context of programme planning, delivery and evaluation, and that there was little institutional support for the linguistic burden carried by multilingual— often in-country— colleagues. The picture that emerged was one in which institutional practices, policies and guidelines largely overlooked the linguistic challenges of listening to local communities, which could have a negative effect on inclusion, project outcomes, and equity in working relationships.

Because of the observed shortcoming of institutionalised listening, some interviewees spoke of the need for a type of listening that can be best described as 'informal'. This listening was a much more hybrid process of mixing and mutuality rather than of one-sided extraction. Interviewees emphasised the importance of trust when engaging in this type of listening, whereby joint efforts of sense-making and co-creation could take place only if trust had been established between NGO workers and the in-country colleagues and local communities they worked with.

The role of language was closely linked to these processes of establishing trust. A variety of NGO workers described ways of working that they had devised, in which they could allow their non-native English-speaking colleagues to use their own language, and some NGO headquarters colleagues made efforts to engage in conversations by using other languages. Devised working practices included allowing colleagues to write in their own language and translating what they had written, or discussing the English content of documents in another language. This behaviour is what we could call 'hospitalité langagière' or 'linguistic hospitality' (Ricoeur, 2004): aiming to host the 'other' without claiming that our own language is sufficient. Linguistic hospitality shows respect and openness, a willingness to learn others' languages and cultures. However, as highlighted in the responses of participants, this type of hospitality relied on the agency and initiative of individual NGO workers and did not seem to be embedded in institutionalised forms of listening.

Overall, this chapter depicts institutionalised listening as one that traditionally remains framed within Western understandings and through English as the lingua franca of development. This largely ignores the importance of listening multilingually and multiculturally to arrive at processes of transnational exchange, and two-way dialogue in which speakers and listeners engage in joint efforts of sense-making. Multilingual listening as two-way dialogue did exist, but generally emerged through the initiative of individual NGO workers who expressed uncertainty about the success of institutionalised forms of listening. In other words, a more radical, risky type of listening (see Chapter 1) did exist, but emerged informally in the in-between spaces as a type of activism on the part of individual NGO workers who were keen to recognise the languages and cultures of the 'other', ready to resist what Ricoeur (2004, p. 4) has called "the pretentions to self-sufficiency" and "the refusal to allow the foreign mediate".

References

Bigelow, M., & Warriner, D. S. (Eds.). (2019). *Critical reflections on research methods: Power and equity in complex multilingual contexts*. Bristol: Multilingual Matters.

Bond (2013). *Principles and checklist for assessing the quality of evidence*. Retrieved from https://www.bond.org.uk/file/17815.

Cornwall, A., & Eade, D. (Eds.). (2010). *Deconstructing development discourse: Buzzwords and fuzzwords*. Rugby: Practical Action Publishing with Oxfam GB.

Crack, A. M. (2013). INGO accountability deficits: The imperatives for further reform. *Globalizations, 10*(2), 293–308.

Ebrahim, A. (2003). Accountability in practice: Mechanisms for NGOs. *World Development, 31*(5), 813–829.

Edwards, M., & Hulme, D. (1996). Too close for comfort? The impact of official aid on nongovernmental organizations. *World Development, 24*(6), 961–973.

Eyben, R. (Ed.). (2006). *Relationships for aid*. London: Earthscan.

INTRAC. (2016). *DFID Beneficiary Feedback Mechanisms (BFM) Pilot. End-point Review: Synthesis Report*. Retrieved from https://www.intrac.org/resources/dfid-beneficiary-feedback-mechanisms-bfm-pilot-end-point-review-synthesis.

Manyozo, L. (2017). *Communicating development with communities*. Abingdon and New York: Routledge.

Ricoeur, P. (2004). *Sur la traduction*. Paris: Bayard.

Roth, S. (2018). Linguistic capital and inequality in aid relations. *Sociological Research Online, 24*(1), 38–54.

CHAPTER 5

Translators and Interpreters in Development

Introduction

The previous chapters have pointed to the omnipresence of translation as a process of linguistic and cultural mediation in many different aspects of development programmes, such as the translation of project-related documents, informal discussions about the meaning of key concepts between NGO staff, or interpreting being provided during meetings with local communities who speak different languages than those of the NGO worker or donor. This chapter aims to explore who the translators and interpreters are that provide linguistic and cultural mediation in INGOs' development programmes.

In the academic literature of Development Studies and Translating/Interpreting Studies, there has been relatively little engagement with the role of translation and translators in contexts of development. A notable body of research exploring the role of the development 'broker' has dealt with this topic to some extent (Bierschenk, Chauveau, & Olivier de Sardan, 2000; Lewis & Mosse, 2006). Within this literature, development brokers are considered as a distinct category of actors who help development agencies to reach the grassroots level, and who are typically embedded both in the local context and in the international development community. To be able to mediate between the local and international level, language skills are of vital importance, and brokers typically master a mix of different languages, including the local and national language, and sometimes additional lingua francas such

H. Footitt et al., *Development NGOs and Languages*,
https://doi.org/10.1007/978-3-030-51776-2_5

as English. Whilst research on development brokers has acknowledged these language skills, there has been little engagement with how brokers conduct translation/interpreting work, how they perceive their role as linguistic mediators, or what translation-related training they may have benefited from.

Another body of work that is related to translators working in contexts of international development concerns research that has investigated 'vernacularisation' processes of human rights discourse, i.e., the process of appropriation and local adoption of globally generated ideas and strategies (Goodale & Merry, 2007; Levitt & Merry, 2009; Merry, 2006). The translators that have been considered as key agents in these vernacularisation processes include lawyers, human rights workers, community leaders and social movement activists (Merry, 2006, p. 42). However, translation in this body of work has largely been conceptualised as a process of transferring ideas from one context to another, with the process of linguistic translation and the figure of the professional translator/interpreter largely remaining absent from these discussions. In sum, the existing research in development anthropology has not yet fully engaged with questions related to the linguistic processes of translation, or with the actors who take charge of these processes and the contextual constraints under which they may be working.

In Translation/Interpreting Studies, on the other hand, the role and agency of these linguistic translators and interpreters, professional and non-professional, has been explored in a variety of contexts as part of the 'sociological turn' in these disciplines (Angelelli, 2012; Fukari & Wolf, 2007) including, for example, in hospitals, courts and asylum seeker settings (Angelelli, 2004; Berk-Seligson, 1990; Inghilleri, 2005). However, the role of interpreters and translators in development contexts has largely passed by unnoticed, although some more recent research has started to address this gap (Marais & Delgado Luchner, 2018; Marais, 2014).

This chapter aims to make a further contribution to this emerging literature by providing more empirical data on the role and figure of the translator/interpreter in international NGO programmes. The chapter describes and contrasts some of the typical profiles of translators/interpreters as well as general trends in translation practice in key locations of INGO operations: firstly, in their UK-based headquarters, and secondly, in their development programmes and in collaborative work with partner organisations in-country, more specifically in Kyrgyzstan,

Malawi and Peru. Considering INGOs as transnational organisations that operate in a decentralised manner through their activities in, above and between the traditional 'container spaces' of national societies (Dijkzeul, 2008), the chapter compares practices across these different contexts, keeping in mind their different political, historical and linguistic characteristics. For each of these locations, the chapter describes who the translators/interpreters are, what their professional background is, and if and how these translation profiles and common translation practices differ from what is generally considered as professional translation/interpreting practice in Western contexts. By providing data that deals with languages and local contexts that have traditionally fallen outside the scope of Translation/Interpreting Studies (Marais, 2014; Tymoczko, 2007), the current chapter aims to extend understandings of translation and interpreting practices in contexts outside the Global North that are of relevance to Translation/Interpreting Studies as well as to Development Studies.

The chapter draws on two key data sets: policy documents relating to language and translation, and semi-structured interviews. The interview data include thirty interviews conducted with translation and communication managers and general NGO staff in INGOs between January and June 2016, as well as eighty-eight in-country interviews held in Kyrgyzstan, Malawi and Peru between December 2017 and January 2018. In addition, the chapter draws on informal conversations with translators in December 2015 during a 'Translating Development' workshop, organised by the Listening Zones research team on 12 October 2017 in London (for a recording of this event, see SchAdvStudy, 2017), and a subsequent key publication, a special issue of the journal *Translation Spaces* (Tesseur, 2018).

The chapter first delves deeper into translation practices at headquarters level, and then moves on to practices in-country. For the in-country data, a succinct overview of the most important tendencies is presented, and references are included to the separate country chapters (Chapters 6, 7, and 8), which explore some of these findings in more depth. It is important to note that we do not claim that these data necessarily represent a generalisable picture, or an exhaustive list of translation/interpreting practices in these contexts, or that the data could be generalisable to any type of development context. Rather, the discussion presents an overview of the practices that were described to us in our specific data set.

Translators and Interpreters in UK-Based Headquarters: Internal Translation Services

Institutionalisation of Internal Translation Services

Although UK-based headquarters of INGOs largely operate in English, some have internal translation departments that handle at least part of the translation needs arising from the organisation's international work. This type of institutionalised translation service at headquarters level was found to be a relatively recent phenomenon. Among the four INGOs with which the Listening Zones research closely engaged, three had internal translation services, all of which had emerged in the last decade or so: Save the Children UK institutionalised the post of translations manager in 2006; Tearfund officially appointed its first translations editor in 2008; and OxfamGB launched an internal translation service in 2011 (Informal interviews, December 2015; 'Translating Development' workshop, October 2017). However, the recent institutionalisation of these posts does not mean that the need for translation was an entirely new phenomenon. Rather, efforts to institutionalise translation and create separate translation departments at headquarters level were intended as a way of enhancing cost-effectiveness and translation quality by streamlining the commissioning of translation work and avoiding duplication.

The existing translation services in OxfamGB, Save the Children and Tearfund were small, consisting of one to four staff members who commissioned the bulk of translation work via a pool of freelancers. The key languages dealt with were similar, with English the source language, and French, Spanish, Portuguese and Arabic the most common languages translated into. Over the years, these INGO translation services had expanded. The amount of words translated, as well as the number of language combinations that translation was provided in, had increased for all three organisations. For example, the demand for translation in Save the Children was described as having increased by eighty per cent since the start of the service (Informal interviews, December 2015). In terms of staffing, too, translation teams had generally expanded. For example, as a result of the increased workload, OxfamGB's service had grown from one part-time translation manager, and one full-time coordinator, to four full-time staff members (Martins, 2018, p. 110). Interpreting tended to be only a small part of the remit of these services, usually restricted to appointing freelancers when interpreting was needed for high-level meetings.

Despite the institutionalisation and expansion of the translation services, the overall sense in interviews with INGO staff (translators and others) was that the need for translation within INGO development programmes remained largely overlooked, with the translation services peripheralised in INGO internal structures. In institutional organigrams, translation was either placed under communication services, making the translation team less visible, or was entirely absent, as was the case in Christian Aid. When translation was structurally placed under communications, this could present a distorted view of the type of work the translation team actually handled, because communication services tended to focus on externally facing communication such as press releases, campaigning materials and branding. Whilst much of the work of the translation services certainly consisted of translating this type of material, translation managers emphasised the breadth of their work, which included translating anything from operational documents, reports and media content to toolkits and training materials such as webinars for staff. On this topic, one translation manager said: "We work with more departments than anyone else does. Translation sits across everything" (Translating development Workshop, 12 October 2017).

Yet despite translators' widespread collaboration within headquarters, languages and translation generally had a low profile in the organisations. Illustrative here was that key documents that relate to INGO translation provision and their statements about official languages in the organisation were generally not well known among staff in various job roles. In twenty-two interviews conducted with staff from Christian Aid, OxfamGB, Save the Children UK and Tearfund whose jobs were not in communication services, only five interviewees (four of which based in the UK) indicated that they were aware that their agency had a language or translation policy. Interviewees tended to respond with uncertainty when asked if their organisation had official languages. For example, one participant replied:

> That's a good question. I've never really been aware… I think all of our offices and all our staff are recruited on the basis of their ability to speak English. It's never really been made particularly apparent to me… I wonder if it's a blind spot perhaps. (NGO 1, manager, UK)

In a similar discussion on the existence of language and translation policies in INGOs, another participant said:

> Well you know honestly if you'd said to me did you have a language policy at Save the Children, I wouldn't know what the answer was. (NGO 27, manager, UK)

Others were aware of institutionalised policies, and expressed an understanding that such policies only covered a handful of languages, although the details were not always well remembered:

> I think Oxfam International has official languages, English, Spanish, French and I think Arabic. So, when a communication is sent out within Oxfam, usually those are the languages it will be sent out in, so it will be in all of those. (NGO 11, desk/advisory officer, UK)

In fact, Arabic is not one of Oxfam International's official languages: whilst OxfamGB currently treats English, French, Spanish, Portuguese and Arabic as its core languages, Oxfam International only has three official languages: English, French and Spanish (Martins, 2018). Nevertheless, the above quotation illustrates that this staff member had a good general understanding of the type of languages covered in existing policies, and what this meant for the organisation's communications. Others indicated they understood the limitations of institutional language policies in terms of financial support:

> I'm aware that there is a language policy, I certainly couldn't quote it. I suspect that it talks about the need to make sure that key documents are translated into, you know, as many functional languages as possible, but there's always a cost issue so I think we do French, we do Arabic, we do Spanish, we do English. (NGO 13, manager, Africa)

Awareness of other documentation related to language and translation work was also limited. For example, some of the NGOs provided guidelines on translation or interpreting, and made these available on the intranet of their organisation, but when staff were asked about these in interviews, they responded that such guidelines did not exist (NGO 22, manager, UK; NGO 16, communications, UK).

Apart from low awareness within the organisation of translation-related policy documents and guidelines, translation needs also tended to be given little consideration throughout the project cycle, all the way from project planning to final evaluations. To begin with, a specific budget for translation and interpreting was generally not included when planning projects. Where it was included: "it [translation and interpreting budget] is not necessarily well quantified. It's just a stab in the dark usually" (NGO 16, communications, UK). Being able to predict the type of outputs that would be produced in a two-year long project and that would need translation, for example, was very difficult. The emergence of translation needs during project implementation was a major challenge for the internal translation teams. INGO translation services were organised in a translation agency model, in which the translation team handled translation requests commissioned by other departments. This placed the initiative for translation/interpreting with other departments, and could leave the translation service in a financially vulnerable position: "So we don't have any central budget for translation and when a team needs a translation they have to consider their whole budget and see what they can allocate to it" (NGO 20, communications, UK).

The need for translation was described by NGO staff as emerging as an 'afterthought' (NGO 6, communications, UK; NGO 16, communications, UK), usually at a point in the project cycle when little funding was left to spend on linguistic provision. An additional challenge was the increased use across the development sector of restricted or ringfenced funding since such monies could only be spent on project-related activities. Translation was often considered as an administrative cost, meaning it would fall outside this remit. Finally, in cases where translation was provided, no feedback tended to be given on how the translations had been received: "we don't actually get much feedback either positive or negative on the translations" (NGO 20, communications, UK). Evaluating the quality of translation provision was not part of monitoring and evaluation, despite the recognition that "in the area of monitoring and evaluation I think the forms and feedback mechanisms are so crucial to get the right information back" (NGO 20, communications, UK).

Overall, the motivations for institutionalising translation services mainly seemed to be concerned with cost-saving measures and streamlining processes, and they were often linked to corporate strategies of growing the organisation's branding, visibility and impact (cf. Bonallack, 2018; Martins, 2018). Ensuring professional translation and interpreting to enhance listening practices, however, did not seem to be part of INGO motivations when creating these services.

Translator Agency

Translation managers openly recognised that the absence of any reference to language and translation throughout the project cycle was a blind spot in their organisation's current policies and working practices. In fact, they described advocating for the important role of translation and interpreting as a crucial part of their job. This type of advocacy involved various aspects. Firstly, translators felt the need to promote their team's services to colleagues in the organisation. The existence of the translation departments and the work they did was felt to be largely unknown, because: "when it [translation] is well done, it is invisible" (Translating Development workshop, 12 October 2017). The invisibility of translation implied that the services were an easy target for funding cuts, all the more so because translation was often considered as an administrative cost, and its added value to successful project implementation was not something that was measured in monitoring and evaluation. Thus, lobbying against potential funding cuts with management was an essential and constant part of the translator's job.

Secondly, an important aspect of translators' internal 'advocacy' work was described as educating colleagues on the processes involved in translation, such as how to commission a translation, what a realistic deadline was, how to decide when a document needed translation, and how to write for translation. Translators argued that staff in headquarters were not fully aware that much of the material they produced would be translated, resulting in source texts that were difficult to translate:

> The material that goes into the translations is not taken sufficiently seriously… So if you're trying to translate something that is not clearly written in English, for example it's got UK-based idioms, play on words, acronyms that aren't explained, maybe some issues with the grammar or so on, so what's going in affects very much how you can translate it. (NGO 20, communications, UK)

Translation teams tried to address these issues by organising awareness raising courses, sometimes as part of new staff induction training, and by including details on translation processes in internal guidelines and in the organisation's translation policy. Despite these efforts, the quality of some of the source texts was reportedly low, and translators argued that one of the crucial but hidden values of translation was in fact its function as a form of proofreading that enhanced the clarity and consistency of the source texts (NGO 20, communications, UK). Thirdly, some translation managers claimed that they tried to raise awareness of the need to plan for translation/interpreting from the early stages of project design, and the importance of seeing language and translation as an integral part of the organisation's strategic approaches to inclusivity, although much work still remained to be done to achieve such a vision (NGO 9, communications, UK; NGO 16, communications, UK).

Whilst their relationships with colleagues in headquarters were largely described in terms of educating and advocating, relationships with colleagues that were based in-country were not characterised by these features. Rather, translators emphasised a desire to collaborate closely with in-country colleagues to be able to produce high-quality translations adapted to the needs of country offices and programmes. Translator's agency varied in this respect: some translators described feeling that the geographical distance from the field meant that they had only a limited understanding of local realities and needs; whilst others described acting as 'connectors' between headquarters and the local level. In some cases, translators argued that, with the existence of the internal translation service, it had become easier to challenge the predominant, and previously largely unquestioned, status of English. For example, one interviewee related that in the past, materials had always been produced with an English-speaking audience in mind, and that translation was expected to be straightforward without making editorial changes to the text. For some material, however, this was now changing: the translations of Facebook posts and tweets in one INGO, for example, were now "presented as an example that they [country offices] can adapt or they can make the choice which ones to use" (NGO 9, communications, UK). According to this interviewee, such change was possible because of the translation service:

> ...because we are the link, many times, between [country offices] and between teams and when we receive a request and we have the materials etc., we are in touch with end-users in other [country offices] or country teams, we both see how some things are hard to translate or wouldn't work. So, they voice their concerns and we talk to the teams here and we tell them 'Actually, that wouldn't work. We need more flexibility here or maybe another image because this picture wouldn't work with the title of the campaign in Spanish because we're changing the approach or something'. (NGO 9, communications, UK)

In Tearfund particularly, translators and editorial teams had worked hard to create a direct line of communication with the target audience of their translations and publications by sending out surveys and requesting feedback from readers. These efforts had started long before the official appointment of a translations manager in 2008. In fact, Tearfund's efforts to translate some of its key publications, including its *Pillars* guides and *Footsteps* magazine, into a variety of other languages, sometimes in collaboration with local communities, was unique in the four INGOs investigated (see also Chapter 2). Tearfund's *Footsteps* magazine, which was first published in the 1980s, has been translated into languages including Bangla, Burmese, Chinese and Hindi, in addition to the organisation's core languages (English, French, Spanish and Portuguese). The key motivation for translating these publications was to increase the publications' accessibility, ensuring that the language remained simple so that people could understand the publications when reading in their second language, or when they had not had the benefit of much education (Hollow, 2008, p. 109). Although Tearfund's efforts to translate these publications in a wide variety of languages has been the victim of funding cuts, and translation of these publications has been scaled down (Informal interviews, December 2015), the organisation remains highly unusual because of the importance it attaches to translating material into a language that is accessible to the people it aims to help. For example, Tearfund's online learning zone (Tearfund, n.d.) is unique among the INGOs in our study in providing guidance and support to people who wish to translate Tearfund's material into other languages.

Overall, our data demonstrate that despite the 'institutionalisation' of the translation services and the growth of their workload, translation managers considered financial and staffing resources to be a constant challenge. The data also showed that the existence of and work conducted by these small and beleaguered services tended to have a low profile, meaning that advocating for the importance of translation was considered a key aspect of translators' jobs. In light of this, it was perhaps understandable that translators were keen to network outside their own organisations and meet other translators and translation managers in order to exchange information on dealing with translation needs in the NGO sector. Evidence of this, for example, is the success of the workshop 'Translating Development' (12 October 2017, London), which was organised as part of the Listening Zones project, with presentations from translation and communication staff from Family for Every Child, OxfamGB and Save the Children UK.

Translators and Interpreters Based In-Country

The linguistic reality of in-country programmes was vastly different from the largely monolingual working culture that characterised UK-based head offices. On a country level, staff tended to be highly aware of the multilingual environment in which they were operating, and of how linguistic challenges could potentially affect project implementation. Paradoxically, professional translation and interpreting tended to be largely absent at country level. Significant in this respect was the low number of interviews that we were able to conduct in our country case studies with professional translators or interpreters working with NGOs. Instead, translation and interpreting were generally provided by multilingual staff from the NGO or from a local partner organisation, or, if the necessary language skills were not present in these organisations, by multilingual speakers recruited in local communities.

The profile of people who acted as translators and interpreters differed slightly between the three country contexts we investigated (Kyrgyzstan, Malawi and Peru) and between the form of linguistic mediation that was required, i.e., translation or interpreting. Table 5.1 presents an overview of common patterns for translation practices from and into English, and at different stages of the project cycle. In the first instance, the table indicates whether translation of specific documents tended to be conducted or not. Secondly, it indicates who generally provided the translations when these were being produced. A more detailed discussion of some of these features is provided below.

Translation vs. Non-translation

The direction in which translation was provided can be interpreted as a pattern that indicates the priorities of NGOs and the direction in which knowledge flows between international and local contexts. Firstly, funding-related documentation such as project applications and reporting materials were translated into English systematically. The motivation for translating these documents into English was generally to satisfy international, Northern-based institutions according to the frameworks and

Table 5.1 Common patterns for translation at in-country level

Translation		*Kyrgyzstan*	*Malawi*	*Peru*
Translation of project applications	Into English	– No translation – Google Translate – A relative/friend translates or edits the Google Translated version	– No translation (mostly written in English)	– No translation – Asking a relative or friend to provide translation – Staff when available, but specialised help on development necessary
	From English	– No translation	– No translation	– No translation
Translation of project material	Into English	– No translation	– No translation	- No translation
	From English	– No translation – Professional translator: but low quality for Kyrgyz	– Translation by professional translator; checked by community member – NGO staff member	– No translation
Translation of (material for) reports	Into English	– INGOs: by multilingual staff. – SNGOs without English skills: no need (because generally unsuccessful in applying for funding in English)	– By INGO or SNGO multilingual staff	– No translation – Asking a relative or friend to provide translation – Staff when available, but specialised help on development necessary

(continued)

demands they had set: funders would often only invite funding applications in English, and, once funding had been granted, they would request local data that could demonstrate accountability in the use of public spending, and value for money. Conversely, project applications and

Table 5.1 (continued)

Translation		*Kyrgyzstan*	*Malawi*	*Peru*
	From English	– Uncommon When it does happen: – Into Russian by professional translator (resourced through INGO) – Into Kyrgyz/Tajik/Uzbek: uncommon	– Uncommon	– Uncommon

Source Author's own creation

reporting documentation were generally not translated from English into local languages, and this type of project documentation was thus generally only available in English. Material that was translated on a more regular basis from English into local languages were training tools and guidelines. As such, information and knowledge tended to flow from Northern, international organisations to the local context, as part of the 'knowledge transfer' that has been central to Western development approaches over the last few decades (Féaux De La Croix, 2013; Narayanaswamy, 2017). Conversely, whilst local organisations often produced their own tools and guidelines in the local context, this type of information and knowledge was generally not translated into English, and it was therefore not made available at a broader, international level.

Absence of 'Professional' Translation

When translation did occur, it was often not provided by a professional translator. One key reason for this was a general lack of financial resources. Thus, when translating project applications or reports, NGOs without the necessary language skills would usually rely on an internal staff member, a volunteer, or a relative who had the requisite language skills. Particularly in Kyrgyzstan, the use of Google Translate to translate project applications was widespread. Usually, these machine-translated applications would then be edited or proofread by a colleague or relative with English language skills, although interviewees readily volunteered that this did not result in quality translations (see Chapter 7, Kyrgyzstan).

For translation into local languages, there was a lack of trained professional translators altogether. The idea of what a professional translator constitutes in the development context challenges the traditional, overtly Western image of the professional translator as someone who has a degree in translation, and who tends to conduct translation work on a freelance basis whilst respecting the codes of conduct set by bodies that aim to regulate the profession, such as the UK's Institute of Translation and Interpreting. In contrast to this image, those who were described as professional translators in the case study countries did not usually have specialised degrees, and translation work would not be their main source of income. In Malawi, for example, a number of interviews were conducted with people who had translated material from English into Chichewa for NGOs before, but none of these interviewees would identify themselves as professional translators. They tended to have other full-time jobs; one was a lecturer in a linguistics department at university, for example. They were recruited by NGOs to translate on an ad hoc, case-by-case basis, usually through their network of personal contacts, or sometimes through local media or specialised newspapers (CBO worker Zomba 1, Professional translator Zomba 29).

In Kyrgyzstan, the idea of professional translation as a specialist service done by freelancers and commissioned through translation agencies was more widespread. However, in the Kyrgyz interviews, several participants described the difficulties they had encountered in finding professionals who would deliver a high-quality service. For example, one SNGO worker said:

> …we had a case when we needed to do a grant application and we hired a translator to translate the project proposal. We paid the translator to translate the project proposal and then the donors called me and asked me: did you translate it yourself? The quality of translation was so poor that they thought that we translated ourselves. But we *paid* for it. (KYR 8, director of national network, Bishkek)

In this particular case, the experience had led the SNGO to revert to a policy of only paying a translator when the project application had been successful. The policy had been devised to counter instances of poor service, but it was also introduced as a cost-saving measure, since professional translation was expensive, and SNGOs could not afford it unless the translated proposal was granted funding. Other interviewees also recounted stories of low-quality translation provided by professionals who had actually used Google Translate for their work. One participant stated that "This translator had used the Google tool" (KYR 8, director of national network, Bishkek), and another shared the following:

> Sometimes we've had problems with some translation agencies, and one time we didn't have time and we sent them a report to translate, and then I understood they just took it from Google, they put it, you know, and all this terminology and all these things [laughs] this is the level of English. (KYR 5, NGO staff member, Bishkek)

These stories also referred to themes of corruption and unprofessional behaviour in which translators had not undertaken the translation themselves. The pool of professional translators in Kyrgyzstan, working with English, Russian and Kyrgyz, was described as consisting of a small number of professionals who provided an excellent service, and a larger group of translators who provided poor, unprofessional work. One interviewee described the 'average' working practice as:

> I give it [the translation assignment] to you and then you give it to your student because the lecturer at the university subcontracts it and won't even check it, okay? So, a whole lot of corruption in this thing, which is tolerated and known by people here in the system, and the whole point is: if you publish something, no one can understand [laughs]. I mean, what's the point? (KYR 11, manager international organisation, Bishkek)

Underlying the challenges described by interviewees seemed to be a wider problem relating to the educational context, and to a lack of professionally trained translators and interpreters. The level of English in education has been described as low in academic literature on Kyrgyzstan (Deyoung, 2011; Korth, 2005). Participants suggested that it was particularly challenging to find professionals who could deliver high-quality translation between English and Kyrgyz, and that it was more common to find occurrences of indirect translation: English-Russian first, then Russian-Kyrgyz (see Chapter 9 for details on how this procedure was also followed for the translation of the Listening Zones final report). The services provided through translation companies were generally also described as low quality, mostly because such agencies tended to work with young English language graduates who were inexperienced and did not have a good understanding of the development sector. This resulted in translations that conveyed the meaning "on the surface but not to the point" (KYR 16, NGO staff, Bishkek). In sum, whilst a professional body of freelance translators existed in Kyrgyzstan, they did not tend to be hired because their services were expensive and they were not considered to have the necessary language skills to provide good quality work.

Key Skills for Successful Translation in Development Settings

One of the key skills that professional translators were said to be lacking was knowledge of the development context. The problem of translating development terminology into local languages was one described at length in all three case studies (see Chapters 6, 7, and 8 for more details). For example, one Kyrgyz SNGO worker related that:

> we see that if the translator is not from our sector, doesn't know, it's very hard for him, even if he knows a lot of words and everything, but the terminology is very important. So that's why we have one or two translators that we are mostly working with. (KYR 5, NGO staff member, Bishkek)

When discussing what was required for successful translation, interviewees prioritised this type of development knowledge, as well as an in-depth understanding of local cultural practices and traditions, rather than experience of professional translation and interpreting. Another area of competence that some interviewees prioritised over professional translation experience was an in-depth understanding of the work of the organisation (see Chapter 8, Peru).

Other translation competences, such as the ability to work with translation technology tools, were entirely absent from participants' responses. One of the aims of using such tools would have been to enhance translation consistency of certain terms, a practice that would be at odds with what was required in certain contexts. For example, Malawian interviewees emphasised the need for translations to be appropriate for a specific community:

> Sometimes you can get a professional translator, but all the same we still get in some people who are closer to communities, who can also maybe facilitate how best a particular concept can be actually translated, so that

> once you go and use it, use it in the community, it is not misunderstood. (INGO worker, Lilongwe 2)

Choosing one translation of a term that would work across development projects in the country or region was thus not always possible or appropriate, and translators needed to have an in-depth understanding of the local context to make appropriate translation decisions (see Chapter 6, Malawi). Related to this, it is noteworthy that the Malawian interviewees who had provided translations for NGOs in the past all emphasised the importance of piloting translations to ensure that they were well received by the target audience, and expressed their desire to receive more feedback from those who commissioned translation work, which was usually lacking (CBO worker Zomba 1; Professional translator Zomba 13; Professional translator Zomba 29).

The overall picture of translation in local development contexts that emerges from the data is thus one in which NGOs rarely rely on professional translators, but seek the services of their colleagues, volunteers or community members. It is important to note that translation work does not tend to be part of the job descriptions NGO staff. In many cases, NGO personnel involved in such activities described how much time and effort these tasks would take, and related that there was little or no recognition from the NGO itself of the importance and the level of complexity of this work (see also Chapter 4). Interviewees articulated a desire for additional linguistic support, such as on English writing, guidance on producing translations and compiling glossaries of terms central to NGOs' work that were understood by local communities. These issues are described in more detail in each of the country chapters. Overall, translation practices in-country have much in common with the type of practices generally referred to as 'activist translation' in Translation and Interpreting Studies, which aims to support political struggles at the local and global level (Boéri & Delgado Luchner, 2020) and where translators "identify with and contribute to concrete political agendas, particularly through volunteer work" (Boéri, 2008, p. 22). The motivations of NGO workers to ensure their message and work is understood by the other can be seen as a political motivation, battling inequality not just as part of the purposes of the development programme but also within the very programme itself and within the internal structures of NGO projects.

Common Patterns for Interpreting Practice

When asked about the use of interpreters for oral translation during meetings with local communities and with donors, participants described similar ad hoc informal language practices. As with translation, professional interpreters were rarely used, and those who assumed the task of interpreting in their absence included NGO staff members, local community members and volunteers (Table 5.2).

As described in Chapter 4, there was a general expectation from NGO headquarters that in-country teams and partner organisations were in a good position to provide linguistic mediation when working with local communities, since many of the staff tended to be nationals from the country. They were therefore assumed to be embedded in the local context both culturally and linguistically. Our in-country interviews confirmed that this was indeed largely the case for NGO workers in Malawi and in Peru. All interviewees in Malawi were at least bilingual with English as their second language. When NGO staff did not speak the local language used in a particular area, interviewees described recruiting a community member who could act as an interpreter (see Chapter 6, Malawi). In Peru, a variety of strategies were described to deal with the need for Quechua speakers if such language skills were not present in the organisation. These included training existing SNGO staff in local languages (although this was uncommon and seldom paid for), recruiting

Table 5.2 Common patterns for interpreting on in-country level

Kyrgyzstan	*Malawi*	*Peru*
Between English, Russian and Kyrgyz – NGO staff (usually INGO staff) *Between Russian and Kyrgyz* – National development experts (Key challenge: not enough experts with Kyrgyz language skills) – SNGO staff, but rare (usually did not have Kyrgyz language skills)	*Between English and local languages* – NGO staff (INGO or SNGO) – Local community member	*Between English and Spanish* – NGO colleague (INGO or SNGO) *Between Spanish and local languages* – SNGO staff – Volunteer from local community

Source Author's own creation

a volunteer from the local community to join the original team (in which case bilingual schools could be a source), or recruiting a volunteer during the implementation stages of a project (see Chapter 8, Peru). In Kyrgyzstan, communication with local communities appeared to be more challenging than in Malawi and Peru. This was mainly because the SNGOs interviewed tended to be Russian speaking with little to no Kyrgyz language capacity within the organisation. This situation is typical for SNGOs in the capital Bishkek, where about half of the interviewees were based. The solution opted for was generally to work with national development experts who would be familiar with the terminology in Kyrgyz relating to their area of expertise. These experts could either deliver training in Kyrgyz themselves or could act as linguistic facilitators if an international expert was delivering the training (see Chapter 7, Kyrgyzstan).

Finally, one interpreting practice that was not fully explored in interviews but was mentioned on a number of occasions by interviewees was that of relay interpreting (Shlesinger, 2010), for example, from English into Spanish and then from Spanish into Quechua. In Translation and Interpreting Studies, the practice of relay interpreting has been described as on the increase. Despite its relevance in a globalised world, in which an increasing variety of languages come into contact with one another, the phenomenon has received relatively little attention in Translation and Interpreting research until now (Maia, Pięta, & Rosa, 2019). This practice is one that merits further research in order to fully understand how the use of a 'pivot language' and working through two interpreters can affect communication and rapport building.

Translation and Interpreting in Development vs. Humanitarian Interventions

The interviews that this chapter draws on specifically focus on the nature of translation and interpreting in long-term development programmes rather than in the humanitarian interventions of NGOs. This section briefly reflects on what could be described as the key differences between providing linguistic mediation in development, as opposed to humanitarian aid, and reflects on how these two contexts have been engaged with differently by international organisations.

Humanitarian interventions are characterised by a sense of urgency, requiring INGOs to respond to a crisis as soon as possible. In this case,

INGOs often intervene in countries and in local communities where they have not worked before. Although the reality of encountering linguistic challenges in emergency response work seems more obvious than in development—where collaborative relationships often last for many years and organisations can be expected to be familiar with local linguistic realities—the recognition that there is a need to plan for translation and interpreting before deploying a humanitarian mission has remained peculiarly absent in the NGO sector for a long time. Awareness of these issues has started to be raised in recent years through interdisciplinary research projects such as INTERACT (EU International Network for Crisis Translation) and by efforts of organisations such as Translators without Borders (TWB), an initiative that started as a network of volunteer translators and has expanded into a full-blown non-profit organisation that delivers training and tools relating to translation in crisis situations.

Despite the difference in humanitarian and development aid in terms of the length of intervention and relationship building with local communities, the challenges of translation and interpreting in these contexts are similar. Policy recommendations that have been produced by the INTERACT team, for example, include the need to consider translation and interpreting challenges early on, and to make addressing these challenges part of disaster preparedness efforts (Federico et al., 2019). In TWB work in response to the Rohingya refugee crisis, recommendations for actors involved in delivering humanitarian aid include training staff in translation/interpreting, including the compilation of glossaries of key terms, and ensuring the use of plain English language (TWB, 2019). Because of the nature of humanitarian intervention, a number of other activities and recommendations that do not fully relate to development contexts have also emerged. These include the potential use of machine translation, which can be useful for contexts in which an immediate response is required and no translators or interpreters with the required language skills are immediately available. Current exploratory topics of research include building and using machine translation systems for lower resourced languages, and the ethics involved in doing so, as well as training 'citizen translators' in the basics of translation as part of disaster preparedness interventions (Baker & Piróth, 2019; Cadwell, DeLuca, & O'Brien, 2019; Cadwell & Federici, 2018; Federici & O'Brien, 2020).

Conclusion

This chapter aimed to provide an overview of common translation and interpreting practices in international development programmes by exploring NGO practices both in UK-based headquarters and in-country. Overall, the data depict an image of translation/interpreting as having a low profile in institutional policies as well as in headquarters, where staff would generally be able to conduct most of their work entirely in English without giving much thought to multilingual needs. Because of this, existing professional translation services at headquarters level in OxfamGB, Save the Children UK and Tearfund were largely working on the periphery of their respective organisations, often at risk of funding cuts. Paradoxically, staff in-country were much more aware of the central role of languages and translation in their work, but the ghost operation of professional interpreting/translation services like those at headquarters tended to disappear altogether at the in-country level. A different skillset than that of professional translators/interpreters working in Northern contexts was sought after: instead of competence in using translation tools, or adhering to codes of professional conduct such as neutrality, NGO staff in the Global South emphasised the importance of local embeddedness, understanding the culture and realities of local communities, and knowledge of NGO work and related development terminology. Whilst this specific skillset cannot be taken for granted, no training or guidelines tended to exist on how to provide successful translation or interpreting, and staff's interlinguistic efforts did not tend to be recognised at an institutional level: language work was generally not part of staff job descriptions. Translators based in headquarters, and participants at the in-country level, considered translation and interpreting to be central to successful communication and project implementation—an observation that tended to be absent in interviews with other staff in headquarters, as well as on a broader institutional level where translation was actually considered as an administrative cost, rather than an integral part of project planning and delivery.

Parallels with the role of languages and translation in humanitarian interventions suggest that, in contexts of crisis and emergency, the importance of languages has started to be recognised through the joint effort of interdisciplinary projects and non-profit organisations such as TWB. It could also be argued that DFID is beginning to recognise the importance of language in humanitarian settings through funding research on these issues. For example, the organisation has recently supported research conducted by TWB, Internews and BBC Media Action on improving access to information for Rohingya communities (TWB, 2018, 2019). However, following Baker and Piróth (2019), some ethical questions may need to be raised about the use of free labour through volunteer translation networks, the fine line between charity work and corporate practices, and who ultimately benefits from the translation work provided (Baker & Piróth, 2019). Moreover, DFID has not, as yet, given the same prominence to translation issues in development settings, a context in which funders potentially continue to assume that INGOs already have the necessary linguistic capacity to listen to the communities they aim to work with, as argued in Chapter 3.

A final self-reflective note on the contents of this chapter and the way it has been structured is in order. As argued at the beginning of this chapter, one of its contributions is to provide insight into non-Western contexts of translation and interpreting, which Translation and Interpreting Studies have traditionally not tended to engage with. It should be noted here, however, that the chapter has not escaped the researcher's own Western background: a conceptual framework of translation as written practice and interpreting as oral mediation has been applied to a context in which this distinction may in fact mean little. Some interviewees, particularly those in African contexts, did themselves not distinguish between translation and interpreting as distinct practices. In cultures in which the spoken word is more valued than the written word, the elaborate discussion in this chapter concerning written translation is perhaps of little value. Whilst the analysis in this chapter has certainly provided new insights into inter-linguistic practices in development contexts, it has not gone as far as to challenge some of the established binaries in traditional Western Translation Studies, such as translation/interpreting or source text/binary text in the context of indirect translation. Overall, the chapter can therefore be understood as pointing to the critical need for Translation and Interpreting Studies scholars to co-create new definitions of what translation may constitute with those living, working and researching in other contexts and locales (see also Chapter 9).

References

Angelelli, C. (2004). *Medical interpreting and cross-cultural communication*. Cambridge: Cambridge University Press.

Angelelli, C. (2012). The sociological turn in translation and interpreting studies. *Translation and Interpreting Studies, 7*(2), 125–128.

Baker, M., & Piróth, A. (2019). *The ethics of volunteerism in translation: Translators without borders and the platform economy*. Retrieved from: http://www.pirothattila.com/Piroth-Baker_The_Ethics_of_Volunteerism_in_Translation.pdf.

Berk-Seligson, S. (1990). *The bilingual courtroom: Court interpreters in the judicial process*. Chicago: University of Chicago Press.

Bierschenk, T., Chauveau, J. P., & Olivier de Sardan, J. P. (Eds.). (2000). *Courtiers en développement: Les villages africains en quête de projets*. Paris: APAD and Karth.

Boéri, J. (2008). A narrative account of the Babels vs. Naumann controversy: Competing perspectives on activism in conference interpreting. *The Translator*, *14*(1), 21–50.

Boéri, J., & Delgado Luchner, C. (2020). Ethical issues in activist translation and interpreting. In K. Koskinen & N. K. Pokorn (Eds.), *The Routledge handbook on translation and ethics*. London and New York: Routledge (in press).

Bonallack, P. C. (2018). Amnesty International Language Resource Centre Overview of current context and vision for the future. *Translation Spaces, 7*(1), 92–105.

Cadwell, P., DeLuca, E., & O'Brien, S. (2019). More than tweets: A critical reflection on developing and testing crisis machine translation technology. *Translation Spaces, 8*(2), 300–333.

Cadwell, P., & Federici, F. M. (2018). Training citizen translators Design and delivery of bespoke training on the fundamentals of translation for New Zealand Red Crossangel. *Translation Spaces, 7*(1), 20–43.

Deyoung, A. J. (2011). *Lost in transition: Redefining students and universities in the contemporary Kyrgyz Republic*. Charlotte: Information Age Publishing.

Dijkzeul, D. (2008). Transnational humanitarian NGOs? A progress report. In L. Pries, L. (Ed.), *Rethinking transnationalism: The meso-link of organisations* (pp. 81–103). Abingdon: Routledge.

Féaux De La Croix, J. (2013). How to build a better future? Kyrgyzstani development workers and the knowledge transfer strategy. *Central Asian Survey, 32*(4), 448–461.

Federici, F. M., & O'Brien, S. (Eds.). (2020). *Translation in cascading crises*. Routledge: Abingdon and New York.

Federico, F. M., O'Brien, S., Cadwell, P., Marlowe, J., Gerber, B., & Davis, O. (2019). *D2.1: Recommendations on Policies*. The International Network on Crisis Translation. Dublin City University.

Fukari, A., & Wolf, M. (Eds.). (2007). *Constructing a sociology of translation*. Amsterdam: John Benjamins.

Goodale, M., & Merry, S. E. (Eds.). (2007). *The practice of human rights: Tracking law between the global and the local*. Cambridge: Cambridge Scholars.

Hollow, M. (2008). *A future and a hope: The story of Tearfund and why God wants the church to change the world*. Oxford: Monarch.

Inghilleri, M. (2005). Mediating zones of uncertainty: Interpreter agency, the interpreting habitus and political asylum adjudiction. *The Translator, 11*(1), 69–85.

Korth, B. (2005). *Language attitudes towards Kyrgyz and Russian: Discourse, education and policy in post-soviet Kyrgyzstan*. Berlin: Peter Lang.

Levitt, P., & Merry, S. (2009). Vernacularization on the ground: Local uses of global women's rights in Peru, China, India and the United States. *Global Networks, 9*(4), 441–461.

Lewis, D., & Mosse, D. (Eds.). (2006). *Development brokers and translators: The ethnography of aid and agencies*. West Hartford: Kumarian Press.

Maia, R. B., Pięta, H., & Rosa, A. A. (Eds.). (2019). *Indirect translation: Theoretical, methodological and terminological issues*. Abingdon and New York: Routledge.

Marais, K. (2014). *Translation theory and development studies: A complexity theory approach*. New York and Abingdon: Routledge.

Marais, K., & Delgado Luchner, C. (2018). Motivating the translation-development nexus: Exploring cases from the African Continent. *The Translator, 24*(4), 380–394.

Martins, A. S. (2018). Development in so many words: The Oxfam GB experience. *Translation Spaces, 7*(1), 106–118.

Merry, S. E. (Ed.). (2006). *Human rights and gender violence: Translating international law into local justice*. Chicago: Chicago Series in Law and Society.

Narayanaswamy, L. (2017). *Gender, power and knowledge for development*. Abingdon and New York: Routledge.

SchAdvStudy. (2017). *Translating development—Translators in development NGOs*. Retrieved from: https://youtu.be/8YVTnRDHUpM.

Shlesinger, M. (2010). Relay interpreting. In L. van Doorslaer & Y. Gambier (Eds.), *Handbook of translation studies* (Vol. 1, pp. 276–278). Amsterdam and Philadelphia: John Benjamins.

Tearfund. (n.d.). *Sharing tearfund's learning and resources across the world*. Retrieved from: learn.tearfund.org.

Tesseur, W. (2018). Researching translation and interpreting in non-governmental organisations. *Translation Spaces, 7*(1), 1–18.
TWB. (2018). *The language lesson: What we've learned about communicating with Rohingya refugees*. Retrieve from: https://translatorswithoutborders.org/wp-content/uploads/2018/12/TWB_Bangladesh_Comprehension_Study_Nov2018.pdf.
TWB. (2019). *Misunderstanding + misinformation = mistrust*. Retrieved from: https://reliefweb.int/sites/reliefweb.int/files/resources/Report_A_Three-Part_Report_-_Cross-Border_Trends_Sep2019.pdf.
Tymoczko, M. (2007). *Enlarging translation, empowering translators*. Manchester: St. Jerome.

CHAPTER 6

Malawi

Introduction

The case studies in the following chapters—first Malawi, then Kyrgyzstan (Chapter 7) and Peru (Chapter 9)—have been chosen as Listening Zones as they present differences in two main variables: the status of English, and the length of development NGO intervention.

English is the official language of government, the law, and higher education in Malawi. Moreover, in 2014 the government announced that English would be the medium of instruction in primary and secondary schools, despite concerns that there are not sufficient resources in terms of teachers and learning materials (Kamwendo, 2016). There are several local languages, and the most widely spoken, Chichewa, is also an official language, serving as a lingua franca in the country. NGO involvement in Malawi expanded considerably in the 1980s and the sector continues to thrive today owing to the considerable availability of donor funds. Several major donors have identified Malawi as a development priority because of its long-term status as one of the poorest countries in the world.

English does not have official status in Kyrgyzstan; indeed, it is spoken by only 0.5% of the population (Aminov et al., 2010). Kyrgyz and Russian are official languages, and the former is spoken by the overwhelming majority of citizens as a first language. NGO involvement in Kyrgyzstan generally expanded in the late 1990s and early 2000s following the collapse of the Soviet Union and the country's subsequent descent into acute poverty, although it has since recovered to become a lower middle-income state.

H. Footitt et al., *Development NGOs and Languages*,
https://doi.org/10.1007/978-3-030-51776-2_6

In Peru, English has no official status, but it is the most widely taught second language with the majority of Peruvians being taught English in secondary school (British Council, 2015). Peru's official languages are Spanish, Quechua and Aymara. NGO presence in Peru expanded considerably in the early 1990s, but is now contracting rapidly, in part because economic growth in recent years has led to it being ranked as an upper middle-income country by the World Bank, which has prompted donor/NGO withdrawal.

A further reason for selecting these case studies was feasibility. Our civil society organisation partner, INTRAC, had a history of support for NGOs in Malawi and Peru, and had a regional office in Kyrgyzstan.

Each of the case study chapters has a similar structure. We begin by providing some context about the NGO sector and the language profile of each country. Then, after detailing our research methods and the characteristics of our interview sample, we move to data analysis. The findings are split between two thematic sections: Communicating in English, and Communicating with Communities. We conclude with some reflections about the contributions of the case study to our understanding of the Listening Zones of development.

The NGO Sector in Malawi

Malawi (formerly Nyasaland) was a protectorate of Great Britain and gained independence in 1964. Malawi's first President, Hastings Banda, led a system of one-party rule for three decades before he was toppled in 1994, and full multiparty presidential and parliamentary elections were held. Regular elections have been held since then and power has transferred between different parties. However, international watchdogs have raised questions about the extent to which these changes reflect genuine competition between rival parties, suggesting that they may be the outcome of rifts between the ruling elites instead (Freedom House, 2018). The country is divided into twenty-eight districts, each presided over by a District Commissioner. Outside of the formal apparatus of government, each village has a traditional leader or Chief who commands considerable authority in the community. Actors leading development interventions have to negotiate this complicated national/district/local authority framework in order to conduct their work. They also have to factor in the all-pervasive presence of corruption, from high-level patronage and nepotism to small-scale bribery by minor officials (Transparency International, 2018).

The overwhelming majority of NGO activity in the country centres on the multidimensional issues caused by poverty. Malawi has been heavily impoverished for decades: according to the most recent data available, per capita GNI was just $320 in 2016 (World Bank, 2018a). It has a population of approximately nineteen million (CountryMeters, 2018), 83% of whom live in rural areas (World Bank, 2018b) and 80% of whom rely on subsistence agriculture (CIA, 2018). According to the World Bank/IMF's assessment, Malawi's economic development has been affected by climate-related shocks and domestic political and governance shocks, which have led to poor performance in poverty reduction (IMF, 2017, p. 1). Recent years have seen some improvement in non-monetary indications of poverty, such as access to primary education, child malnutrition and under-five mortality (National Statistical Office, 2017), and these achievements resulted in Malawi partially or fully achieving four out of eight of the Millennium Development Goals (MDGs, the international development goals for 2015 contained in the UN Millennium Declaration).

However, monetary poverty remains a serious issue, particularly for rural dwellers who constitute 57% of Malawi's poor (compared to 17% of urban dwellers who are classified as poor) (National Statistical Office, 2016). In recent years, levels of monetary poverty have worsened due to extreme weather events such as floods and droughts, and fluctuations in market prices for agricultural produce, affecting the ability of farming households to sustain themselves and earn a living. According to the latest household survey, 99% of households experienced at least one such shock in the preceding twelve months (World Bank, 2018c). The most recent Gini co-efficient data for Malawi from 2011 (0.45) underlines the stark disparity in income distribution between the rich and poor (National Statistical Office, 2016). Inequalities in wealth are most pronounced in the Southern region, and female-headed households (57% of total households) are poorer than their male-headed counterparts (43%) (IMF, 2017). Pressures are exacerbated by the high birth rate and young population: 46% of whom are aged under fifteen (CIA, 2018). Moreover, 46% of Malawian children are stunted, which has an impact on their physical and intellectual development (UN, 2015). The country therefore fell significantly behind some of the MDG targets, and the likelihood of meeting the more ambitious 2015 Sustainable Development

Goals is doubtful (SDGs, 17 international development goals set by the UN General Assembly in 2015).

Malawi has long been a 'donor darling'. Over a five-year period (2010–2015), the largest donors in order of proportion have been the USA, the UK, the World Bank, the EU and the Global Fund (Amusden, 2017, p. 15). The majority of aid has gone to health, education, agriculture and governance. New donors are emerging on the aid landscape, such as Brazil and the Arab world, but their presence is 'negligible' compared to donors from the Global North (Amusden, 2017, p. 16). China is increasingly important, but it mainly channels its funds to Chinese companies and infrastructure development (Amusden, 2017, p. 16). Over forty bilateral and multilateral donors contributed an average of 40% to the national budget in the decade preceding the 'Cashgate' scandal in 2013 (Malawi Government, 2011). The revelations of 'Cashgate' included evidence that politicians and senior civil servants had embezzled over $32 million over six months, an amount equivalent to one per cent of Malawi's GDP (Kayuni, 2016). Audits of the government's ledgers between 2009 and 2014 revealed $356 million to be missing (Strasser, 2016). The scandal precipitated the firing of the entire cabinet by President Joyce Banda, a series of high-profile prosecutions, and an investigation by Malawi's anti-corruption bureau, leading to the implementation of various reform measures. Donors from the Global North suspended budgetary support worth approximately $150 million annually (Strasser, 2016). In contrast, China has been willing to pursue a 'non-interference' approach to giving aid.

The Malawian Government with the World Bank has drawn up a Growth and Development Strategy (termed MGDS III) to guide its medium-term development plans, with a view to attaining the SDGs. This includes five priority areas: agriculture and climate change management; education and skills development; energy and industrial development; transport and Information and Communication Technology (ICT) infrastructure development; and health and population management (Malawian Government, 2017). The World Bank and IMF have cautioned that achieving these ambitions will depend on the strengthening of public sector institutions so that it is better able to "absorb the impact of future shocks and maximize the impact of available domestic and foreign resources" (IMF, 2017, p. 5). Moreover, they continue to press for the strengthening of governance and accountability frameworks, especially concerning public procurement, in order to ward against the corrupt practices that led to Cashgate.

Since the 'blip' of Cashgate, the net official development assistance and official aid received by Malawi has risen to a historic high ($1.515 billion in 2017) according to the latest available figures (World Bank, 2017). The aid is directed to sectors that mirror the international and national development priorities outlined above. Western donors have utilised ways of giving funding other than budgetary support, such as pooled funds (Chasukwa, 2018). However, the actual aid received by Malawi is even higher than this, since official figures do not include the aid delivered by NGOs. The Council of Non-Governmental Organisation in Malawi (CONGOMA) has 914 NGOs officially registered (Chasukwa, 2018, p. 21), although it has been alleged by the NGO Board that there are thousands more in existence (Face of Malawi, 2013). Thus, the amount of aid that is not captured by official accounting mechanisms may be quite substantial.

Malawi attracts the attention of INGOs due to several factors. Firstly, it's persistent position at the bottom of several international indicators of economic development and poverty. The IMF has ranked it the third poorest country in the world (IMF, 2018), which is notable since—unlike many others among the world's poorest countries—it has not been embroiled in war or conflict. Secondly, Malawi's colonial-era links with Britain (notably Scotland) has helped to establish long-term British government/NGO involvement in development activities (Ross, 2013). Thirdly, the country is peaceful and politically stable. As per the official travel advice of the Foreign and Commonwealth Office, "most visits to Malawi are trouble-free" (Gov.uk, 2018). Fourthly, it boasts a decent road network that enables easy travel around the country, even to far-flung rural areas (Swidler & Watkins, 2017, p. 1). An added advantage is that the country is relatively small compared to many others on the continent, meaning that it is more manageable to travel the length and breadth of the country to deliver programmes and projects.

Policies about NGO regulation in Malawi shape the operating environment for NGOs in significant ways. CONGOMA is the largest umbrella organisation in the NGO sector. Its stated mission is to "provide a sharing and reflection platform for NGOs to influence government and development processes… and enhance their operating environment" (CONGOMA, n.d). One of its most important contributions has been to assist with NGO registration law, both in terms of facilitating meetings between NGOs and government officials and feeding into the drafting of key clauses. There was widespread controversy and dismay in the sector when the NGO Act, enacted in 2000, designated CONGOMA as the official coordinating body for NGOs and required all organisations to join (Gugerty, 2016, p. 84). NGOs were also required to register with the NGO Board, a body that was established by the Act. This development precipitated fears of a more intrusive state-sponsored approach to NGO regulation, and a loss of faith in CONGOMA's ability to represent NGOs as an independent voice (Gugerty, 2016, pp. 85–86). In recent years, the government has repeatedly threatened hundreds of NGOs that were not registered with the NGO Board with closure. International bodies have voiced considerable concerns about the erosion of civic space. In April 2017, the government introduced amendments to the NGO Act (the main legislative instrument pertaining to NGOs) that stoked fears that intrusive and arbitrary controls could be used to silence organisations that are critical of the political authorities. There have also been attempts by the government to introduce significant fee hikes for NGO registration and other operational necessities (ICNL, 2019). Moreover, the mooted amendments would endow the NGO Board with the power to approve NGO funding applications to donor agencies, in order to ensure that they align with government policies and "advance the public interest" (Amnesty International, 2018). If approved, these legal requirements may be expected to shape the ways that NGOs 'listen' in significant ways. They would increase the disincentives for NGOs to engage with actors and issues that would be likely to attract the adverse attention of the authorities.

Languages in Malawi

English arrived in Malawi with the British colonialists and Christian missionaries. In contrast with some other European powers, the British generally favoured linguistic indigenisation to facilitate the exercise of power over the colonised (Matiki, 2001, p. 202). They developed an English–Chichewa bilingual language policy, with English used in official domains and higher education, and Chichewa reserved for lower levels of primary education. Post-independence, Hastings Banda designated English the official language during his time in office; a status that it has retained ever since. Chichewa (also known as Chewa, Nyanja and Chinyanja) was chosen as the national language in an attempt to assimilate all other linguistic groups in the name of national unity. This was met with considerable discontent by some minority language speakers. To this day many Malawians have an aversion to Chichewa because of its association with Banda's repressive regime (Williams, 2014). The stated intention of Banda's bilingual policy was to promote a dual role for English and Chichewa in politics, administration, the law and commerce. However, the direction of language policy ever since has 'heavily favoured' English over all local languages, to the extent that English has established strong dominance over Chichewa (Matiki, 2001, p. 201).

Thirteen local languages exist, including Chilomwe, Chiyao, Chitumbka and Chisena. Malawi contains several ethnic groups and there is a close link between language and ethnic identity. Unfortunately, census data on language speakers in Malawi is quite dated (UNData, 2009) but shows that 6,500,000 citizens (from a total population at the time of 13,000,000) speak variants of Chichewa. The census did not survey speakers of English, but a 2003 study suggested that there were 540,000 English speakers in the country.

English has an elitist status in Malawi. It is the language of politics, administration, the law, commerce and education. Indeed, it is necessary to pass English in order to complete high school and enter university. This education policy determines the linguistic hegemony of English and the privileged life opportunities of English speakers. Central Malawians with an eye on social mobility are said to insist that their children only speak English (Englund, 2006); "For many Malawians, economic success is predicated on one's ability to speak, read and write English" (Matiki, 2001, p. 207). English competency is almost directly correlated to the level of affluence of all Malawian ethnic groups, even rural dwellers (McNamara, 2015a, p. 460). The one exception is the Tumbuka (an ethnic/linguistic group mainly located in northern Malawi) who are disadvantaged due to discriminatory practices, migration patterns and politically motivated underdevelopment (McNamara, 2015a). In short, the privilege associated with English in Malawi and its hegemony over local languages cannot be overstated.

Participants

Organisations were visited in Lilongwe, Blantyre and Zomba in December 2017 to January 2018. Thirty-five interviews were held in English. Interviewees were selected through pre-existing professional contacts and the snowball method. They included ten participants from INGOs (mainly programme managers/officers and one Country Director/National Secretary). There were nine participants from SNGOs (mainly programme officers and three CEOs). SNGOs included those involved in sexual/reproductive health, human rights, agriculture, civic education and development communication. There were also four participants from community-based organisations (CBOs) (including two Directors). Outside of the civil society sector, there were three participants from international organisations/donors. Five academics were interviewed who had experience of translating materials for NGOs, and there were four miscellaneous participants who had relevant background experience in the development sector (one a former DFID officer).

The overwhelming majority of the participants had university degrees, and many had postgraduate qualifications. Also, nearly all of them (bar the academics) had many years of experience in working for multiple NGOs in different capacities. They therefore had experience with receiving funds from the most active donors in Malawi, including anglophone donors such as DFID and USAID. They were all bilingual, and many were multilingual. All but six were men. This is perhaps not surprising given that I/SNGOs provide a thriving sector for employment for highly qualified Malawians, who are mainly men, particularly in older generations. Malawi's gender gap in primary education is still significant (USAID, 2016), which restricts the educational/job opportunities and earning capacity for females in later life.

Communicating in English

English has a high status in Malawi and carries connotations of education and privilege. As a participant from an international NGO observed, English is closely associated with conceptions of international development: "when you use English, or development – your argument is that you need to move people from traditional society to modernity and in our thinking modernity is associated with English" (INGO worker, Lilongwe 21). The strong association of English with 'development' is reinforced by the default use of English by the largest donors in Malawi (e.g., DFID, USAID) and high-profile INGOs.

Participants were keenly aware that the cultural capital of English shaped the way that they are perceived in the development sector:

> English is a language and not an indication of somebody's competence, it's a language just like any other, but in the development world it doesn't really that much, that English is just a language, because it's like when you're able to speak English then oh yeah you're very competent. (SNGO worker, Lilongwe 7)

> People trust someone who fluently speaks English, and if they go into the community, they will trust someone because they will say: "I think he knows what he's doing. He seems to be learned because he fluently speaks English." (Former INGO worker, Lilongwe 14)

However, workers within organisations can have differing levels of English competence. Therefore, a series of translation challenges arise for an INGO when a message filters down from HQ, to the national office, then to the community:

> And if it's an international campaign, maybe I go to the meeting, I understand the concept, but I have to bring it back to my team, which means I cannot use the same English, the same language, as I was using as international. I have to bring it to this level now, to localise it, and further localise it when we're going to the field. (INGO worker, Lilongwe 9)

For example, a senior executive from an SNGO explained how the organisation's work had been affected in the past when staff members had not fully understood the purpose of the project:

> …there was a time when we had a certain project and I discovered that half of the project staff members in my institution didn't understand it, and they were busy running up and down, always busy, busy, busy, and later on we discovered that these people didn't know exactly what this project was about. (SNGO Senior Executive, Lilongwe 10)

Relatedly, it is interesting to note that no examples were found during the fieldwork of successful project applications written in English being translated into Chichewa. National or local staff without English language skills typically rely on a verbal briefing from their line manager about the purposes of a project but cannot read the funding application themselves to cross-check their understanding of the aims and objectives and key terminology.

It can also be problematic to translate messages in the reverse direction to ensure that donors have a good sense of what is happening on the ground:

> ...definitely the insistence will be that [an NGO worker] needs to know English. Particularly... where it interacts with the donors, because the reports have to be written in English. So, one has to be able to understand properly some of the concepts that they will be using at reporting time, what the demands of that particular project are. But also, there comes another example of where we lose something in translation because most of the communities which we interact with are in Chichewa. So, how they describe an impact they have seen with the project in Chichewa and how you translate it into English, sometimes it can lose the real sense of what the impact of the project has been. (INGO worker, Lilongwe 6)

Professional help is generally only sought when translating material at the organisational level or for donors (e.g., training manuals, funding proposals). High-quality translation was said to be expensive. Therefore, if an organisation was seeking to streamline its budget proposal or spending, translation may be one of the things that is neglected or economised on. A problem that was said to often occur is that linguists are employed as translators who have no background in development, and they often struggle with translating development jargon and produce work of uneven quality.

Participants expressed frustration that these translation problems are compounded by the lack of standardisation for frequently used English terms in the development field. Different NGOs use different definitions for similar 'buzzword' concepts, which render them vague and imprecise (Cornwall & Eade, 2010). 'Resilience' is a notorious example; in the words of one participant: "even if you talk to ten people in different NGOs, they will all interpret it differently, because they see nothing like one thing which is to say 'this is resilience'" (Donor official and former NGO worker, Lilongwe 8). Jargon is perpetuated by the need for NGOs to comply with the donor's preferred terminology:

> There's no need for bringing in the word resilience, just talk about "Put a dyke here" in the local language, you see what I mean? But because they have to report to a donor, they have to use the word resilience. Which means they have to translate it and talk about it. (INGO worker, Lilongwe 9)

For this participant, donors are the key source of a bewildering array of 'buzzwords':

> I think the donors do perpetuate this language disease, by the tools that they give to their beneficiaries of their grants, their grantees. So, for example, you have templates, reporting templates, you have M&E frameworks, those are specific to each donor. Their own language, their own definitions of those languages, and therefore the grantees have no choice but to adopt those languages… But at the end of the day it's confusing to the local donors, even more confusing for the communities, but particularly for participatory monitoring and evaluation. (INGO worker, Lilongwe 9)

It was suggested that NGOs have another interest in preserving the ambiguity surrounding development jargon. One participant from a major INGO noted how she had observed that organisations tend to coin their own terminology in order to distinguish themselves from their competitors. This led to the proliferation of English jargon, spearheaded by organisations that are more interested in claiming they are unique than promoting cross-cultural understanding. Another participant from an SNGO observed that development jargon served to flatter the ego of the development worker rather than facilitate the inclusion of poor people:

> Yes it's to keep professionals like me, to satisfy me, if I'm a doctor I need to be satisfied by the acronyms and abstract and kind of methodologies, but the poor person does not require this, the poor person does not require the acronyms, the jargons, but I require jargons, it's part of my speciality, I feel good when I talk to you in a professional manner to convince you. (SNGO Executive, Lilongwe 3)

Participants said that donors had different expectations about the need for language support. For example, there was a clear expectation from the European Union that language requirements would be written into the proposals for Malawian civic education programmes. However, for other international donors, questions were generally not asked about the costings for translation/interpretation, nor about the language capacity of staff. NGOs were said to be reluctant to share language-related problems or to open up discussions about the resources needed to fund language support sufficiently. One participant from an INGO was particularly direct in explaining his motivation to acquire and protect funding: "I will be frank with you: as a NGO, what I want is money from the donors. I want money to pay salaries, I want money for my NGO to move" (INGO worker, Lilongwe 21). In the context of this financial pressure, NGOs may be disinclined to admit to problems with the ways that projects are being delivered, for fear that donor support would switch to a competitor NGO:

> ...more and more resources are becoming scarce and NGOs are really having to look for resources to fund their projects... So, "don't tell the donor very much about how you make sure communities are participating but tell them about what you have achieved and what you are capable of achieving with this money." (INGO worker, Lilongwe 6)

Another INGO participant described the position of NGOs and communities in the aid chain as being entirely reactive to the desires of the donors:

> ...there will be a call, for example from DFID, and they'll ask for people to apply, that means the concept is there already. Like, the DFID wants to do this. So, you respond to the call. So already there you have defined the parameters, ok? And the moment you define parameters... means you're also defining the kind of communication and the language that is going to be used within those parameters. So, already you know that the conceptualisation of projects, particularly if they are donor funded, the communities, or the citizens, or the recipients they are not involved at that level. That's already defined, you just have to respond. (INGO worker, Lilongwe 21)

In this rendition, listening is unidirectional: the donor establishes a conceptual and financial framework that compels NGOs and communities to listen to them.

Communicating with Communities

The INGO/SNGO/CBO participants claimed that listening to communities was key to their organisation's approach to development work. They attested to the importance of eliciting feedback from communities and understanding and responding to their needs and preferences. Listening to the words that the community uses to describe sensitive subjects was seen as absolutely essential by the INGO and SNGO participants during the needs assessment stage to design a culturally appropriate project.

The main problem with communicating with communities, which was volunteered by every participant with direct experience of development work, is that there are few direct translations for English development buzzwords in the local language. Chichewa was variously described as a 'shallow', 'poetic' language, 'deficient in terminology' in comparison with English. Development jargon is difficult to translate, particularly abstract concepts and technical words. Terms that were commonly mentioned as challenging to translate included accountability, advocacy/influencing, climate change, empowerment, gender, resilience and sustainability. These are words that are the common currency of Anglocentric development discourse. They articulate key principles and targets that are found in the SDGs, among large anglophone donors and in the policy documents of leading INGOs. Not being able to easily translate the core concepts of mainstream development presents a significant challenge to staff on the ground. Participants all explained how the meaning of the word can often get 'lost in translation'; the message can be 'diluted', 'generalised' or distorted in the attempt to communicate it to non-English speakers. The complexity of the language challenge is not just due to the multiplicity of local languages in Malawi, but also the different dialects. Even communities that share the same mother tongue and live relatively close together may have distinct dialects that mean that an interpretation that works in one location does not work in another. Therefore, development workers who are keen to build meaningful listening relationships will have to invest time in adjusting to the local context and finding ways to interpret them that are appropriate in the local vernacular (Makoni, 2012). Challenges can be heightened when interacting with people who are illiterate and cannot read NGO literature in any language, much less English (approximately 35% of the population) (CountryMeters, 2018).

In order to convey the meaning of these words to speakers of local languages, it is often necessary to engage in extended explanations using metaphor, simile, euphemism and local proverbs. It is essential to use lots of illustrative examples to convey a message: "You have to tell a story in order for people to understand the concept… And the use of practical examples, the use of pictures…" (INGO worker, Lilongwe 9). Participants described this as a cumbersome process. Those who were engaged in a short field visit or a project with a tight time frame often felt that they did not have the space to ensure that the purpose of the intervention was fully understood by the community:

> And the projects when they start nowadays don't allow much space… so that it makes sense in terms of whether you translate the proper way or whether you understand the concepts or what you understand by the outcomes. So, the moment sometimes you are granted [money] and sometimes a quarter of the implementation time has gone so you have to hit the ground running and you have to do it very quick. In those respects, I think it also makes people not value investment very much in these things like language. (INGO worker, Lilongwe 6)

Participants who had longer-term engagement with the community maximised the advantage that this extra space afforded them to talk to the community and felt that this contributed to the success of their project. In the words of an SNGO worker associated with a democracy promotion project funded by the EU: "You find the first day of the project people won't understand anything because of the words that we're using, it's into the second day or third day that they grasp what we really wanted to communicate" (SNGO worker, Zomba 25).

INGO/SNGO/CBO participants described liberally employing euphemisms where the topic might be culturally sensitive. Examples of taboo topics include genitalia, sexual intercourse, sexual health and reproduction, contraception/abortion, HIV/AIDS, LGBT+ issues and sanitation (particularly defecation):

> …the challenge which I've seen over time is that most of the English words… you can't just translate them, even if it's a correct translation, because they have a negative connotation. So, like, in Chichewa you may not easily just say "I'm here to talk about sex." Ok? Because that word automatically would lead some people to withdraw. (Donor official and former NGO worker, Lilongwe 8)

Commonly used euphemisms are different from one locale to another (even when the communities share the same tongue) so it is necessary to have 'local intelligence' on how messages should be crafted. To further complicate matters, euphemisms that have currency among the older generation are falling out of use for younger people, thus necessitating organisations to tailor their communication strategy to different groups *within* the community, as well as *between* communities. Young and old are often separated into groups to discuss issues relating to sex, as the former are thought to be willing to have candid discussions.

Respecting the local culture is paramount. One of the most important considerations is working with the gatekeepers in the community—primarily the village Chief. Most rural dwellers in Malawi are exposed to the formal rule of the state and the indirect rule of the Chief (Eggen, 2011). Malawi was described as a 'subservient' culture where those in authority expect homage and respect. An SNGO participant working on civic education explained that her organisation employs careful nuances in their terms to build good relations with the community. In the Central region and in the South, her organisation holds discussion groups that can be translated in English as 'citizens' forum'. However, this term has been judged as inappropriate to use elsewhere:

> ...but in the North it's like, the term that they use in Chitumbuka in English it may translate as 'the forum of elders'... because for them in the North they have strong paternal tendencies, so they do respect the elders a lot and most of the elders are men and so the understanding is definitely a bit different. (SNGO worker, Lilongwe 7)

In addition, issues that challenge embedded relations of power, particularly regarding gender equality, can be met with a hostile reaction from the community (particularly from male powerholders, but also from women). As Biruk and Ntata (2009) have also found, the concept of 'gender' is regarded with suspicion by some rural Malawians who perceive it to be a Western import that threatens commonly accepted social norms. Similarly, Dodson and Riley (2016) found that some urban Malawians associated 'gender' with Westernisation, and that the word carried negative connotations of a long history of social change imposed by outside forces. A common way that participants dealt with some of the gender-related problems that arose with culturally sensitive topics was to separate men and women into different groups, thus allowing for less inhibited discussion. This approach requires some delicacy:

> [Men] get suspicious: "What are you telling our women?" But then the tactic we have used sometimes was to have also a man with the men separately and even though your primary goal is to hear the women's stories, but just to make sure that they're not very suspicious, they have a man meeting with the men and a woman meets the women, or you explain to

> the village Chief exactly what you're doing, so they understand that there needs to be that space for women. (INGO worker, Lilongwe 9)

Adapting their approach to suit different audiences is a constant challenge for development workers.

Development workers may not be fully conversant with the full range of languages and dialects that encompass the regions to which they are deployed; in which case, it is common practice to enlist a local community member as a language intermediary: "the people themselves are the engines, the people themselves can help you to find the right terms that you can use in your development work" (SNGO worker, Lilongwe 19). However, the Chief of the village could be expected to select the local interpreter, as he is the key gatekeeper for the community. The Chief was said to be likely to choose someone loyal to him and therefore questions could be raised about the reliability of the information provided. Any feedback that reflects poorly on the Chief may not be volunteered or accurately communicated. One INGO seeks to address this problem by asking the community to elect an interpreter.

Participants perceived translation and interpretation matters as especially salient to their work because poor communication on the ground can lead to project failure. An SNGO participant believed that donors were not always appreciative of this consideration:

> Also, sometimes we have the challenge of "one size fits all" approach. You know people speak Chichewa, but comprehension of Chichewa, the dialect differs from area to area. So, it's good to understand the context in where the project will be implemented and what are the cultural issues as they relate to language. For instance, I'm thinking of these multilateral donors, they will have a project to be implemented—in Zambia, Malawi, Mozambique—sometimes they will design a framework which is the same. But it's very important to consider that because of the language issues, cultural issues in Malawi it may not be the same as it will be in Mozambique. (SNGO worker, Lilongwe 19)

Also, three of the participants felt that international staff (who were not from Malawi) were not sufficiently appreciative of these issues. Firstly, because they do not speak the language themselves and so do not have the capacity to listen to those affected by their aid projects:

> ...they go on the ground they want to see what is happening. But they have to be told in the local language and someone has to translate, and they assume that things are working, but had they been able to listen directly to what the communities are saying, they would have known that this guys have missed the point. (SNGO Executive, Lilongwe 10)

Secondly, because of an arrogant conviction that they have the 'monopoly over knowledge' and are reluctant to immerse themselves in the local context to grasp understandings on the ground, rendering them distant from the communities (INGO worker, Lilongwe 4). For example, one of the participants recounted his experience of trying to explain the community understandings to international staff:

> ...there are moments where I have tried to clarify to say, "this is what it means in the context of the people" to say what they're saying. This is the background why they're saying it. And to someone, who does not understand that background, it's very difficult to be convinced that it's the right reason for people to think like that, because they are somehow conceptually distant from that context. They're coming from a different background, where that is simply not making sense to them. It just doesn't make sense. And because it doesn't make sense to them, no matter how much you explain it, it's like a dichotomy that you can never solve... I think a lot of internationals do not come with that spirit of saying "Let me immerse myself..." (INGO worker, Lilongwe 4)

Without community 'buy-in', NGOs may take the initiative and "start doing things for the community rather than engaging with communities to understand properly what it is that they want to do and move them with the project" (INGO worker, Lilongwe 6). However, communities cannot be expected to value the motivations and outcomes of a project if they have not had a meaningful opportunity to participate in its design and implementation. One Chairperson of an SNGO reflected upon how his long career in development had revealed the centrality of communication for project success:

> So communication is actually at the centre of any NGO's work, it should be there, without communication they should not be expecting any results, they will keep on doing the same things for twenty years, for thirty years, for decades and decades, they will not see any results, and they will start

> blaming the communities. Why? They did not put communication at heart. (SNGO Executive, Blantyre 33)

There is an alternative possibility to this interpretation of the participants that the community are unable or have difficulty in understanding their message—a problem that they claim could be fixed with better efforts at communication. McNamara's (2017) ethnographic research with Tumbuka Malawians provides a salient insight into the power dynamics that underpin a project conceived amidst contested narratives. He argues that his case study shows that rural Malawians and NGO fieldworkers construct different discourses of sustainability, and that fieldworkers dismissed villagers' criticisms of their projects as ignorance of the meaning of sustainability. Fieldworkers only accepted that Malawians understood sustainability when they accepted the terms of the NGO project. Thus, the claims made by our participants about the problems associated with 'poor communication' should be treated with some caution. It is possible that communication difficulties not only stem from interpretation issues, but also refusal from I/SNGOs to acknowledge the different understandings and narratives of the community as valid (see also McNamara, 2015b).

Despite the problems outlined above, there are numerous examples of innovative practices to bridge the communication divide between NGOs and the people. These included the use of local languages in community radio stations broadcasts, jingles and popular songs (albethey methods that facilitate unidirectional communication, rather than interaction). Participatory methods are also used by some organisations to open up conversations with the community, particularly on sensitive issues. These include community cinemas, where screens and projectors are taken to villages to show dramatised films about health and social issues. At opportune points, the SNGO facilitator pauses the film to ask the audience what action they think the protagonist should take. This was said to be an effective method to foster dialogue on issues in a way that is inclusive and tailored to the local context. Some organisations also use participatory 'street theatre' for similar purposes, and one INGO formulated a slogan for a maternal health campaign that was suggested by women from the community, which ensured that it was appropriate for local cultural norms.

There were also examples of good practice with regard to intra-organisational issues. Knowledge management is a persistent problem with NGOs (Hayman, King, Kontinen, & Narayanaswamy, 2016), partly due to high staff turnover, and 'short-termism' induced by the fast turnaround time of projects. To deal with this problem, one SNGO has devised a method to share and capture learning about language within the organisation. It promotes reflective practice among its volunteers and facilitates discussions between them so that they can pool their knowledge. In the participant's words:

> …volunteers collect terms from the communities they work in…So they pick on the words that people are using in the village; when they go to another village they also try to use the same terms that the community members were using, and if people understand things differently in this community then they also pick out some words in there, and later on the officers bring all those variations together in a series of workshops and they come up with agreed upon terms. So, whenever there's a new concept that is being introduced, they will go through a similar process. (SNGO worker, Zomba 25)

Other examples included a team of INGO workers who collectively created a M&E manual in Chichewa that incorporated translations for key terms based upon their experiences of interacting with communities. It continues to be revised and updated after fieldtrips so that knowledge can be retained and shared.

Conclusion

The importance of listening appears to (at least rhetorically) be an area of consensus in the development sector in Malawi. All of the INGO/SNGO/CBO interviewees claimed that listening to communities is one of the most important aspects of their work, and this is also reflected in the literature produced by their organisations. Listening in practice, however, is shaped by a number of factors. English acts as a form of cultural capital because it is associated with modernity and privileged knowledge, and so it is imbued with power. Development buzzwords that have common currency in NGO/policy circles in Malawi are invariably English, but participants noted that the definitions of these buzzwords are not standardised, which further complicates the business of translation. Participants variously portrayed the promotion of jargon as in the interest of different actors in the aid chain: it enables the fieldworker to reinforce his/her professional status, it enables the NGO to preserve a competitive edge over its rivals, and it enables the donor to set the conceptual terms of their development agenda.

The listening relationship between NGOs and communities is shaped by linguistic and cultural issues. There are many different languages and dialects in Malawi, and few direct translations for commonly used English words in development work. Those who directly interact with communities therefore find it challenging to accurately convey their meaning, often having to engage in long explanations, making copious use of locally appropriate euphemisms, idioms and metaphors. Participants commonly acknowledged that it was crucial to respect cultural norms, especially in terms of powerholders such as the village Chief. Fieldworkers must adapt their messages to account for the taboos surrounding topics that are a common concern of development work, such as sexual health and reproduction, and sanitation. They often attempt to divide villagers into similar social groupings (by age or gender, for example) to facilitate less inhibited discussion. They frequently have to negotiate sensitivities about interventions that are perceived by the community as threatening to existing gendered power relations. This task is made more difficult when the project has a short timeframe.

It was said that the impact of failing to listen and communicate could be substantial. Participants identified poor communication as a key factor in project failure, not least because it impedes relationship building with the community. Local people are disempowered by poor communication because they cannot fully participate in the design and implementation of projects. Participants felt that donors and international staff, who are remote from the field, do not fully appreciate these considerations. Although numerous examples of innovative practice were encountered during fieldwork, there was a common call from the participants for more sharing of learning.

A key theme that emerged from the interviews is how relationships are structured by asymmetrical power in all variants of the Listening Zones. The listening relationship between donor and NGO was characterised as unidirectional: the NGO listens and responds to the donor's agenda but there is little reciprocity. The donor–NGO Listening Zone was portrayed as heavily circumscribed, but not just because projects are funded by donors. Projects are also conceived by donors, framed by their preferences and articulated in their jargon. Listening is conducted on the donors' conceptual, linguistic and procedural terms. NGOs are compelled to adopt the language of the donor (ordinarily in highly specialised English) to access funds and to comply with reporting requirements. The financial power of donors over NGOs inhibits the latter from offering honest feedback about the implications of underfunding translation/interpretation work. However, this one-sided listening relationship is one that NGOs venture into knowingly and voluntarily. NGOs co-create a Listening Zone where they are selectively mute about difficult issues because it is to their financial benefit. NGOs could choose to enter into a robust discussion with donors about the importance of prioritising language in development projects, or they could explore other sources of income that could enable them to conduct their projects differently. Instead, many self-censor and submit funding proposals that minimise or omit the importance of language support in building respectful relations with the community.

Thus, the foundation is laid for the creation of a Listening Zone between NGO and community that is highly distorted and exclusionary, where the purpose of listening and the language used largely reflects the donor's agenda. NGOs conduct 'listening exercises' with the community at conventional points in the project cycle, such as needs assessment, and monitoring and evaluation. The listening is sporadic and instrumental. The projects are framed by development buzzwords that act as a form of symbolic capital but are not easily translatable or well understood by non-English speakers. The Listening Zone between NGOs and community is enabled by the powerful local gatekeeper, the village Chief. This (usually male) figure permits entry into the community and can select local interpreters who can be expected to be loyal to him (and so may tailor their interpretations according to the Chief's preferences). The Listening Zone between NGO and community is shaped by a complex interaction of relationships of power at the macro-level (international donors) and the micro-level (village) gendered hierarchies. Future research could explore the community's perceptions and experiences of the Listening Zone. It should not be assumed that they are unable to exercise agency in shaping the Listening Zone to their advantage. As Anderson and Patterson (2017) argue in their study on AIDS discourses in Malawi and Zambia, local people can resist top-down approaches by instrumentalising NGO discourses to gain status, power and resources.

Finally, the Listening Zone between NGO management and their subordinates was also portrayed as largely unidirectional. The power of NGO management over their staff members may lead the latter to be reluctant about admitting to knowledge gaps about the organisation's work, for fear of being labelled inept or ignorant. This may especially be the case where staff members are not sufficiently fluent in English to understand the relevant official documents. There is a strong association in Malawi (informed by its colonial history) of English with modernity, education and professional competence. It is understandable that some local staff may find it embarrassing to admit that they find translation a struggle. In contrast, participants claimed that some international staff internalise a cultural and professional arrogance about the superiority of their ways of thinking, and therefore it is difficult to explain the local context to them. The (perceived) confidence of international staff contrasts markedly with the discomfort of local staff in negotiating the multiple Listening Zones of development.

References

Aminov, K., Jensen, V., Juraev, S., Overland, I., Tyan, D., & Uulu, Y. (2010). Language use and language policy in central Asia. *Central Asia Regional Data Review, 2*(1), 1–29.

Amnesty International. (2018). *Malawi 2017/2018*. Retrieved from: https://www.amnesty.org/en/countries/africa/malawi/report-malawi/.

Amusden, I. (2017). *NORAD evaluation department* (Report 4/2017 Country Evaluation Brief). Malawi. Retrieved from: https://norad.no/globalassets/publikasjoner/publikasjoner-2017/evaluering/4.17-country-evaluation-brief_malawi.pdf.

Anderson, E. L., & Patterson, A. S. (2017). Instrumentalizing AIDS empowerment discourses in Malawi and Zambia: an actor-oriented view of donor politics. *International Affairs, 93*(5), 1185–1204.

Biruk, C., & Ntata, P. R. (2009). The challenges of doing gender research in developing countries: Focus on Malawi. *Journal of Comparative Social Work, 4*(1), 1–15.

British Council. (2015). *English in Peru: An examination of policy, perceptions and influencing factors*. Retrieved from: https://ei.britishcouncil.org/sites/default/files/latin-america-research/English%20in%20Peru.pdf.

Chasukwa, M. H. M. (2018). *The political economy of pooled development funds in Malawi—The case of local development fund* (Unpublished PhD thesis). Leeds: University of Leeds.

CIA. (2018). *The world factbook. Africa: Malawi*. Retrieved from: https://www.cia.gov/library/publications/resources/the-world-factbook/geos/mi.html.

CONGOMA. (n.d). *Vision & mission*. Retrieved from: http://www.congoma.mw/about-us/vision-mission/.

Cornwall, A., & Eade, D. (2010). *Deconstructing development discourse: Buzzwords and fuzzwords*. Rugby: Practical Action Publishing.

CountryMeters. (2018). *Malawi population*. Retrieved from: https://countrymeters.info/en/Malawi.

Dodson, B., & Riley, L. (2016). 'Gender hates men': Untangling gender and development discourses in food security fieldwork in urban Malawi. *Gender, Place & Culture, 23*(7), 1047–1060.

Eggen, Ø. (2011). Chiefs and everyday governance: Parallel state organisations in Malawi. *Journal of Southern African Studies, 37*(02), 313–331.

Englund, H. (2006). *Prisoners of freedom: Human rights and the African poor*. Oakland: University of California Press.

Face of Malawi. (2013, April 23). Malawi has 5,000 NGOs operating illegal—NGO board. *Face of Malawi*. Retrieved from: http://www.faceofmalawi.com/2013/04/malawi-has-over-5000-ngos-operating-illegal-ngo-board/.

Freedom House. (2018). *Freedom in the world 2018. Malawi profile*. Retrieved from: https://freedomhouse.org/report/freedom-world/2018/malawi.

Gov.uk. (2018). *Foreign travel advice: Malawi*. Retrieved from: https://www.gov.uk/foreign-travel-advice/malawi/safety-and-security.

Gugerty, M. K. (2016). Shifting patterns of state regulation and NGO self-regulation in sub-Saharan Africa. In M. Fremont-Smith (Ed.), *Regulatory waves: Comparative perspectives on state regulation and self-regulation policies in the nonprofit sector* (pp. 69–91). Cambridge: Cambridge University Press.

Hayman, R., King, S., Kontinen, T., & Narayanaswamy, L. (Eds.). (2016). *Negotiating knowledge: Evidence and experience in development NGOs*. Rugby: Practical Action Publishing.

ICNL. (2019, 14 June). *Civic freedom monitor: Malawi*. Retrieved from: https://www.icnl.org/resources/civic-freedom-monitor/malawi.

IMF. (2017, July 5). *IMF economic development document*. Retrieved from: https://www.imf.org/en/Publications/CR/Issues/2017/07/05/Malawi-Economic-Development-Document-45037.

IMF. (2018). *GNP per capita: Current prices*. IMF DataMapper. Retrieved from: https://www.imf.org/external/datamapper/PPPPC@WEO/OEMDC/ADVEC/WEOWORLD/ZMB/MWI.

Kamwendo, G. H. (2016). The new language of instruction policy in Malawi: A house standing on a shaky foundation. *International Review of Education, 62*(2), 221–228.

Kayuni, S. W. (2016). Running to stand still: Reflections on the cashgate scandal heist in Malawi. *Journal of Money Laundering Control, 19*(2), 169–188.

Makoni, S. B. (2012). Language and human rights discourses in Africa: Lessons from the African experience. *Journal of Multicultural Discourses, 7*(1), 1–20.

Malawian Government. (2011). *Malawi aid atlas 2010/11FY.* Retrieved from: http://www.mw.undp.org/content/dam/malawi/docs/capdev/AID%20ATLAS%202010-11%20-%20Malawi.pdf.

Malawian Government. (2017). *The Malawi growth and development strategy (MDGS) III (2017–2022).* Retrieved from: https://www.afidep.org/download/policy_guidelines/Malawi-Growth-_-Development-Strategy-MGDS-III-2017-2022-Final-Version-copy.pdf.

Matiki, A. J. (2001). The social significance of English in Malawi. *World Englishes, 20*(2), 201–218.

McNamara, T. (2015a). English, community and opportunity in northern Malawi. *The Australian Journal of Anthropology, 26*(3), 456–469.

McNamara, T. (2015b). *A village and its NGOs: Community embedded utilisations and understandings of NGO presence in rural northern Malawi* (Unpublished PhD thesis). University of Melbourne.

McNamara, T. (2017). "They are not understanding sustainability": Contested sustainability narratives at a northern Malawian development interface. *Human Organization, 76*(2), 121–130.

National Statistical Office. (2016). *Malawi in figures 2016.* Retrieved from: http://www.nsomalawi.mw/images/stories/data_on_line/general/malawi_in_figures/Malawi%20in%20Figures%202016(1).pdf.

National Statistical Office. (2017, February). *Malawi demographic and health survey 2015–2016.* Retrieved from: https://dhsprogram.com/pubs/pdf/FR319/FR319.pdf.

Ross, K. R. (2013). *Malawi and Scotland together in the talking place since 1859.* Oxford: African Books Collective.

Strasser, P. G. (2016). An anti-corruption bureau's inexorable endeavor: A study of Malawi's Cashgate Sandal. *Washington & Lee Law Review Online, 73,* 303–367.

Swidler, A., & Watkins, S. C. (2017). *A Fraught embrace: The romance and reality of AIDS altruism in Africa.* Princeton, NJ: Princeton University Press.

Transparency International. (2018). *Malawi.* Retrieved from: https://www.transparency.org/country/MWI#.

UN. (2015). *Sustainable development goals: Localisation, opportunities and challenges for Malawi.* Retrieved from: https://mw.one.un.org/sdgs-malawi/.

UNData. (2009). *Population by language, sex, and urban/rural residence.* Retrieved from: http://data.un.org/Data.aspx?d=POP&f=tableCode:27.

USAID (2016, September 26). *Malawi gender equality factsheet.* Retrieved from: https://www.usaid.gov/malawi/fact-sheets/malawi-gender-equality-fact-sheet.

Williams, E. (2014). *Bridges and barriers: Language in African education and development.* London: Routledge.

World Bank. (2017). *Net official development assistance and net official aid received (current US$)*. Malawi. Retrieved from: https://data.worldbank.org/indicator/DT.ODA.ALLD.CD?locations=MW&most_recent_value_desc=false&view=chart.

World Bank (2018a). *Malawi*. Retrieved from: https://data.worldbank.org/country/malawi.

World Bank. (2018b). *Rural population (% of total population)*. Retrieved from: https://data.worldbank.org/indicator/SP.RUR.TOTL.ZS.

World Bank. (2018c, August 2). *Malawi—Fourth integrated household survey 2016–2017*. Retrieved from: http://microdata.worldbank.org/index.php/catalog/2936.

CHAPTER 7

Kyrgyzstan

The NGO Sector in Kyrgyzstan

Kyrgyzstan is a mountainous country with a strong nomadic tradition located in the heart of Central Asia. Its six million inhabitants live mainly in less mountainous areas. These are located in the north, in and around the capital Bishkek, and in the south, including the cities Osh and Jalalabad. International NGO intervention in the country started after the collapse of the Soviet Union, when the newly independent Kyrgyz Republic was faced with the task of building a viable economy, which was to be characterised by a liberal system with privatised markets. The abrupt collapse of the USSR meant a withdrawal of social and economic state provisions as well as a sudden reduced need for economic production for the wider Soviet economy. These changes led Kyrgyzstan into acute poverty in the early 1990s (Buxton, Earle, & Giffen, 2005, p. 35).

The country's economy gradually recovered, and by 2014, Kyrgyzstan was upgraded from a low to a lower middle-income country (World Bank, 2018). Nevertheless, Kyrgyzstan is currently ranked as the second poorest country in Central Asia and is 122nd out of 189 countries on the Human Development Index with a score of 0.672 (UNDP, 2018). Extreme poverty, defined as living at US$1.90 per day, decreased from 42.2% in 2000 to just 1.4% in 2016 (World Bank, 2018). Poverty figures show a relapse between 2010 and 2013, generally seen as a consequence of political upheaval in the country and of the global financial crisis, but

H. Footitt et al., *Development NGOs and Languages*,
https://doi.org/10.1007/978-3-030-51776-2_7

figures have improved since then (IMF, 2016, p. 3). Despite the reduction in people living in extreme poverty, overall poverty remains relatively high in comparison to neighbouring countries, with an estimated 67.1% still living below US$5 per day (World Bank, 2018). Almost three quarters of the poor live in rural areas, where income is highly dependent on agricultural harvest and remittance flows (IMF, 2016, p. 3). Remittances are a critical part of Kyrgyzstan's economy and constitute 32.9% of GDP, the second-highest percentage worldwide (World Bank, 2018). Kyrgyzstan's economy has been described as narrow and dependent on such remittances as well as on foreign aid. Economic progress made in the decades after independence is generally considered as not consolidated and at risk of reversal, particularly in light of political instability and civil conflict (DFID, 2018; IMF, 2016).

Kyrgyzstan's political history has been turbulent, with its first two presidents being ousted after national demonstrations in 2005 and 2010. After the 2010 revolution, Kyrgyzstan established a parliamentary democracy, the only one in former Soviet Central Asia. Yet democratic gains have been described as unstable because of pervasive corruption and because political parties are considered as not sufficiently familiar with the new system to make it work effectively (DFID, 2018; Freedom House, 2018). These issues as well as the fact that the ruling political party has sought to consolidate power by suppressing opponents and civil society critics through the judicial system are among the factors that have led Freedom House to rate the country as only 'partly free' (Freedom House, 2018).

Western understandings of development generally consider a strong civil society sector as a key component of a democratic political system. Partly because of this conviction, early international development interventions in Kyrgyzstan focused strongly on the promotion of civil society (Buxton et al. 2005). Western governments, such as the USA, considered the end of the Soviet period to be an opportunity to contain Soviet international influence, and as a way to introduce democracy in formerly socialist territory (Aksartova, 2005, p. 16). Donors implemented democracy building programmes and encouraged the establishment of NGOs based on Western models (Aksartova, 2005, p. 3). The availability of large amounts of international funding led to a proliferation of NGOs in Kyrgyzstan, which quickly became known as the country with the highest NGO density per population in Central Asia (Garbutt & Heap, 2002). The exponential increase in the number of NGOs was seen as a positive sign for the country's democratisation and the country was referred to as an 'island of democracy' in Central Asia (Anderson, 1997). However, the tide turned in the mid-2000s, when hopes of democratisation and liberalisation started to fade. Donor funding priorities changed as a consequence of unmet expectations and in light of changing approaches to development, which now gave increasing responsibility to developing countries' governments to organise development aid. Many civil society programmes were closed, and others faced significant limitations in their funding (Bayalieva-Jailobaeva, 2018).

The climate in which Kyrgyz civil society organisations currently operate was described by participants in our study as challenging and competitive. Lack of government funding, partly due to corruption and misappropriation of funds, has been described as one of the reasons for this (Wilkinson, 2014). In addition, the space for civil society to debate and challenge the political and economic agenda has been shrinking. Under the influence of Russia's 'foreign agent' law, Kyrgyz parliamentarians have undertaken efforts to pass a similar law in Kyrgyzstan that would place restrictions on foreign assistance (ICNL, 2018). Although this has not been successful, NGOs that participated in our study reported that local communities often distrust them and question whether ulterior motives are at play ('Why would anyone do anything for nothing?'). Despite these setbacks, Kyrgyzstan's civil society sector has been described as one of the strongest in Central Asia by various international watchdogs and experts (Bayalieva-Jailobaeva, 2014; Buxton et al. 2005; ICNL, 2018), with NGOs active in a wide range of areas, including human rights, support to vulnerable groups, culture and art, health, protection of the environment, education and advocacy.

The USA has been an important funder of NGO work in Kyrgyzstan since independence, and it continues to be one of the major donors. In 2016, the largest DAC donors in order of proportion were the European Commission, the USA, the World Bank, Germany and Switzerland (Trading Economics, 2017). Together, these donors provided a budget of US$177.7 million. DFID's spending in the country was at £3 million in 2016–2017 (DFID, 2019b), with the United Kingdom contributing 0.04% of total net Official Development Assistance (ODA) to the country (DFID, 2019a), a stark contrast to its 14% contribution to Malawi (see Chapter 6, Malawi). According to the OECD's Development Cooperation report (2018), the Russian Federation, a non-DAC member, is in fact one of Kyrgyzstan's largest donors: in 2016, it provided US$198.8 million, which is more than the 2016 budget provided by the five largest DAC donors mentioned above. Kyrgyzstan was Russia's second-largest recipient, preceded only by Cuba. The Russian Federation mostly provided its development assistance in the form of debt relief (OECD Development Assistance Committee, 2018), which may be one of the reasons why Russian donors were not mentioned by our interviewees. Another country in close geographical proximity to Kyrgyzstan that one might expect to invest in the country is China, yet its assistance seems limited at the moment, with no mention in interviews and little evidence in the academic literature. However, as part of China's Belt and Road Initiative (BRI), it is expected that China will increase its provision of development aid in future to countries that participate in the BRI, including Kyrgyzstan (Overland & Vakulchuk, 2019).

As mentioned above, donor priorities in the region have changed since the 2000s, with more emphasis being placed on the government's responsibility to organise and provide development aid and ensure sustainable growth and good governance. The focus on state building and the need to enhance public sector effectiveness, accountability and transparency are central to the Kyrgyz government's own development priorities, as described in its development programme plan titled 'Unity, Trust, Creation' (Kyrgyz Government, 2018). The plan emphasises that the order of Kyrgyzstan's development programme is determined by "the practical need to solve first and foremost the issue of effective development management (public administration)", which it considers as necessary to trigger economic growth, and finally to allow addressing "the basic needs of the Kyrgyz people" (Kyrgyz Government, 2018, p. 6). Whilst the programme identifies gender, environmental and technological aspects as cross-cutting issues, its main focus lies on countering challenges presented by political and economic instability, including corruption and ethnic tensions. The role of civil society is defined as one of 'partnership' and is referred to explicitly in the context of sustainable social protection and development, in order to enhance the quality of life of the country's residents.

The re-definition of the role of civil society over the years, i.e., from acting as a counterbalance to the state to working with it, has had an effect on the funding mechanisms of overseas development aid, as explored in the work of Jailobaeva (2011) and Bayalieva-Jailobaeva (2014, 2018). Bayalieva-Jailobaeva's findings demonstrate that as a consequence of shrinking funding to NGOs directly, particularly for efforts related to capacity building, competition for NGO funding has become fiercer and those NGOs that have professionalised are in a stronger position to obtain international donor funding. Such professionalisation is described as having experience, technical skills and a material basis such as having a bank account, a structure including a board of trustees, and qualified staff (Bayalieva-Jailobaeva, 2018, p. 289). Her findings imply that small grass-roots organisations, who may not have the experience or infrastructure required to work with donors, are excluded from international funding streams. In addition, her work also shows that some NGOs have expanded and diversified their funding sources, for example, through membership fees. These organisations have thus become less donor dependent, while at the same time increasing the need for accountability to and connection with communities. These findings thus have potentially important implications for the listening relationships of NGOs with their funders.

Languages in Kyrgyzstan

Kyrgyzstan's official languages include Kyrgyz, referred to as the 'state language' and spoken by 71.4% of the population as a first language, and Russian, which is the first language of 9% of the population (CIA, 2017). Uzbek is spoken as a first language by 14.4% of the population, mainly in the South of the country, while other languages such as Tajik account for 5.8% (CIA, 2017). As a second language, Russian continues to hold a dominant position, with 34.50% of the population adopting it in such a way. English, on the other hand, is still only spoken by a fraction of the population, with statistics around 0.5% being reported (Aminov et al., 2010). Along with French and German, English is offered in some schools as a 'third' or foreign language, although teachers are not widely available (Aminov et al., 2010).

Kyrgyz became an official language in the region in 1989, after years of Russification in pre-Soviet and during Soviet times. Kyrgyz has a short history as a written language, which was developed in the 1920s, and the language has been strongly influenced by Russian during the period of Russian rule (Korth, 2005). As will be discussed below, this history is often considered as a key reason for the lack of technical vocabulary and standardisation of the language.

Because of various socio-economic and political reasons, Russian was granted some rights again in 1994, such as allowing the use of Russian in the workforce in predominantly Russian-speaking regions (Tarbox, 2016, p. 17), and it acquired the status of 'official language' in Kyrgyzstan in

2003 (Korth, 2005). The last few years have seen a push for the use of Kyrgyz in official settings, with a law passed in 2010 that requires embassies, consulates and other diplomatic representations of Kyrgyzstan in foreign countries to use Kyrgyz as their working language (Aminov et al., 2010). The enhanced demand for Kyrgyz in governmental institutions has exacerbated Kyrgyzstan's lack of professionally trained translators in the state language (Kim, 2010). In fact, Kyrgyzstan's Poverty Reduction Strategy for 2014 includes as an objective "to develop and introduce the program of training, retraining and certification for the state language translators" to address this situation (IMF, 2014). Data from population census show that the number of people who can speak Kyrgyz has increased by 17% between 1989 and 1999, although this data should be treated with caution, as people may indicate they speak Kyrgyz for political reasons, with Kyrgyz now being closely linked to Kyrgyz national identity (Korth, 2005). Our interview data does correlate with the trend noted in the census: there was a general sense among interviewees that Kyrgyz was now more widely spoken in rural areas.

Nevertheless, Russian retains a dominant position as a first language in urban areas. It also continues to be a popular second language as it allows speakers to find employment opportunities in other Russian-speaking countries (Tarbox, 2016, pp. 37–38). The importance of Russian should not be underestimated: over one quarter of the country's GDP comes from remittances from citizens working abroad, mainly in Russia and Kazakhstan (CIA, 2017).

The language situation in Kyrgyzstan is further complicated by the status of minority languages and the link between language and ethnicity. In 2010, interethnic violence between Uzbeks and Kyrgyz broke out in the south of the country, mainly in the cities of Osh and neighbouring Jalalabad (CIA, 2017). These events continue to shape the work of civil society in the country, many of whom are working on conflict prevention and community relations, and for whom language is a critical and sensitive part of the discussions they are having with local communities.

Participants

Fieldwork was conducted in January 2018 in the capital Bishkek and in Osh, Kyrgyzstan's second city. Discussions and interviews (34) were held with SNGOs (20), INGOs (5), coordinators of national networks (3), international donors (3), and development consultants, language mediators and academics (3). Twenty-four participants were female, ten were male. Eighteen of these interviews were conducted in English, while sixteen were held with the help of an interpreter: thirteen in Russian and three in Kyrgyz. A general trend was that English language interviews were held with staff at INGOs and in some cases coordinators of national networks. While the researcher could plan these interviews independently, the role of the interpreter as a broker was pivotal in reaching out to SNGOs. The researcher did not speak Russian or Kyrgyz, so relied on the interpreter to arrange interviews. Having worked as an interpreter in the Kyrgyz civil society over the last ten years, she had an extensive network of contacts and this provided access to local SNGOs. As a general approach, the researcher and interpreter selected SNGOs that worked on a broad range of issues, including advocacy (human rights, women's and girls' rights), peacebuilding and community relations, health issues and people with disabilities, and supporting civil society. The interpreter had worked with some of these organisations before; others were selected on the basis of their reputation and using the snowball method.

Twenty-five interviews were conducted in Bishkek, where a large proportion of Kyrgyz NGOs is based, while an additional eight interviews were conducted in Osh during a shorter visit of four days. This means that the interviews present the experiences of urban-based organisations rather than rural ones. The choice for these two cities was mostly practical: as the research was conducted in January, a period of heavy snow and cold in the country, it was virtually impossible to visit SNGOs based in rural communities. As with the interview sample in Peru (see Chapter 8), a large proportion of participants were female. The civil society sector in Kyrgyzstan is reportedly heavily female-led, although the reasons for this have remained unexplored (Jailobaeva, 2011; Féaux De La Croix, 2013; Simpson, 2010). In the interviews we conducted, all but one interviewee from INGOs and donors were male, whereas women typically held positions as directors of SNGOs or national networks. The high number of women in the research data should be approached with some caution and should not be interpreted as representative of SNGOs throughout the country, as previous research has stated that urban SNGOs tend to be led by women, whereas leaders of rural SNGOs are often men (Jailobaeva, 2011).

Communicating in English

English was reported as playing a key role in Kyrgyzstan's development sector, particularly in SNGOs' survival strategies. Participants asserted that as little funding for development programmes was now available through the Kyrgyz government, especially for advocacy and rights-based work, securing international funding was critical for organisational survival, and for this, the use of English was seen as critically important. Of the twenty SNGOs interviewed, only four reported having some English language capacity. All twenty SNGOs encountered difficulties with communicating in English with international donors, even those who had some English language skills. The first obstacle SNGOs encountered was writing grant applications, the process of which was complicated further by difficulties in gaining access to the internet, the complexity of application forms, and the need for a highly specialised English that included development buzzwords and donors' preferred terminology (KYR 23, Director of SNGO, Osh). Some donors required applications both in English and in Russian, which typically entailed submitting two complete applications prepared in separate 'packages', making the 'burden' of translation even heavier (KYR 9, Director of SNGO, Bishkek). NGO workers described these requirements as "just not realistic" (KYR 30, Director of SNGO, Osh), particularly for small, rural NGOs with very limited financial means to pay for translation (KYR 6, SNGO workers, Bishkek).

The need for English in engaging with international donors occurred from the very beginning of the funding process, starting from donors' publishing their call for applications in English, and consequently accepting applications and any follow-up reporting monolingually in English. Unsurprisingly, this meant that "in the end, we cannot afford all this work, and most of the time, we just don't make any grant applications" (KYR 6, SNGO workers, Bishkek). The cost of translation could to some extent be spared by the use of Google Translate, which at least six of the organisations interviewed relied on frequently. The introduction of Kyrgyz as one of Google Translate's languages in 2016 has helped some organisations in improving their access to information, but there was a feeling that Google Translate, either from/to Kyrgyz or Russian, could not serve as a solution in producing and translating information related to NGOs' work, including project applications: "…the translation is not good. So, the reader will not get the idea, the way that I want to express it" (KYR 25, SNGO worker, Osh). Participants argued that translation costs related to project applications and reporting should be supported by international donors, but that this was not the case: "…you already are reading in the instructions that 'we do not support any costs related to grant application'. So, I understand that if I have to translate the grant application, then I have to pay for it myself" (KYR 24, Director of SNGO, Osh).

SNGO workers expressed particular frustration regarding the widespread practice of international donors and INGOs not sharing final reports and evaluations in local languages, meaning the information in these publications could not contribute to local capacity building: "Not all final monitoring reports are translated [into Russian or Kyrgyz]. The wider public does not have access to them. We have very little understanding of what's going on there" (KYR 2, Director of national SNGO network, Bishkek). Some SNGOs had lobbied with their international donors and partners for the use of Russian in application forms and reporting, but the success of these lobbying activities had been limited (KYR 2, Director of SNGO, Bishkek; KYR 7, INGO worker, Bishkek). A solution that some international donors, like the European Union, had opted for was to allow a system of sub-granting, "allowing 25% of the grant money to be regranted to smaller NGOs" (KYR 7, INGO worker, Bishkek).

The system of sub-granting was deemed helpful by some SNGOs, as it meant they were not confronted with linguistic barriers to accessing funding (KYR 29, Director of SNGO, Osh). However, it did result in a very distant relationship between SNGOs and international donors where the only direct contact between the two would be "in training or workshops, where the communication was through an interpreter" (KYR 29, Director of SNGO, Osh). Organisations that provided sub-grants were presented by interviewees as examples of good practice: they would accept funding applications in local languages (i.e., Russian and Kyrgyz), they would be open to funding translations costs as part of project work, and they would often provide training in response to local organisations' needs, such as sessions on monitoring and evaluation, grant writing, and reporting (KYR 23 and 29, Directors of SNGO, Osh). These organisations were typically INGOs or international private organisations that had an office in Bishkek and that had been working in the region for several years. In the international aid chain, their position as mediators between the international donor and local organisations and communities also implied a position as linguistic mediators, acting as translators of information between local and international levels. One SNGO worker explained that they were part of several networks, and that "our partner organisations accept applications in Russian. Or they say: you can write reports in Russian, we'll translate them into English" (KYR 3, SNGO, Bishkek). Some INGO workers emphasised their role as translators. In many cases, they were the only partner in the development collaboration who mastered all languages involved: English, Russian, Kyrgyz, in some cases Uzbek and Tajik. For one INGO, these multilingual requirements meant that:

> [We] usually develop a communication plan with the local partner, which we will sign and then we start the partnership. So, which person will contact, and in which language, and how they do reporting, particularly narrative and financial reporting, so we clarify in the beginning, so... if they ask us to do in Kyrgyz, we do translation in Kyrgyz. (KYR 28, INGO worker, Osh)

This institutionalised type of multilingualism that led to formalised contracts was rather an exception, but the practice of informal oral and written translation by multilingual NGO workers was widespread: "many of our colleagues they do translation when our expat staff for example come from other countries or from partner organisations in the fieldwork, and in office work also we do translation" (KYR 16, INGO worker, Bishkek). These processes of translation were described as challenging: when reporting back to donors, colleagues sometimes spent hours trying "to find the appropriate vocabulary to express ideas, or to convey the information they get from the field" (KYR 16, INGO worker, Bishkek).

The language of development was heavily associated with 'the West'. Conveying concepts related to human rights and sexual health, for example, was particularly difficult:

> For a lot of people in the country, if you say human rights, these are just two empty words for them. And normally... they think that, it's not here, it's somewhere else, and some people will say: "ah, human rights, it's there! These are European values." And let alone the concepts like sexual rights or reproductive rights... So, if you want to have a dialogue with someone about these concepts, then you have to unpack these words for this person.

> You need to explain exactly what is meant by that. (KYR 10, Director of SNGO, Bishkek)

Some NGO workers reflected critically on the influence of Western concepts and ideas on their own work. This terminology was described as a specific 'academic' type of development language that was being constantly updated, further adding to the challenge for development workers to explain their work to rural communities (KYR 16, INGO worker, Bishkek). In some ways, English- and Russian-speaking NGO workers, who had mastered this terminology, were seen as living in conceptually different worlds than those living in rural communities, working with new methodologies "designed for Western mentality" (KYR 31, SNGO worker, Osh). Mastering this terminology and the methodologies that came with it could be a process of years: "the first time I attended a workshop on 'Theory of Change', it was difficult for me to understand… only later, with years of experience, I got the idea, Theory of Change" (KYR 23, Director of SNGO, Osh). For some of the international organisations active in the sector, explaining or teaching this terminology through workshops to local civil society workers had been one of their core goals in the early years of intervention:

> …it was about 'What is a modern language of development?' Replacing communist and Marxist ideas, which most people knew about quite well, and replacing them with a sort of international development terminology, within our market economy and so on… And it was very valuable because this was the talk that people had to learn so as to be able to interface with the development agencies. (KYR 7, INGO worker, Bishkek)

The import of Western models and terminology of development in former Soviet territory is an issue that has been widely debated in the literature on the region (Aksartova, 2005; Buxton, 2009; Dunn & Hann, 1996; Howell, 2000; Kandiyoti, 2002; Roy, 2002). In our interviews, participants raised particular questions on the usefulness of some of the activities funded by international donors, when these events were constructed around concepts that local communities were unfamiliar with (KYR 31, SNGO worker, Osh; KYR 29, Director of SNGO, Osh). Such events were often run in English, with interpreting into local communities' languages, thus decreasing the probability that participants would understand and retain the information provided to them (KYR 16, INGO worker, Bishkek). According to participants, international organisations, who organised these events in English, had little understanding of the fact that much of the translated terminology was not part of local communities' worlds, and that such training would therefore run the risk of being ineffective.

English as a language was omnipresent in the international development sector in the country. English language knowledge was a prerequisite to be able to work for an INGO in Kyrgyzstan, with fluency in English often being the sole selection criterion in INGO recruitment processes. This means that whilst INGOs were seen as highly supportive in offering translation support to SNGOs, interviewees also expressed frustration at the negative implications of INGO recruitment strategies for local NGO capacity and career advancement:

> [Donors], for example, they want to hire an expert from an NGO sector, but they want this person to speak very good English... I have all the other skills that the donors want for a certain job, but because I don't speak English... I am not eligible for some of their jobs. (SNGO staff member)

The requirement for English meant that these jobs were primarily accessible to those who were more privileged and had had the opportunity to learn English. In some cases, SNGOs felt that they were making considerable investment in the training of young graduates, who had often graduated from English language departments but did not have any knowledge of the development sector, only to be left emptyhanded when these young people then left to take up better-paid positions in INGOs (KYR 31, SNGO worker, Osh). As this often left SNGOs without any English language capacity, learning English was a recurring theme in nearly all of the interviews with these organisations. Although English language skills would, in the first instance, often be seen as a tool to access funding, they were also strongly associated with access to knowledge and information:

> ...most of our library [in the NGO], we have very amazing books in English ... and that's why I started to read in English too. It was my own efforts, and trying, ambition and motivation, because it's really the desire to get knowledge, it made me go forward... you start to see it's an international language, you cannot always speak Russian or Kyrgyz, you need to try. (KYR 15, SNGO worker, Bishkek)

Moreover, English would allow SNGO workers to share their work internationally. One Kyrgyz-speaking SNGO recounted how they had had a visit from a UN worker who had then published an English article on the SNGO's work, which had been "disseminated into thirty-six countries around the world" (KYR 6, SNGO staff, Bishkek). This had been an incredibly positive experience for this small SNGO, for whom this international visibility was a way of sharing their work outside their own country and linguistic circles. Thus, English was seen as a way to access international debates, to share experiences with others and participate in a wider dialogue. Yet the insistence on English meant that many continued to be excluded from such events. One participant related that her organisation had received an invitation for a conference in Amsterdam and was asked to "nominate your candidates from the youth who are infected by HIV, but they should know English. [We have] no one!" (KYR 4, Director of INGO, Bishkek). An SNGO worker whose organisation was part of an international network recounted that they were usually assigned an interpreter, but argued that working through interpretation lessoned their capacity to contribute:

> ...when we have group discussions, by the time the interpreter translates, by the time I think about it, and for example I want to react and express my opinion, but by the time I am ready to speak, someone else, who speaks English, is already speaking the same thing that I wanted to say, and all I have to do is, like, I agree with what has been said. (KYR 26, Director of SNGO, Osh)

As one participant summarised it, the insistence on English in the sector "is limiting capacity of civil society activists, to be fruitfully engaged, a. [and] b. it's also disempowering the relations, because you can have no voice if you don't understand all the details" (KYR 9, Director of national network, Bishkek). There was thus a general feeling that if donors were to support English language development among NGOs, this would contribute to more equitable relationships in which a truly bidirectional dialogue could emerge. However, participants also expected considerable efforts from international donors and partners to speak their languages:

> ...first of all, if the organisation has a serious intention to work in this country, in a certain area, they *must* learn the local language... and traditions. On the other hand, English language is an international language

> and donors could invest in local people… learning English. (KYR 8, Director of national network, Bishkek)

Learning local languages could be part of "annual performance appraisal", so that international staff would be "motivated to learn the local language… so they must be motivated and say that: if you don't learn the local language, then goodbye!" (KYR 8, Director of national network, Bishkek).

Language learning would not just demonstrate respect for local communities but would also help in developing development projects that were more attuned to local communities' needs. Participants argued that, at present, a disconnect existed from the early stages of programme design, and that international partners "already came to us with the programme that had already been designed… we have never been consulted" (KYR 8, Director of national network, Bishkek). This led to programmes that were not relevant to rural communities, but that would nevertheless "be implemented, in the end, but it will be done just kind of, to tick off, to say that it is done" (KYR 8, Director of national network, Bishkek). In the experience of this interviewee, 'listening' had actually improved, as donors were now more ready than in the past to do needs assessments and consult experts, but:

> …they consult with ministries, they consult with government agencies at the central level. But they don't normally consult with beneficiaries at the local level. They don't consult with local self-governments at the district level or the rural, village municipalities. (KYR 8, Director of national network, Bishkek)

Donors were thus seen as listening to the wrong people: those who were from elite backgrounds, spoke different languages (English or Russian, but no Kyrgyz) and who were not representative of local communities and did not understand their culture or daily challenges. The problem, in the end, seemed to at least partly boil down to one of language and of international donors and partners not understanding local realities, not least the fact that there is a mismatch between the languages spoken by many NGO workers, i.e., Russian, and those of local communities, i.e., Kyrgyz.

Communicating with Communities

In the local development context, Russian and Kyrgyz, and to a lesser extent Uzbek and Tajik, are the languages NGOs use to work with communities. Participants reported an increase in the need for Kyrgyz, firstly, to work with rural communities who were described as now increasingly speaking Kyrgyz rather than Russian, and secondly, to work with national governmental institutions. For example, one SNGO reported recently being asked for the first time to submit project applications and reporting to a national governmental institution in Kyrgyz (KYR 3, SNGO worker, Bishkek). Some civil society organisations seemed to be better equipped to deal with the increasing need for Kyrgyz than others. From our interview data, a varied picture emerged in terms of organisational linguistic capacity: INGOs that had offices within the country had succeeded in attracting staff who were multilingual, speaking Russian, English, Kyrgyz, and in some cases, Tajik and Uzbek. Some of their staff had grown up in rural, Kyrgyz-speaking areas, and were among the few who had had access to English language training (KYR 12, Director of INGO, Bishkek; KYR 16, INGO worker, Bishkek; KYR 18, INGO worker, Bishkek; KYR 20, INGO worker, Bishkek; KYR 28, INGO worker, Osh). Most of these staff members had been able to attend university in the USA or the UK, some of them through funded educational and cultural exchanges (see also Aksartova, 2005, pp. 138–139). SNGOs in Osh tended to be multilingual, using Russian, Kyrgyz and Uzbek, and in some cases Tajik, which contrasted sharply with the SNGOs based in Bishkek, nearly all of which were monolingual Russian. In Osh, the city where ethnic violence broke out in 2010 between Kyrgyz and Uzbeks, being multilingual as an NGO worker was seen as a necessity, as speaking someone else's language was considered as important to be able to establish trust with local communities (KYR 12, Director of INGO, Bishkek; 27, SNGO worker, Osh; KYR 28, INGO worker, Osh). A sensitivity to linguistic and ethnic tensions was key to being able to work with communities in southern areas, especially for those working on conflict prevention.

SNGOs based in Bishkek, however, ran into linguistic problems when aiming to work with rural communities. Staff in these organisations were often part of Russian-speaking elite groups, and generally spoke no or little Kyrgyz. The problem with Bishkek-based SNGOs' lack of Kyrgyz skills was conceived as a deeper societal issue. Participants described

SNGO workers in this context as being recycled in and out of government, UN, and other INGO bodies, and as concerned with advancing their careers rather than benefiting the lives of local beneficiaries (KYR 1, INGO worker, Bishkek; KYR 14, international donor, Bishkek; KYR 21, Director of SNGO, Bishkek) (see also Simpson, 2010, pp. 284–285). This grim disconnect between Bishkek SNGOs and Kyrgyz-speaking communities was seen as being further exacerbated by the fact that international organisations did not always insist on Kyrgyz-language knowledge, "show[ing] the arrogance of the elite of Bishkek... and it's just not right, you know, not to have this capacity" (KYR 14, international donor, Bishkek). According to one participant, the tide had begun to turn under the influence of the government's increasing emphasis on the use of Kyrgyz in governmental positions. Whereas ten years ago, women from Bishkek would, according to this interviewee, say "they were proud that they don't speak Kyrgyz... because it meant that they are not riff-raff from the countryside, but they are the cool girls from the city" (KYR 14, international donor, Bishkek), but Kyrgyz was now a requirement for some posts in international organisations in the country, because "it's a job skill, that person needs to talk to people in the communities" (KYR 14, international donor, Bishkek). In Bishkek-based SNGOs as well, there was a recognition that having Kyrgyz language capacity had become increasingly important, particularly because "when you go to the region, this new generation, they speak more Kyrgyz" (KYR 12, Director of INGO, Bishkek). Some SNGO workers had taken to learning the language for their work, openly recognising that learning Kyrgyz also meant to "come to learn the culture" (KYR 21, Director of SNGO, Bishkek). These views chime with Korth's (2005) findings, whose study of language use and language attitudes in Kyrgyzstan describes an enhanced status of the Kyrgyz language since independence.

The SNGOs in our interviews that were not well equipped to deal with the increased need for Kyrgyz tended to devise ad hoc solutions that were often insufficient. For example, one such solution was to organise workshops run by two trainers, one who typically spoke Russian, in some cases English, and one who spoke the local language. However, it was difficult to find professionals who mastered the necessary terminology, and "sometimes there are some topics where we don't have trainers in Kyrgyz... we try to translate some handouts into Kyrgyz, but the training is in Russian, and we ask like in Osh to invite people who have a knowledge in Russian language" (KYR 5, SNGO worker, Bishkek). The Kyrgyz-Russian language barriers between urban NGOs and the local communities they work with illustrate how information and knowledge is often only accessible for Russian-language speakers. When SNGO workers made an effort to use Kyrgyz in their work to listen to communities, this was described as challenging, particularly because of the various dialects of Kyrgyz and the lack of a standardised written language. A Russian native speaker from Bishkek with some Kyrgyz language skills explained how the Kyrgyz used in Osh, close to the border with Uzbekistan, is:

> some Kyrgyz-Uzbek, like literally mixed... and when I go to monitor in Osh, it's sometimes very hard to listen, because some words I can understand but other words they talk like in Uzbek. And I ask somebody from the NGO to sit together and sometimes explain me what is going on. (KYR 5, SNGO worker, Bishkek)

Equally, when SNGOs aimed to produce materials for communities, such as handbooks and guidelines, it was difficult to make these texts understandable for everyone. Much of this work was produced in Russian and then translated into Kyrgyz by freelance translators or translation agencies (see also Chapter 5), but the fact that there was no standardised Kyrgyz language caused a plethora of issues:

> We produced special instruction for police officers for this project, and we started trainings in all regions of our country, and we translated our presentation into Kyrgyz language... our trainer, he was... from Bishkek... and when we go to the regions, people are listening and listening and they say: "who translated this?" They are very angry, because in our country, we have seven regions, and we can say that we have seven dialects of the language, and they said "we don't understand!" (KYR 4, Director of SNGO, Bishkek)

The SNGO had hired an official translator from the president's team. Yet the example shows that producing a translation that is accessible to a broad Kyrgyz audience remains challenging, even when working with governmental Kyrgyz translators, who can be expected to have knowledge of the appropriate terminologies. This illustrates the extent of the challenges involved in providing suitable translations: even when hiring professionals with appropriate language skills, NGOs' efforts to communicate with local communities may be hindered by language issues.

A related problem was the reported lack of technical, business and development terminology in Kyrgyz, as alluded to in the introduction. Despite governmental efforts to increase the presence and importance of the Kyrgyz language in all facets of society, Russian continues to be the language associated with science and technology, as well as higher education, giving rise to a diglossic situation in which Russian is still often seen as the 'high language' and Kyrgyz as the 'low language' (Huskey, 1995). In the case of development terminology, many terms would often either be transposed from English into Russian and then into Kyrgyz as loanwords. According to one interpreter, the reason for this non-translation practice was that, firstly, "sometimes the translation is longer than in English, and it doesn't really reflect the exact meaning of the English word" (KYR 11, freelance interpreter, Bishkek), and secondly, because "some people think they will sound smarter" when using English words (KYR 11, freelance interpreter, Bishkek). For newcomers to the NGO sector, this would result in having to decipher a whole new vocabulary and the methodologies that came with it, because even if people "don't speak English, they know these words: actor, stakeholders, and then they would say 'SWOT analysis' in Russian: 'analiz SWOT'" (KYR 11, freelance interpreter, Bishkek). For professional translators and interpreters, the challenges involved were manifold:

> ...when donors started using the word advocacy... we still struggle with that. And for example, when I do a translation, if it's NGO workers who know the word, I just say 'advokatze', because it's easier for them to understand, if I say 'advokatze' rather than I start explaining. But if it's, if these are not professionals who know the word, then I have to almost explain like, what that means. (KYR 11, freelance interpreter, Bishkek)

Because these were foreign words, they were often described as empty vehicles without any real meaning (KYR 13, freelance consultant, Bishkek; KYR 34, academic, Bishkek). When having to translate handbooks and training materials that would be full of development buzzwords, entire texts would run the risk of becoming meaningless: "People can understand this handbook the way they like, because they are all outside words" (KYR 13, freelance consultant, Bishkek).

Despite the many challenges involved for SNGOs to speak about their work in Kyrgyz, interviewees also shared positive experiences of material they had produced in Kyrgyz, which were considered as key achievements.

A Kyrgyz-speaking NGO, for example, had produced a methodology on one of the main topics it was working on:

> ...based on our many years' experience as an NGO in a rural area. It's written in a very simple Kyrgyz language, and where we tell about the best practice including, like, what we learned from international best practice, and it's all written in a very accessible Kyrgyz language, and that's why it's quite popular with rural NGOs. (KYR 6, SNGO, Bishkek)

One INGO worker related how their INGO had produced guidelines for local carpenters in Kyrgyz in the aftermath of an earthquake in one of the districts in which the NGO was active. The handbook on construction norms and how to behave in emergency situations was the first of its kind to be available in the Kyrgyz language and was seen as a key publication to make this knowledge available for Kyrgyz people. An interesting development was that the international donor then asked to have the book translated in Russian because it was difficult to find this kind of handbook in the language. Thus, the project intentionally set out to produce knowledge in the local language, embedded in the local culture and context, and in doing so contributed to developing terminology of key development topics in the local languages.

Alongside the language issues described so far, participants also spoke of cultural differences which could exacerbate listening challenges. Some participants (KYR 11, freelance interpreter, Bishkek; KYR 16, INGO worker, Bishkek) explained that people in rural areas would not ask questions to guests, because it was considered as disrespectful and as a sign of ignorance: "their kind of culture is that if you ask a lot of questions it might look like they don't know anything" (KYR 16, INGO worker, Bishkek). This meant that it was not only NGOs' listening practices that could be problematic, but also their speaking: "when [NGO people] go to the field, we keep using the terminologies, which is unusual for local people, and because local people would not mostly speak out to explain, to clarify this terminology, I think the barrier between the two will remain there" (KYR 16, INGO worker, Bishkek).

Misunderstandings because of culture would arise on many occasions and in many forms, and there was a general feeling that international partners left little room for SNGOs to organise their work in a way that was suitable to the local cultural and political context. For example, one interviewee related that international donors did not always show an understanding of the different political climate in which SNGOs in Kyrgyzstan are working:

> ...we were starting a project, and we were working with local self-governments and with the police, and there we have a very strict hierarchy and subordination. And when we talk about accountability, our foreign... our partners, it means one thing and they take it seriously. Our international partners wanted the police to report to the local community, like every three months. But for us... we don't have power over the police. So, we cannot tell the police to go and report... it is very difficult. And it was very difficult to persuade our international partners that it's almost like mission impossible. (KYR 31, SNGO worker, Osh)

This example not only shows how international partners may not be willing to negotiate their terms of work and what 'accountability' could imply, but also that there was little understanding of the different socio-political context. Before Western donors' involvement in Central Asia and the establishment of NGOs according to a Western organisational model, civil society type organisations would have only had a social role, not a political one. Though NGOs have now been present in the country for several years, their position is often described as tenuous, as they represent an organisational template that is unfamiliar to local society (Aksartova, 2005; Jailobaeva, 2011).

However, not all international partners are the same, and some NGO workers recounted very positive collaborative experiences. Some reported that the INGOs they were working with had a Russian-speaking staff member in their headquarters in the UK, the Netherlands or France. Because of the shared history of former USSR countries, a Russian-speaking staff member was seen as extremely helpful because they "already knew the problems. It was similar in Russia and in Kyrgyzstan" (KYR 18, INGO worker, Bishkek). In this particular case, the participant related how this shared language and history also meant there was a better understanding of what a culturally appropriate way of working would constitute:

> ...we have this tradition, seeking advice from elders, from our parents, talking to our brothers and sisters and that kind of thing, so it seemed natural that we talked to people about their needs. But it was a real contrast for example when we met other, one other project, we had a few other projects funded by [name of international donor], I am talking about

> [name of international donor] because it was more a business-approach, a more top-down approach, so just, maybe it would be written down on paper that it was sort of more... sort of participatory approaches, but they wouldn't really care about that. (KYR 18, INGO worker, Bishkek)

For the INGO that this interviewee worked for, the importance of the family, seeking advice from elders, and of taking the time to "dedicate several days just [to] sit with people and hear" (KYR 18, INGO worker, Bishkek) was understood as central to its work in order to show respect when listening and working with people. Throughout the interviews, the donors that participants felt were more open to different approaches of doing development and accommodated a listening that was more culturally appropriate tended to be private organisations rather than governmental institutions. Examples included the UK's Big Lottery Fund, the Stars Foundation, and the Soros Foundation (KYR 6, SNGO staff, Bishkek; KYR 15, SNGO worker, Bishkek; KYR 18, INGO worker, Bishkek; KYR 23, Director of SNGO, Osh).

Rather than using international donor's approaches to accountability, which were largely related to paperwork, software and complicated methodologies for data collection, the key to successful listening and building respectful relationships with local communities seemed to be:

> [to] just listen, speak to people, and feedback... eat their bread, and drink their tea... bring our biscuits and sit there for a whole day and speak with them, just speak with them, these kind of things, their concerns, their problems, and... would also ask "what could you do yourself?" (KYR 18, INGO worker, Bishkek)

For this, of course, speaking the local language was critical, and various interviewees precisely articulated this as a key recommendation to international donors and partner organisations. Speaking the local language meant being "closer to the Kyrgyz people... local communities will trust them more" (KYR 21, Director of SNGO, Bishkek) and "local people they will see the efforts of the donor representative and their attitude will be different... there will be more trust, because language is a bridge of trust" (KYR 8, Director of national network, Bishkek).

Indeed, speaking the local language, or at least working with local experts who are familiar with the local context and needs, would help in addressing the observed disconnect between international donors and urban-based NGOs on the one hand and rural communities on the other. This disconnect was reported in the majority of interviews in various ways and from various perspectives, and is recognised in the literature (Jailobaeva, 2011; Buxton, 2009; Howell, 2000; Simpson, 2010). One interviewee argued that donors were "not prepared to make the necessary compromises to work with smaller organisations", with "considerable security measures to move around Bishkek it seems and… won't travel on any local airplane to Osh" (KYR 7, INGO worker, Bishkek). One originally rural-based NGO expressed its concern that "unless donors and international organisations they change their policy, unless they pay more attention to rural areas, rural NGOs, unless they adopt a language policy, then rural areas are getting more and more marginalised" (KYR 6, SNGO staff, Bishkek), thus underlining the limited ability of international donors and organisations to access rural areas and realities if they cannot speak the local language. Overall, participants argued that continuing to disregard the importance of (speaking) local languages would contribute to a development sector in which NGOs are busy with their own urban daily realities and survival but overlook the realities of the rural communities they aim to support.

Conclusion

In Kyrgyzstan, the listening relationships between SNGOs and international donors were distorted because of the preferred use of English among donors, and the lack of such skills among SNGOs. Because funding applications often had to be submitted in English, SNGOs either did not apply for funding, or they used tools such as Google Translate, which tended to be inadequate for qualitative translation and therefore usually did not result in successful funding applications. In light of Bayalieva-Jailobaeva's (2014) finding that professional NGOs in Kyrgyzstan are in a better position to obtain international donor funding, our country case study findings add that a critical asset in this professional skillset is English language proficiency, including knowledge of development terminology. Because SNGOs did not have these linguistic skills, the Listening Zones between SNGOs and international donors were frequently shaped indirectly by INGOs and international private organisations who acted as linguistic mediators and as channels for funding through a system of sub-granting. Whilst some SNGOs were positive about this mediating function of international organisations, the perceived downside was that these organisations caused a brain drain in the local NGO sector because of their preference for English language skills.

The listening relationships of SNGOs with local communities were equally characterised by language barriers, mainly because of urban-based SNGOs' lack of Kyrgyz language capacity. This finding contradicts international donors' assumptions that NGOs have the necessary linguistic skills to listen to communities, as described in Chapter 3. The disconnect between urban-based NGO workers whose native language is Russian and that of Kyrgyz-speaking communities described in some of the literature on Kyrgyzstan was generally acknowledged in our research data. Those participants from INGOs and international private organisations that took part in the study, however, were more successful in acting as (linguistic) mediators between international donors and local partner organisations and communities, as most of those interviewed were multilingual in English, Russian and Kyrgyz.

As mentioned in the introduction, Bayalieva-Jailobaeva's (2014) findings on the Kyrgyz NGO sector indicated that NGOs have diversified their funding sources, which may have important implications for the accountability of NGOs and their relations with local communities. This apparent new reality was not one that was encountered in our interviews, yet this may be due to a bias in the interview data, which mainly consisted of Bishkek-based SNGOs, for whom language was a key obstacle in creating close working relationships with local communities. These SNGOs showed awareness of the increasingly important role of Kyrgyz in their work with communities, but they continued to struggle with finding adequate solutions to address this emerging new reality. Time will tell if enhanced Kyrgyz language learning in the NGO sector, which was described as a necessary effort by various interviewees, will become the solution that is opted for.

Overall, the Listening Zones of Kyrgyz NGOs were characterised by their translation processes, or in fact, the absence of them, and the consequent non-communication or miscommunication. Language barriers were described as daily realities by interviewees, but it was felt that this was ignored by international donors and in guidelines or policy documents relating to development. The implications of a listening that lacked the effort to engage in translation efforts led to development projects that were arguably decontextualised, often not corresponding to the needs and cultural context of local communities, or that did not effectively engage with local communities, because the language that information or training was provided in was inaccessible to them. This created situations in which development efforts were conceived as tick-box exercises rather than as opportunities for dialogue that demonstrated respect and showed an interest in the lived realities of local communities. Interviewees conceived of this a-linguistic approach as a type of listening that granted power to certain groups and excluded others from access to information, training activities, funding and engaging in a dialogue with other development actors.

References

Aksartova, S. (2005). *Civil society from abroad: U.S. donors in the former Soviet Union* (Unpublished PhD Thesis). Princeton University, Princeton.

Aminov, K. V., Jensen, V., Juraev, S., Overland, I., Tyan, D., & Uulu, Y. (2010). Language use and language policy in Central Asia. *Central Asia Regional Data Review, 2*(1), 1–29.

Anderson, J. (1997). *The international politics of Central Asia*. Manchester: Manchester University Press.

Bayalieva-Jailobaeva, K. (2014). A new look: Professionalization of NGOs in Kyrgyzstan. *Central Asian Survey, 33*(3), 360–374.

Bayalieva-Jailobaeva, K. (2018). New donor strategies: Implications for NGOs in post-Soviet Kyrgyzstan. *VOLUNTAS: International Journal of Voluntary and Nonprofit Organizations, 29*(2), 284–295.

Buxton, C. (2009). NGO networks in Central Asia and global civil society: Potentials and limitations. *Central Asian Survey, 28*(1), 43–58.

Buxton, C., Earle, L., & Giffen, J. (2005). *The development of civil society in Central Asia*. Oxford: INTRAC.

CIA. (2017). *The Central Intelligence Agency World Factbook: Central Asia. Kyrgyzstan*. Retrieved from: https://www.cia.gov/library/publications/the-world-factbook/geos/kg.html.

DFID. (2018). *DFID Central Asia: Kyrgyzstan and Tajikistan profile*. Retrieved from: https://assets.publishing.service.gov.uk/government/uploads/system/uploads/attachment_data/file/723131/Central-Asia-Tajikistan-Kyrgyzstan-July-2018.pdf.

DFID. (2019a). *Department for International Development annual report and accounts 2018–19*. Retrieved from: https://assets.publishing.service.gov.uk/government/uploads/system/uploads/attachment_data/file/815787/ARA-2019.pdf.

DFID. (2019b). *Kyrgyzstan*. Retrieved from: https://devtracker.dfid.gov.uk/countries/KG. Accessed 2 January 2020.

Dunn, E., & Hann, C. M. (1996). *Civil society: Challenging Western models*. London: Routledge.

Féaux De La Croix, J. (2013). How to build a better future? Kyrgyzstani development workers and the knowledge transfer strategy. *Central Asian Survey, 32*(4), 448–461.

Freedom House. (2018). *Freedom in the world. Kyrgyzstan profile*. Retrieved from: https://freedomhouse.org/report/freedom-world/2018/kyrgyzstan.

Garbutt, A., & Heap, S. (Eds.). (2002). *Growing civil society in Central Asia*. Occasional Papers Series. Oxford: INTRAC.

Howell, J. (2000). Making civil society from the outside: Challenges for donors. *European Journal of Development Research, 1*(1), 3–22.

Huskey, E. (1995). *The politics of language in Kyrgyzstan*. Washington, DC. Retrieved from: http://www.ucis.pitt.edu/nceeer/1995-810-28-4-Huskey.pdf.

ICNL. (2018). *Civic Freedom Monitor: Kyrgyz Republic*. Retrieved from: http://www.icnl.org/research/monitor/kyrgyz.html.

IMF. (2014). *The Kyrgyz Republic: Poverty reduction strategy paper* (IMF Country Report No. 14/247). Washington, DC.

IMF. (2016). *Kyrgyz Republic: Selected issues* (*IMF Country Report No. 16/56*). Washington, DC.

Jailobaeva, K. (2011). *The return of the state to development: The state, donors and NGOs in post-Soviet Kyrgyzstan* (Unpublished PhD Thesis). University of Edinburgh, Edinburgh.

Kandiyoti, D. (2002). How far do analyses of post-socialism travel? The case of Central Asia. In C. M. Hann, (Ed.), *Postsocialism: Ideals, ideologies and practices in Eurasia* (pp. 238–257). London: Routledge.

Kim, Y. (2010, May 2). *Speak Kyrgyz, not Russian, diplomats told*. Institute for War and Peace Reporting. Retrieved from: https://iwpr.net/global-voices/speak-kyrgyz-not-russian-diplomats-told.

Korth, B. (2005). *Language attitudes towards Kyrgyz and Russian: Discourse, education and policy in Post-Soviet Kyrgyzstan*. Berlin: Peter Lang.

Kyrgyz Government. (2018). *The development program of the Kyrgyz Republic for the period 2018–2022: 'Unity, Trust, Creation'*. Bishkek. Retrieved from: https://www.un-page.org/files/public/the_development_program_of_the_kyrgyz_republic_for_the_period_2018-2022.pdf.

OECD Development Assistance Committee. (2018). *Development co-operation report 2018: Joining forces to leave no one behind*. Paris: OECD.

Overland, I., & Vakulchuk, R. (2019). China's Belt and Road Initiative through the lens of Central Asia China' s Belt and Road Initiative through the lens of Central Asia Roman Vakulchuk and Indra Overland. In F. M. Cheung & Y. Hong (Eds.), *Regional connection under the Belt and Road Initiative:*

The prospects for economic and financial cooperation (pp. 115–133). London: Routledge.

Roy, O. (2002). Soviet legacies and Western aid imperatives in the New Central Asia. In A. Sajoo (Ed.), *Civil society in the Muslim world: Contemporary perspectives* (pp. 123–148). London: I.B. Tauris.

Simpson, M. (2010). Unpacking East/West tensions: Women's NGOs and Islam in contemporary Kyrgyzstan. *Anthropology of East Europe Review, 28*(1), 268–301.

Tarbox, L. K. (2016). *Language and foreign policy : The Kyrgyz experience* (Unpublished Master's thesis). University of South Carolina, Columbia. Retrieved from: http://scholarcommons.sc.edu/etd/3322.

Trading Economics. (2017). *Kyrgyzstan: Net official development assistance and official aid received*. Retrieved from: https://tradingeconomics.com/kyrgyzstan/net-official-development-assistance-and-official-aid-received-us-dollar-wb-data.html.

UNDP. (2018). *Kyrgyzstan human development indices and indicators: 2018 statistical update*. Retrieved from: http://hdr.undp.org/sites/all/themes/hdr_theme/country-notes/KGZ.pdf.

Wilkinson, C. (2014). Development in Kyrgyzstan: Failed state or failed state-building. In A. Ware (Ed.), *Development in difficult sociopolitical contexts* (pp. 137–162). London: Palgrave Macmillan.

World Bank. (2018). *Poverty and equity data portal: Kyrgyz Republic*. Retrieved from: http://povertydata.worldbank.org/poverty/country/KGZ.

CHAPTER 8

Peru

The NGO Sector in Peru

Whereas INGO activity is longstanding and continuous in Malawi, and is relatively recent in Kyrgyzstan, Peru provides an insight into a changing international aid architecture. In what has been called a 'post-aid' environment (Appe, 2018), relations in Peru are being reshaped between international aid actors, donors, INGOs, civil society organisations and governments and private corporations. Peru is officially ranked as an upper middle-income country, with World Bank data suggesting that the poverty rate (the percentage of the population living on US$5.50 a day) fell from 52.2% in 2005 to 26% in 2013 (World Bank, 2018). Consistent economic growth, combined with investment in infrastructure, education and health, have resulted in significant reductions in hunger and poverty, including a diminution in chronic malnutrition from 29% in 2007 to 13% in 2016 (World Food Programme, 2017).

The reallocation of Peru from the lower middle-income category, in which it had been positioned since 1996, to the upper middle-income list in 2011 (OECD, 2019) has had major repercussions for international donor support. OECD figures suggest that whilst there was a 37% increase in contributions to NGOs in Latin America between 2005 and 2008, the increase was just 3% between 2008 and 2011 and subsequently fell further. Among the ten recipient countries in Latin America, Peru is in ninth place in terms of Official Development Assistance (ODA) aid, receiving only 3% of the total aid (OECDStats, 2017). The UK's bilateral

H. Footitt et al., *Development NGOs and Languages*,
https://doi.org/10.1007/978-3-030-51776-2_8

commitment to the continent of Latin America has also markedly diminished in this period. In the OECD's 2018 report, 29.9% of bilateral aid went to the UK's top ten recipients, none of whom were in Latin America (OECD, 2018). DFID has now reduced its Latin America Regional Unit and has closed its regional offices in Central America and the Andes.

Given the changed status of Peru, large UK-based INGOs have tended not just to scale down their commitments, but rather to exit the country altogether. Christian Aid, for example, had an established programme in Peru since the 1980s but made the decision in late 2012 to withdraw from the country:

> The need to reduce our geographical footprint to "do more in less places" and the increasing demands on a very small office (including complex donor requirements) led to a decision to phase out the Peru programme. Other factors taken into account included comparative niche between countries. (Buttner, cited in Edussuriya, Lewis, Orengo, Raharimanana, & Selliah, 2017)

Some international and multilateral agencies are still active in Peru, most notably USAID and the World Bank, and American members of INGO federations like Oxfam America, or long-established Catholic groups like Cafod remain, but the participation of INGOs has greatly diminished. As one Director of an SNGO in Lima explained: "you invest time and energy, and the majority of the responses are negative, because they say, 'No, we're not working in Peru', or 'we're leaving Peru now'" (Director of SNGO, Lima 1).

Peruvians who had previously worked for or been supported by INGOs described the whole NGO sector in Peru as having noticeably changed in the past few years. One SNGO reported that it had formerly had five offices which were now reduced to two, with staffing down from fifty to fourteen: "I think that what NGOs have to do is to find new work, new forms of organisation, re-establish themselves, recycle themselves" (Director of SNGO, Arequipa). The international aid that is still flowing tends to be concentrated in very specific areas, like women's rights, or child trafficking, or advocacy connected to conflicts in new mining areas, or climate change related projects: "I think there are themes which… international cooperation has prioritized, and other themes that they no longer support" (SNGO worker, Lima1). The pattern within Peruvian organisations interviewed in this project was to seek funding from as wide a range of potential international donors as possible: France, Germany, Switzerland, the USA, Belgium and the EU, were all noted as providing funding, whereas the UK tended to be mentioned only in the past tense, a finding which accords with recent ODA figures on comparative donor funding to Latin America: major donors are the USA, Germany, France and Spain, with the UK the seventh largest, alongside Switzerland, at 3% of the total (OECD, 2018).

In some cases, the state—whether at national, regional or municipal level—has stepped in to supplement or replace shrunken international cooperation resources. In emergency aid, for example, one participant compared the number of agencies (some twenty-five) involved in supporting victims in the 2001 earthquake in the Andes, with the relative absence of NGOs after the 2017 earthquake where the government took primary responsibility for organisation (Director SNGO, Arequipa). Major bilateral donors like USAID have increasingly sought to reposition their development initiatives away from direct support for local agencies towards a channelling of resources through the Peruvian government (USAID, 2012–2016). With the resultant diminishing job opportunities in NGOs, some experienced staff have moved to work in state-funded projects which SNGOs argued often had a very different modus operandi and ethos. NGOs and civil society organisations frequently felt they were regarded as ancillary to government, or that they were being used as convenient window dressing in official discussions with international bodies like the OECD (Director of national network, Lima 2).

With the contribution of foreign bilateral and multilateral donors receding, the role of government agencies and private companies and corporate foundations is rising. Cruz and Pousadela (2016) argue that there has been a marked shift in Latin America towards a hybrid pattern of funding for civil society organisations (CSOs). As the government steps into supplement or replace shrunken international cooperation resources, many CSOs are in effect morphing into service providers and thus putting advocacy work to one side. In addition, and despite a history of mutual distrust, there has been some cooperation between the private sector and CSOs, although the level of volunteerism in Peru is relatively low.

Whilst this new aid environment clearly presents challenges to those who work in Peru, some SNGOs pointed to the opportunities it offered, in particular in terms of an expanded South–South dialogue. Appe (2016) argues that there are now examples in South America of civil society networks which are beginning to shift traditional development discourse, positioning their activity in potentially new ways. As the Director of one of the South American networks explained:

> it's a network which brings together organisations which are very focused on access to legal and safe abortion. ...it's a global problem, the problems in Chile, Peru, Ecuador, Columbia, are crosscutting... what we do is create spaces for meeting.... (Director of national SNGO network, Lima 1)

In some cases, the formation of these national and Latin American alliances might be seen as a way of defending the sector against government monopoly.

Despite the upper middle-income designation of Peru, there are still high levels of inequality in the country. One experienced SNGO worker argued that infant mortality in some areas was comparable to that in parts of Africa (Director of SNGO, Lima1). The World Food Programme (2017) points to persistent and deep pockets of food insecurity, especially in rural areas. The World Economic Forum's Global Gender Gap report (2016), using an index of women's participation, economic opportunities, education, political empowerment and health, found that Peru had fallen from 45th to 80th of 144 countries. Poverty affects more urban dwellers in absolute terms—corresponding to 14.5% of the urban population—but is more prevalent in rural areas, affecting 45.2% of the rural population. It is particularly high in the Sierra and Amazon regions, among indigenous and Afro-descendent communities, especially women. Whilst the economy is expected to grow between 2016 and 2021, a major challenge remains the fact that a large percentage of the labour force is employed informally, with employment precarity particularly high among women. The Oxford Poverty and Human Development Initiative (OPHI, 2018) index of multidimensional poverty which seeks to go beyond monetary poverty by including aspects such as poor education, health care provision, housing and access to basic services, places Peru below other countries in Latin America like Haiti, Guatemala, Nicaragua, Honduras and Bolivia. According to the report, 12.4% of Peruvians live in conditions of multidimensional poverty. This type of poverty is ten times higher in rural Peru than in urban areas.

The Government's own priorities, set out in its Bicentennial Plan concluding in 2021 (World Food Programme, 2017), concentrate on the elimination of social, gender and cultural barriers. One of its four policy guidelines focuses on eliminating extreme poverty by promoting differentiated and inclusive policies for the poorest populations and establishing social protection strategies for children, adolescents, the elderly, women heads of households and disabled and other vulnerable populations. National policies relating to SDG 2 include a National Plan for Disaster Risk Management, a Plan for Food Security and Nutrition (2015–2021), a Social Development Policy and a National Plan for Gender Equality (2012–2017). The World Food Programme (2017) contends that decentralisation remains a major problem in translating these national policies into actions on the ground, with uneven local capacities exacerbating inequalities in districts and municipalities with high levels of poverty and malnutrition.

Historically, in a context of military rule, democratic instability and corruption, NGOs have played an important role in Peru, largely in two distinct phases: firstly, in the 1970s under the government of Juan Velasco Alverado, and secondly, in the 1980s with the re-emergence of a democratic government which focused on grassroots issues. The Civic Freedom Monitor (ICNL, 2018) suggests that the political environment in which many of these organisations emerged shaped a sector which has been strongly committed to forms of development that are explicitly bottom-up in character. High levels of corruption, particularly under the Fujimori government of the 1990s, coupled with a politically left NGO community, led to frequent tensions between NGOs and the government with crackdowns on NGO activities. A recurring controversy in the sector is the scope of state supervision of NGOs, with an important legal-political debate contained in the Constitutional Court judgement (2007), which set out the role of civil society organisations and that of state supervision. This is an issue that continues to be prominent today with the Peruvian Agency for International Cooperation, *Agencia Peruana de Cooperación Internacional* (APCI), modifying its directives on the requirements for the renewal of NGO registration in 2016. Groups within Peru, like the *Asociación Nacional de Centros* (ANC) and those outside, like the UK-based Peru Support Group, have argued that such government initiatives are specifically aimed at controlling tensions and conflicts that arise around the development and exploitation of valuable mining resources. The Civicus Monitor (Civicus, 2016) sees Peru as being an "obstructed" site for CSOs, pointing to a lack of consultation with peasant and indigenous community groups over mining initiatives, a 'dependent judiciary', and widespread discrimination against women, indigenous peoples and

LGBT+ groups. NGO advocacy activity more recently has been particularly focused on the mining areas of Peru and the perceived failure of the government to adhere to its legal requirements to consult communities before allowing extractive industries to move in. The campaign '*Consúltame de verdad*' ('consult me for real'), for example, was spearheaded by CooperAcción (2018) and Oxfam America, citing the findings of a study of eleven consultations in the mining and oil sectors in which the process had seemed to be treated as a formality and given inadequate time.

Languages in Peru

Unlike Malawi, where English is an official language, and Kyrgyzstan, where it is spoken by a very small minority of the population, English in Peru is the main foreign language taught within the educational system. Peru is formally a multilingual nation. The official language is Spanish, spoken by over 82.6% of the population (INEI, 2017). In the areas in which they are predominant, Quechua and Aymara also have official status. Quechua is spoken by 13.9% of the population, mainly concentrated in the central and southern highlands. There are several dialectal variants of Quechua, and the language has markedly influenced Peruvian Spanish which includes a number of Quechuan words in its vocabulary. Aymara is spoken by around 1.7% of the population, based around Lake Titicaca and along the Peru–Bolivia border in the south. 'Other native languages' account for 0.8% of the population—in the Peruvian Amazon, it is estimated that around forty languages are currently spoken. In addition, 0.8% of the population speak 'other languages', including a small immigrant population whose mother tongues include Japanese, Chinese, Italian, German, Arabic and Urdu (INEI, 2017).

Whilst the status of the official languages of Peru was originally established in 1975, the provision of intercultural bilingual education has been a more uneven process (García, 2004). In 2011, the *Ley de Lenguas Indígenas* (Peruvian Indigenous Languages Act) set up institutional structures to implement the provision of language rights, and in particular the right to translation and interpreting in these languages. This resulted in the Ministry of Culture launching a series of courses to train bilingual speakers to operate as language mediators both in public service settings and in the consultation processes with communities before the launch of mining activities. Between 2012 and 2016, 307 translator–interpreters, representing some thirty-six languages, were trained in nine basic courses held in Lima and in the department of Cusco. Andrade Ciudad, Howard, and de Pedro Ricoy (2018) argue that this programme raised awareness of language rights in Peru and increased the self-worth of the indigenous trainees concerned.

Incorporating indigenous languages in this way has, however, had implications for the teaching of other languages like English. The British Council's report on English in Peru (2015) suggested that whilst there had been government moves to encourage bilingualism with English as the main second language, policies to implement this were fragmented, and indigenous languages and cultures had been given much greater priority. Around 57% of Peruvians study English in secondary school, with 46% learning it at university (2015 figures). According to the British Council, however, it has been acceptable for English language teachers to have no formal qualifications, and there have been high drop-out rates from English language teacher training programmes. Whilst it is thought that the burgeoning tourist market encourages more interest in English, an ability to speak the language is still closely linked to household income. Though English is certainly the most widely taught foreign language and is prized as a tool for improving employability, it is by no means widely spoken in Peru, as indeed is the case in much of the rest of Latin America: a recent report, the English Proficiency Index (see Barnés, 2018), found that the region as a whole was the only place in the world in which English language competence had gone down since 2017. Significantly, perhaps, whilst half of the organisations visited in Peru had translated their websites into English, only one participant sought to conduct part of our conversation in English.

Participants

Identifying potential Peruvian participants in the research project was initially done through discussions with UK INGOs and funding groups. This early list was then extended as contacts in Peru suggested colleagues who might be interested in being involved. Given the desire to include organisations whose headquarters were located in regions of greater poverty, two SNGOs in the Andes were directly approached on the basis of what was generally known about their work in the area. Ultimately, organisations and projects were visited in Lima, Arequipa and Cusco in January/February 2018, with detailed discussions (twenty individuals) held in Spanish (with the one exception noted above) lasting between two and five hours. Participants were directors of SNGO national networks, workers in SNGOs, development consultants, ex-partners of UK-based INGOs and cultural specialists. SNGOs included those involved in advocacy (women's rights, child trafficking and exploitation), in projects with disadvantaged groups in suburban and rural areas, in environmental development and protection and in supporting local cultures. Six of the SNGOs were working in the Andes, one in the Amazon, and three had projects focused on poverty in urban areas. Eight of the participants were bilingual Quechua/Spanish speakers. The agencies varied in size from fourteen full-time staff to three full-time equivalents. In many ways this group of Peruvian participants reflected the particular contemporary aid architecture of the region. Only one SNGO was currently being project funded by UK organisations, although six had previously worked with major UK-based partners, and one participant was able to discuss in detail the exit strategies of the particular UK INGO. What was evident was the wide range of nationalities of donor bodies with whom the SNGOs were now working: the USA, Germany, France, Italy, Switzerland, Holland, Spain, Belgium and Dubai were all specifically mentioned as recent or current funding sources. The gender imbalance of participants (fifteen female, five male)—which reflects that of the Kyrgyzstan case study, but contrasts markedly with the Malawian sample—may be related to the relative precarity of the NGO sector in Peru at this time. Discussions with the SNGOs focused on the participants' own listening experiences on the ground, firstly in relation to external donors, and secondly in their contact with the local communities with whom they were working in the Andes, in the Amazon region, or in areas of urban poverty. Quotations from their comments in Spanish have been translated by the author.

Communicating in English

The current situation of English in the development sector in Peru is somewhat paradoxical. On the one hand, English is still seen to be necessary as a vehicular language in which to seek funding from across the world. It also provides much of the key original vocabulary (sometimes in translation), which multilateral and INGO donors use in constructing the terms of their projects and in evaluating progress. In this context, global development English presents major challenges to Peruvian groups. Firstly, they have to acquire the necessary resources to translate international calls for funding and submit credible applications in English. Secondly, the dominance of English in the overall development sector is seen as a major contributing factor in creating relationships of inequity between donors and partners. On the other hand, the changing aid landscape in Peru has brought into the country a wide range of non-anglophone (especially European) donors whose apparently respectful approach to languages was felt to contrast markedly with former experiences of dealing with English-language funders.

For participants, the English language was largely associated with the necessity to find sources of international funding. Without English, the range of sponsors potentially available could be radically reduced: "…we don't speak English, and it's a real limitation, because if you speak English you can go and convince people, you can sell them your project, but when you can't speak English, it limits you" (Director of SNGO, Andes 1). If EU calls for funding were published in a number of languages, the perception was still that you would need to be an anglophone in order to be a successful applicant (SNGO worker, Lima 2). English, in this context, was framed as a written language relating to the paperwork connected with funding calls, applications and contracts. Whilst some participants felt able to send and understand short emails in the language, the formality and length of international donor processes represented a much greater linguistic challenge for which they received little external support. One participant had managed to persuade an INGO to translate an original project idea coming from their SNGO (Director of SNGO, Arequipa), and another agency had been invited to include a formal budget line for professional translation in their project application. On the whole however, SNGOs were left to make their own arrangements for translating calls and applications. Using professional translators was so expensive that the process of successful project application usually depended on finding willing volunteers who had an adequate level of English: "When we've had to make applications in English… when everything has to be in English… In that case we've had to get help, we did it with my son, or [X]'s son… because they know English and can help us with the translations" (Director of SNGO, Lima 1). One SNGO still working with a UK-based INGO described the long process of identifying a suitable and supportive linguistic mediator:

> …for several years [X] did it which meant a huge amount of time for him, a drag on his health because he was helping a number of institutions

> which were applying for funding. It was really exhausting… and then two years ago [Y] was a volunteer here, she knew… she could write and she could imagine and know what she was talking about… she has the capacity to speak English and Spanish well, and she knows the project…. (SNGO worker, Lima 1)

What was important in this situation was to find volunteers who understood the work of the organisation and could transmit the SNGO's distinct vision of development rather than simply translating the words in the application: "It's like using Google Translate and everything comes out translated, but 'That word isn't what we wanted to say'" (SNGO worker, Andes 1).

After a successful application, relationships with donors tended to be paper-based, in English, with a linguistic formality which was seldom conducive to open dialogue and discussion. One Director of a national SNGO network described how they were obliged to ask a Dutch colleague to read through all the documentation coming through in English and then summarise it: "I told her, 'everything that comes in, you read and do me a summary, and then I'm going to tell you which interests me'… and then I'd tell her to translate that" (Director of national network, Lima 2). If participants had made unsuccessful applications, they were left unsure as to whether their failure had been essentially a linguistic inadequacy—a case of not understanding and using the English terms incorrectly (Director of national network, Lima 2). The whole process of applying for funding and initiating contractual relationships in a foreign language was "stressful, it's a bit stressful that everything comes in English, and we're always left feeling insecure" (SNGO worker, Andes 1).

The English being used in these paper exchanges was understood to be a specialised technical language: a global development English. Participants noted however that this terminology was inherently unstable and dynamic, differing from one INGO to another: "The problem of language isn't just translating a word. It's how each individual agency understands it. Each agency has its own particular set of concepts… Of course, it gets confusing" (SNGO worker, Lima 4). Given the diversity of donors to which Peruvian SNGOs now apply, one single agency might well find itself manipulating a range of different English 'development buzzwords' (Cornwall & Eade, 2010) at the same time:

> they all manage the projects on the basis of results but each of them gives a different name to the dynamic they use... and so we're talking about the same thing but using different words and things get more and more confused... we've got different donors here, so, for example, there's "Theory of Change," which is another methodology and perhaps some of them don't use "Theory of Change", so with these we'll talk about "indicators", or something like that.... (SNGO worker, Lima 2)

In practice portmanteau neologisms were often used in Spanish (*monitorear*, for example), with SNGO workers left to interpret the exact meaning of the INGO's particular usage among themselves, a process that took time and could result in their realising, after signing the contract, that they had failed to budget for all the implications of the new requirements. Some of the basic vocabulary of global development English was cited as being difficult to translate. One participant talked at length about problems in understanding the meaning of 'empowerment' for example: "words like 'empower' have a very important meaning which we translate as *empoderamiento* but which in reality is a neologism which doesn't exist and therefore doesn't necessarily translate its full English meaning" (SNGO worker, Lima 4). A common way of handling this sort of difficulty was simply to leave the word in English, accepting that it was not going to be clearly understood by the receiving partner or by the community: "They put it over to us as a whole word... in English... often you never know what it is, there's a lot of that here..." (Director of SNGO national network, Lima 2). In some cases, though, different interpretations of a keyword lay at the heart of a project's rationale. One participant who worked in child protection noted that the term 'exploitation' in this context had different technical meanings in the USA and in Peru:

> We make a distinction between two [different] phenomena, so when we talk with them, we have to be sure to emphasize the distinction, that we're talking about two different concepts, because if not, they're going to understand it as one single concept. (SNGO worker, Lima 3)

Inevitably, this global development English was associated with what several participants viewed as straitjacket assumptions underlying development processes. A development consultant with considerable experience in the field argued that there was often a circularity in projects: "the format does violence to the richness of the real situation and transforms it into 'indicators' which have not been established on the basis of this reality but come in a pre-set form" (Development Consultant, Lima). The time constraints of project-based development, and the pressure to produce quantitative data as proof of results, were seen as alienating development work from those to whom it was intended to aid, in situations where progress might best be measured in a longer time frame, and with an emphasis on individual biography (SNGO worker, Andes 4). Significantly, when participants were asked to suggest their own examples of successful listening, they overwhelmingly alluded to particular instances of face-to-face contact at the micro level—a meeting when women demanded a different approach to what the SNGO was proposing to do, one-to-one discussions with children, the life history of young people who had changed direction and ambition. SNGOs pointed out that some of their own specific ways of working, drawn from the Latin American tradition of development, might, in their untranslatability into English, provide some challenges to the global English-language development praxis:

> ...there's a concept which is vital for us in our work, vital, important, which we can't translate which is the word *acompañamiento*... our work is *acompañamiento* of the communities so that they can achieve their own development. In English we don't know how to explain *acompañamiento*. (SNGO worker, Lima 1)

As with problematic English terms, it was assumed that these distinct Spanish-named concepts would become comprehensible to foreigners if they observed their actual implementation in projects:

> ...the term *acompañamiento*... we understand that the relationship of the adults... is a horizontal relationship with the young... now let's say translating it, it's not complicated because it can be explained by the context and it's basically understood by the things which are done in that process. (SNGO worker, Andes 4)

For many participants, the perceived dominance of global development English demonstrated a sharp inequality in relationships between donors and Peruvian recipients, symbolised for one Director of an SNGO network by the number of Northern-based organisations that made the long journey South, in comparison to the relative lack of travelling the other way round (Director of national network, Lima 1). At a basic level, there was a sense that international donors were coming to Peru with their own agendas which were often not clearly expressed to potential partners:

> ...what is called Hidden Agendas, because very often someone will come with an agenda with preestablished ideas and approaches to spread here. Then, they'll say to you, "No, you have to participate," and I say to them, "How can we participate if you're not moving from your point of view, your wishes, your proposal?" So here there's a lot of cooperation which comes with an already set agenda. (Director of SNGO national network, Lima 2)

In some programmes, the language of the donor predominated at each stage of the partnership, establishing the terms of the programme and conditioning project implementation on the ground:

> When the negotiations take place in the language of the donor, then the NGO has its directives which it understands, and they speak that language, and things are set up in this way. Then it's immediately translated into the organisation of the whole NGO in order to fulfil requirements and the flow of resources. (Development Consultant, Lima)

Underlying much of this concern about the dominance of English in development was the view that by speaking a different language from the community, donors would find it difficult to engage in any real dialogue of equity with local groups. For some SNGOs, the global development dynamic itself militated against any awareness on the part of donors of the multilingualism of Peru, and the diversity of its different cultures: "I say that globalization is done for the majority, and this, one way or another, has the effect of extinguishing minorities, above all as regards language" (SNGO worker, Andes 1). In this scenario, funders in general, it was felt, tended to relate local languages negatively to poverty, rather than positively to cultural capital: "when agencies do finance language it's because they relate it to poverty... Why is it minority? ...What makes it minority? ...they will be poor in monetary terms, but culturally very rich" (SNGO worker, Andes 1). One SNGO that dealt principally with local cultures, related this inequity of donor/recipient relationships to a neoliberal positioning of development which deliberately prioritised the economic over any engagement with and respect for cultural diversity:

> There are no projects for culture… I think it's a system which comes from… the powerful and is imposed on governments and we are above all consumers. To develop productive projects so that it's certain that we have to buy their technological packets, whether they're seeds, fertilizers, chemicals, everything. (SNGO worker, Andes 6)

In the distinct aid architecture of Peru, SNGOs were now seeking and receiving funds from a variety of sources, largely European and North American. Linguistic relations with these agencies were perceived as being noticeably different from those which they had formerly enjoyed with UK-based INGOs. To begin with, donors with offices in Peru appeared to employ Spanish speakers, often Peruvians: "Now the Cooperation agencies in the vast majority have project directors, if they're going to work in Latin America, they have to know Spanish… I think about 98 percent are Peruvian" (Director of SNGO, Arequipa). One SNGO outlined a roll-call of organisations that had requested funding applications in Spanish: "Kinder Mission… in Spanish. So I said, 'What joy!' because CESAL in Spanish, UNICEF helped the process in Spanish, Adveniat in Spanish, Kinder Mission in Spanish" (SNGO worker, Andes 3). SNGOs characterised these non-anglophone donors in positive terms, seeing their linguistic openness as a sign of a desire to establish more equal relationships. Participants talked about agencies "making the effort to speak Spanish to… understand better how we work here… they make the effort'" (SNGO worker, Andes 3). This readiness to speak Spanish on the part of donors was interpreted as demonstrating respect for Peruvian partners: "Really you could say that [non-anglophone] European organisations… are very respectful of the language. The people with whom we have contact speak Spanish very well" (Director of SNGO, Lima 1).

Arguably, the changed aid environment in Peru appeared to bring with it a more robust linguistic self-positioning on the part of some SNGOs who were looking towards a potentially profitable South–South dialogue (SNGO worker, Andes 4). The experience of INGOs exiting from Peru could thus be represented as an opportunity to define a distinct Peruvian/Latin American style of working: "I think that Latin America is also an area which has had to demonstrate why it's important to invest since our countries are not preferentially poor or needy and what we've had to put on the label 'Latin America' is competence, expertise, our capacity to transform" (Director of SNGO, Lima 1). Whilst some SNGOs were still seeking to recruit staff with an intermediate level of

English, the dominance of development English seemed more questionable: "[European donors] they come but they speak Spanish so there's no problem. English for me, it's important, but I'm not going to die if I don't speak English" (Director of SNGO, Andes). Indeed, SNGO workers in the poorer regions of Peru argued that the major linguistic need for them was Quechua or Aymara: "[English] is no use for where I'm working, however much English is important, it's not going to be useful for me if I want to work in Ayacucho" (SNGO worker, Andes 1).

Despite these signs of change, however, the evidence of this study suggests that an absence of interlingual translation in SNGO relationships with donors creates a development norm dominated by global development speak English with its specialised and changing vocabulary. This linguistically untranslated vision produces a decontextualised development reality in which donor/SNGO relationships are perceived as unequal from project inception to implementation, and one in which the responsibility to understand, learn and adapt clearly rests with the agencies in the South, rather than with the funders in the North.

Communicating with Communities

If participants saw English as the written language of formal development cooperation with multilateral or bilateral funders, they viewed the languages of the Peruvian Andes and Amazon as related to oral face-to-face dealings with communities. With one exception, all the SNGOs in this project conducted their management and headquarters operational procedures in Spanish. Spanish, as the majority language of the country, associated with the wealthy and more populous coastal regions and the capital, holds considerable cultural capital. It is seen as a means of social and economic progress by first language Spanish speakers and often by parents whose mother tongue is not Spanish but who are ambitious for their children (Development Consultant, Lima; SNGO worker, Andes 2). Much as global English has traditionally been represented as signifying modernity, bringing progress from the rural to the urban (Crack, 2018), a capacity to speak Spanish was linked overtly to improved job prospects and greater economic autonomy, encouraging some 'escape' from the poverty of more isolated areas (Director of SNGO, Arequipa; SNGO worker, Andes 4). Several participants mentioned the ways in which their own fluency in Spanish contributed to establishing a hierarchical relationship with the groups they were seeking to support:

> In fact, when the Andean people see someone coming from Lima, who comes with qualifications, has a job, they make themselves smaller and smaller and rush away. So if you work there, you have to take off the mask of the Masters degree, take off the mask of Lima, take off the mask of leader, and the mask of language, and that's the most difficult to take off because it's the only one you have. (SNGO worker, Andes 1)

Despite the official recognition of Quechua and Aymara, and government awareness of the languages spoken in the Amazon, the link between indigenous languages and poverty was the background against which relations between SNGOs and local communities were largely sited.

Peru's linguistic diversity was seen as a relevant factor for SNGOs wherever they were working. In one project in which radio messages were relayed across the whole country, these were translated into Quechua or Aymara, or into a very localised form of Spanish. As the participants noted: "…you really become aware how different, completely different, they are because in Iquitos they speak this way…, in Cusco even if you use Spanish, they use different words, in Lima too" (SNGO worker, Lima 4). In large cities like Lima or Cusco, SNGOs might be dealing with groups who had recently emigrated there from rural Peru, and whose first language was not Spanish. Looking after street children who were bilingual could involve meeting and talking with their families who came in from the countryside: "They come in to find them, and in general they speak Quechua so we need to understand them in their mother tongue… we can establish a relationship with them in Quechua" (SNGO worker, Andes 3). Development projects in the Amazon would have to engage with very considerable linguistic complexity at a micro level: "In NGOs, there isn't this much more territorially-based project… in the Amazon it's much sharper because they're linguistic families which are based in particular basins of the river, 'I'm from Morona', 'I'm from Pastaza', 'I'm from Tigris'" (Development Consultant, Lima). In the Andes, a population might be ostensibly bilingual: "in the zone of Puno and the high parts, they speak Quechua or Aymara, but the language is not exclusive, there's a duality, a bilingualism" (Director of SNGO, Arequipa). In practice, however, development workers suggested, the language spoken was often influenced by demographic factors like gender or age, which could very well include the target populations of the projected activities (SNGO worker, Andes 1). At times, too, one experienced worker in the Andes suggested, a bilingual group might choose to use Quechua rather than

Spanish as a protective device before agreeing to invite the SNGO representative more fully into their discussions (SNGO worker, Andes 2). It was crucial however to be aware of the distinctive structures, tone and body language of Quechua and Spanish. One bilingual participant argued that Spanish was a much more diffuse language, "…it has a lot of words to express the same. So when you say a word, you really have to be a good Spanish speaker to know exactly what you are saying… it depends on the circumstances… the tone", whereas Quechua, she suggested, was more intimate, personal and corporeal (Director of national network, Lima 2).

The development agencies dealing with these mixed linguistic contexts had adopted a range of organisational approaches: teams comprised solely of Spanish speakers, mixed teams of Spanish and Quechua-speaking personnel, and project groups that had been designed at the outset as entirely Quechua speaking. Ensuring that they had some Quechua-language capacity for work in the Andes led some organisations to target the linguistic skill at recruitment stage, or to consciously retrain existing staff. One SNGO, for example, provided access to a Quechua course for the particular staff member involved, though without any direct financial support. Two more discussed the dilemma of finding Quechua-speaking personnel who were also professionally qualified:

> our workers… speak Quechua. But it's not easy to recruit them, because there aren't many professionals who speak Quechua. They need to be local professionals, and sometimes these local professionals aren't at the best level, because these are the most isolated areas from the town. (Director SNGO, Lima 1)

Other participants talked about forming alliances in the community with key workers who could then act as intermediaries. One SNGO working in the Amazon suggested that useful insiders for them could be teachers in the bilingual schools (SNGO worker, Lima 4). The director of a large and long-established environmental organisation argued that when you were working in a community it was always possible to identify an appropriate intermediary for the project and then to build on their skills:

> …in the community, when one's working, you always know people who have some characteristic, who are not just answering some immediate requirement, but are also seeing the future of their community, a vision.

> And then, with these people we can strengthen their capacities. (Director of SNGO, Arequipa)

In another case, the SNGO had found a suitable volunteer mediator as the project was actually under way:

> ...we contracted a lady who... comes from the community, who understands the reality of her people, which has helped us to know more about what's happening, and at the same time, as she knows what [the organisation] is doing from the inside, she can transmit what we're doing to the community. (SNGO worker, Lima 1)

As SNGOs discussed their experiences and programmes, languages were cited as being important at each project stage: when activities were originally designed and early information was sought, during the implementation phase, during feedback and monitoring and evaluation, and in diffusing the results and messages within the communities. Establishing accurate information about the context of a group before embarking on projects was difficult but crucial. One SNGO working in the Amazon region talked about the effort needed to engage with the way in which groups actually understood and framed a specific problem the SNGO had started identifying: "there is a hidden part here... in communities which still have [their native language] or don't have much contact with Spanish" (SNGO worker, Lima 4). Achieving this knowledge through a professional intermediary who was not native to the community would not necessarily provide access to how people in the region envisaged their needs: "You can have a consultant, an adviser with a lot of academic knowledge, but if this academic knowledge is not tested against what the communities have to say, and against what they see as useful, it will be of no use at all" (SNGO worker, Andes 1). A dialogue was needed at the outset so that the intended beneficiaries were able to express themselves, and this discussion would be considerably more rewarding if it were conducted in the same language. If this stage was omitted, there was a fear that projects could start running on the basis of mutual incomprehension and, in the long term, waste valuable time (Director of national SNGO, Lima 2).

Participants raised a number of issues relating to the ways in which implementation would be affected by a lack of awareness of language and culture. One very experienced SNGO Director, herself a Quechua speaker, described how the first steps of a development programme could be blighted by cultural ignorance:

> …there can be misunderstandings and also there can be abuse. For example, if I'm from the city, I can go somewhere, I can say "Hi!", I can go in, sit down, and someone's going to come up and ask me something. But in the countryside, I can't do that, so I've got to go in, greet everyone, make my presence known, and explain why I'm there. And a lot of people act like that, and obviously, it's a shock. From then on, the relationship is already slightly broken, and then when you want to work with them, talk together, you end up saying "why aren't they understanding me?", but it's a case of cultural matters that we have to take account of if we want to enter into a relationship. (Director of SNGO network, Lima 2)

Real community ownership of a programme on the ground came, a development consultant argued, from accepting that there were a variety of possible interpretations of issues and that the key to success was to realise that it was the community who were defining the parameters of the exercise: "there is a heterogeneity, huge cleavages in the discourse on both sides, and if you want to construct a shared discourse, it's hearing, 'This is my project, says the community, the district, the population, and they're going to help me to execute it'" (Development consultant, Lima). One participant recounted what she saw as the classic case of a large international development initiative which had failed to ensure joint ownership and understanding of the objectives of their intervention from the outset. The project aimed to address poor nutrition in an Andean community by providing its members with additional economic resources gained from outside investment in the commercial production of guinea pigs (Worldark, 2017). The model being followed was that of a community making money from selling this locally prized delicacy and thus being in a position to feed their families a more nutritious diet. Results from the project, however, indicated that people in the community were more poorly nourished when the project finished than before it had begun. Food poverty had grown. Follow-up work to investigate this failure, she claimed, concluded that the community's interpretation of a diet which was less conditioned by poverty was one in which an increased purchasing power would permit them to buy high-status western food and drink, a diet which did not accord with the principles of good nutrition espoused by the funders (SNGO worker, Andes 1).

What was at issue here was not simply communication and the passing of messages, but rather an understanding of the cultural conceptions of the Andean and Amazonian peoples, an understanding which was basic to achieving successful outcomes:

> It isn't an intercultural problem, it's not a problem of whether you speak a language or not, it's whether you understand the world from which they are speaking, and if they understand the world from which you're speaking… it's not that scientific knowledge is better, but that these are forms of knowledge, of origins and constructions which are very different. (Development Consultant, Lima)

One SNGO with projects relating to criminal abuse pointed out that they were sometimes dealing with communities that had no equivalent word for the Spanish *justicia*, with its implications of impartiality and being supported by an independent judiciary (SNGO worker, Lima 4). *Infancia* ('childhood') was another word that had served to complicate development practices in the Andes. Two SNGOs spoke about the problems they had encountered in working with children and families without there being some commonly shared sense of what 'childhood' actually meant: "No… yes, well there is 'childhood' …if what we understand the words to fully mean in Quechua… because a lot of the time we understand what we believe it to be without having investigated it" (SNGO worker, Andes 2). Given that Quechua is primarily an oral language, it was difficult to find manuals which might help to explain where these differences in views lay. Instead, one worker suggested from experience that a way in was to listen to the songs that the parents sang to their children, and to try to observe how children were represented in the festivals of the community (SNGO worker, Andes 1). In practice on the ground, however, these development workers were still uneasy as to whether they had really managed to bridge the gap of conceptual uncertainty: "I'm never sure about what I'm understanding" (SNGO worker, Andes 1).

Beyond the practicalities of delivering effective development interventions, there was a general feeling that important values were at stake. Three quarters of the participants made a direct link between an awareness of languages/cultures and the cultivation of broader values like trust and mutual respect. A director of an SNGO national network argued that development practitioners who were not sensitive to language issues could cause considerable and serious upset in a community:

> ...of course, when you don't understand this [language differences], there are things you express which appear to be saying something, but in reality they're not. So, there is a great deal of unease, so there's distrust which is not only generated at this level, but right across the whole population... people think that the person speaking Spanish has absolutely nothing to do with this culture.... (Director of SNGO national network, Lima 2)

Speaking the language of the community was an important sign that the agency was seeking to establish a context of respectful and equitable relations, getting beyond the straitjacket of the development project. The marked cultural capital of Spanish meant that a conscious decision on the part of an agency to speak in the language of the locality could be interpreted, according to SNGOs, as a clear sign of respect: "...if you learn Quechua, you're showing them that you have respect for their language, that it's really important to you" (SNGO worker, Andes 1). This valuing of languages within a development project re-imagined the relationship between NGOs and communities as a personal one, putting oneself in the shoes of the recipients, a process that implicated development professionals themselves in reflecting on, and possibly changing, their traditional practices.

Participants working in the Andes who were bilingual tended to talk more than colleagues in Lima about the ways in which development sustainability could be specifically related to languages. On the one hand, there were linguistic legacy issues arising from past development initiatives. One participant pointed out that, despite the lengthy history of interventions in the Andes, she had been unable to draw on any development glossaries in Quechua which could be useful to her in the present project:

> I long for... a glossary or some interpretation of the terms of project language adapted to Quechua. It would be great, so that we can make relationships with the population...because there are glossaries of development language in Spanish, so get them into Quechua, Aymara, Awajún, in other dialects..., it's necessary. (SNGO worker, Andes 1)

More generally, there was a sense that the interface between development and the continued preservation and sustainability of minority languages in Peru was not really being thought through:

> …the fact of not investing in the rescue of these knowledges through their languages [in the Amazon], we're achieving things, lowering malnutrition, giving children access to school… but there's something here which we haven't gained in terms of development, the sustainability of a language. (SNGO worker, Andes 2)

This argument about linguistic sustainability was closely related to a perception of indigenous cultures as having perspectives and ways of being that were very different from Spanish-derived cultures. Several participants, all bilinguals, described for example the Quechuan *cosmovisión* (worldview) in which Western distinctions between animate and inanimate beings were replaced by a belief that everything has life. In this worldview, the *chakra* (small holding/farm) was a fundamental of Quechuan life, a meeting place for mutual help across the community:

> …the *chakra* is a space where we work, we go back to it again to look at the earth, to respect it. When you sow maize and accompany it as it grows, you understand the value of life and it's more, we meet together, we sing, dance, we sing to the plant, to life. (Director of SNGO, Andes)

For some participants, there had been a failure in development practice to recognise the contributions that such cultural differences had made historically and might still make today. As one Director of a national SNGO network suggested:

> …recuperating the culture, recognizing their culture. It's not as if there's nothing there, it's not as if you're taking something which is so innovative and so new. There are many things which were already known and are known, and by forgetting we've gone back and caused harm. (Director of national SNGO network, Lima 2)

The extent to which there was real bidirectional learning, with development practitioners adapting their own knowledges to these indigenous ways of living and of doing development, was perceived as being relatively slight by those in the areas engaged in supporting local cultures. One SNGO argued passionately that Quechuan ways of being had a great deal to teach society in relation to the key problems faced by the world today, and could conceivably contribute concrete solutions to climate change, food insecurity and mental health:

> ...we're told we have to be modern, live in this other way, leave all these things and live here, but we've had fifty years of modernity... we're not living better, we're worse. We've contaminated our rivers, we've lost our bio-diversity, we've lost our values, there's a lot of violence in the world, there's a lot of emotional illness. (Director of SNGO, Andes)

At the root of the controversy about cultural sustainability was an assimilationist critique, a fear that the activities of government and NGOs, though ostensibly respecting local languages, were in practice designed to subordinate indigenous cultures to a broader national agenda. Thus, for some participants, the fact that the government was now teaching the Quechua language in its schools in the Andes might actually become an impediment to understanding and sharing aspects of the Andean imaginary. Writing down Quechua, an originally oral language, within the education system, was simply, they argued, translating words into Spanish, without any accompanying sense of the Andean culture and cosmography that the words expressed. From this perspective, external intervention by NGOs without an acute and respectful awareness of cultural specificity could actively damage communities rather than sustaining them: "Development isn't culture. Development is killing culture" (Director of SNGO, Andes).

Conclusions

In Peru, the designation of 'upper middle-income country' has brought major changes to the NGO sector, with multilateral and bilateral donors scaling down their work, and large UK-based INGOs gradually exiting. In the resulting aid landscape, direct government intervention in development has grown, and SNGOs have found themselves having to seek finance from a broader range of donors, and to explore the possibilities of South–South dialogue and alliances. What is evident is that the English language is still largely perceived as the global language of development. SNGOs listen to their anglophone donors largely through written English, in calls for funding, applications for finance and contractual relationships. In this situation, agencies struggle with translating funding calls into Spanish, and then translating their subsequent applications into English. By its absence, interlingual translation thus plays a key role in creating these Listening Zones of development on the ground as donors, partners and communities meet. The evidence from this case study in Peru suggests that, in the contact zones of funders and Southern partners, the failure to integrate translation into project cycles leaves the hegemony of global development English largely unchallenged, with consequences for the ways in which the meanings of development are created, and initiatives implemented. The onus for understanding the considerable paperwork associated with calls for funding, applications, donor contracts and monitoring normally lies with the Southern NGOs. On the whole, such organisations lack the financial resources to employ professional translators to assist them. Instead, they rely on volunteers—preferably insiders working within the agency—to translate the calls, write the applications and explain the terminology. Given the fluidity of the technical vocabulary of global development English, partners often import specific English words into their documents, or use agreed neologisms. The result of this is that projects can be operating with quite serious, but unrecognised, misunderstandings or misapprehensions. The absence of translation produces a development reality that is a technical time-limited, largely decontextualised, process, and one that inevitably establishes relationships of inequity between anglophone donors and Spanish-speaking partners. In a situation in which the aid architecture of Peru is starting to change, these development inequalities are thrown into sharp relief by the translation practices of some of the wider range of funders with whom Peruvian NGOs are beginning to engage.

In the contact zones of Southern partners and their communities, attenuated forms of the anglophone donor/partner development realities are often replicated. Despite the officially recognised multilingualism of Peru and initiatives to train community interpreters, the cultural capital of the Spanish language is strong, and there is an a priori tendency to identify indigenous languages unproblematically with development-defined 'poverty'. Nevertheless, SNGOs in this case study were aware that they needed to include some form of translating in face-to-face meetings with the communities. The provision of translation, however, tended to be ad hoc, varying between the recruitment or training of their own personnel on the one hand, and the identification of suitable community mediators on the other. In this situation, language skills and community/cultural knowledge were the key competences expected, rather than any experience of professional interpreting/translating. Unlike the decontextualised development speak of donors, SNGOs on the ground perceived their work with communities as locally situated, within a dialogic process in which there was an emphasis on the translation of key messages coming from development practitioners. The sense of any bidirectional encounter where Spanish-speaking SNGOs, external to the community, listened and learned from the communities themselves, was however much less evident. In creating the meanings of development realities, this largely unidirectional encounter could produce a homogeneous vision of development, different from that of the external donors, but still one in which the mutual exchange of visions, and hence the modification of practices, were not generally prioritised. In these Listening Zones in Peru, interlingual translation, both by its absence in donor/SNGO relationships, and in the characteristics of its presence in SNGO/community meetings, was a key creator of development realities on the ground, establishing dominant contexts, attributing power to certain groups and potentially marginalising the voices of others.

References

Andrade Ciudad, L., Howard, R., & de Pedro Ricoy, R. (2018). Translation policy and indigenous languages in Hispanic Latin America. *International Journal of the Sociology of Language, 251,* 19–36.

Appe, S. (2016). Shifting the development discourse: A narrative of a civil society network in Ecuador. *Journal of International Development, 28,* 666–682.

Appe, S. (2018). Directions in a post-aid world? South-South development cooperation and SCOs in Latin America. *VOLUNTAS: International Journal of Voluntary and Nonprofit Organizations, 289*(2), 271–283.

Barnés, H. (2018, October 31). English proficiency index, 2018. *El Confidencial.* Retrieved from: https://www.elconfidencial.com/autores/hector-g-barnes-120/. Accessed 2 November 18.

British Council. (2015). *English in Peru: An examination of policy, perceptions and influencing factors.* Retrieved from: https://www.britishcouncil.pe/sites/default/files/english_in_peru_may_2015.pdf.

Civicus. (2016). *Monitor: Tracking civic space.* Retrieved from: https://monitor.civicus.org.

CooperAcción. (2018). *Consúltame de verdad.* Retrieved from: http://cooperacción.org.pe/consultame-de-verdad.

Cornwall, A., & Eade, D. (2010). *Deconstructing development discourse: Buzzwords and fuzzwords.* Oxford: Practical Action Publishing.

Crack, A. (2018). Languages, power and inclusion: The donor's perspective. *Development in Practice, 29*(2), 159–169.

Cruz, A., & Pousadela, I. (2016). The sustainability of Latin American CSOs: Historical patterns and new funding sources. *Development in Practice, 26*(5), 606–618.

Edussuriya, K., Lewis, S., Orengo, Y., Raharimanana, H., & Selliah, A. (2017). *What's it like to be on the receiving end of exit? A partner and country office view* (INTRAC Learning Paper). Bond, London.

García, M. (2004). Rethinking bilingual education in Peru: Intercultural politics, state policy and indigenous rights. *International Journal of Bilingual Education and Bilingualism, 7*(5), 348–367.

ICNL. (2018). *Civic Freedom Monitor*. International Centre for Not-for-Profit Law. Retrieved from: http://www.icnl.org/research/monitoring.

INEI. (2017). *Census: Perfil sociodemográfico*. Peru: Instituto Nacional de Estadistica e Informatica. Retrieved from: https://www.inei.gob.pe/media/MenuRecursivo/publicaciones_digitales/Est/Lib1539/index.html.

OECD. (2018). *Development cooperation report: Joining forces to leave no one behind*. OECD Development Assistance Committee: Enabling Effective Development.

OECD. (2019). *History of DAC lists of aid recipient countries*. Retrieved from: http://www.oecd.org/development/financing-sustainable-development/development-finance-standards/historyofdaclistsofaidrecipientcountries.htm.

OECDStats. (2017). *Disembursements to countries and regions*. Retrieved from: https://stats.oecd.org/Index.aspx?DataSetCode=TABLE2A.

OPHI. (2018). *Global MPI country briefing: Peru (Latin America and the Caribbean)*. Retrieved from: https://ophi.org.uk/wp-content/uploads/CB_Per-2.pdf.

USAID. (2012–2016). *USAID Peru: Country development strategy*. Retrieved from: https://usaid.gov/peru.

World Bank. (2018). *The World Bank in Peru: Country overview*. Retrieved from: https://www.worldbank.org/en/country/peru/overview.

World Economic Forum. (2016). Retrieved from: https://www.weforum.org/reports/the-global-gender-gap-report-2016.

World Food Programme. (2017). *Draft-Peru country strategic plan (2018–2022)*. (WFB/EB.2/2017/7-A/3Rev.1). Retrieved from: https://executiveboard.wfp.org/meeting/72.

Worldark. (2017). *Tiny Guinea pigs give a big boost*. Retrieved from: https://www.heifer.org/join-the-conversation/magazine/2017/spring/tiny-guines-pigs-give.

CHAPTER 9

Learning from the Listening Zones

Learning from Listening in International Development

NGOs are an inherently interdisciplinary topic. That is why journals that focus on NGO and civil society research have an explicitly interdisciplinary remit, such as *Voluntas* and *Nonprofit and Voluntary Sector Quarterly* (Brass, Longhofer, Robinson, & Schnable, 2018). Influential works on NGOs have stemmed from International Relations (IR) outlets, but Development Studies journals have been the source of most relevant publications over the last thirty-five years (Brass et al., 2018). There is much overlap between these disciplines. NGO-related work in IR and Development Studies both draw upon a similar body of literature and are preoccupied with similar themes. Both disciplines are interested in the interaction of NGOs with extant power structures, and their contribution towards challenging or reifying such structures. They are also equally interested in the accountability and legitimacy of NGOs (Edwards & Hulme, 1996; Gugerty & Prakash, 2010; Steffeck & Hahn, 2010). The IR scholarship on NGOs largely concentrates on questions surrounding the influence that NGOs wield over political discourse and political outcomes (Davies, 2019), ontological debates about how to define and conceptualise NGOs (DeMars & Dijkzeul, 2015; Götz, 2008; Martens, 2002) and the potential of NGOs as norm-diffusing agents (Ahmed & Potter, 2006; Betsill & Corell, 2008; Yanacopoulos, 2015). In Development Studies, the focus tends to be on the effectiveness of

H. Footitt et al., *Development NGOs and Languages*,
https://doi.org/10.1007/978-3-030-51776-2_9

development interventions and the issues faced by NGOs that reflect the tensions between fulfilling their mandate of empowering the poor and satisfying donor priorities (Edwards & Hulme, 2013; Lewis & Kanji, 2009). However, in both disciplines there is little research on the way that language and language mediation shape the relationships between NGOs and communities.

In this chapter, we discuss the implications of our research for the ways that scholars in IR and Development Studies understand NGOs and their language and listening practices. We identify the key themes in NGO scholarship, and suggest ways in which our findings invite an expansion of the research agenda. We argue for the importance of integrating within IR and Development Studies a more linguistically informed understanding of international encounters. We then discuss what the implications of the research might be for the other disciplines involved: Listening Studies, Intercultural Studies and Translation Studies. Finally, we offer some critical self-reflections on the challenges involved in researching multilingually.

NGO Research in IR and Development Studies

Several classic works on NGOs and transnational civil society were produced around the turn of the century, which have been criticised in recent years for presenting an idealised or superficial account of NGOs (see e.g., Kaldor, 2003; Keck & Sikkink, 1998; Matthews, 1997; Scholte, 2004). NGOs and transnational activists are portrayed in this literature as a largely homogenous group that embody Western ideals of democracy and human rights. In Keck and Sikkink's famous definition, the NGOs that form part of transnational advocacy networks (TANs) work internationally on issues and are bound together by "shared values, a common discourse, and dense exchanges of information and services" (1998, p. 2). Their shared norms are inspired by liberal values and a desire to amplify the voices of those who are poorly represented, or unrepresented, by decision-makers in government (Keane, 2003). NGOs are portrayed as advocates of grassroots participation in governance at the local, national and international stage (Korten, 1987). They are said to be particularly concerned with the poor, the vulnerable and the underprivileged, and to seek to empower those who face difficulties in asserting their claims on a non-responsive state. In this reading, NGOs are essential components of a civil society that is a crucial counterweight to the contemporary state in an era of globalisation (Price, 2003). They operate across state borders to mediate between people and sites of political authority and economic power. For the purposes of this chapter, we call this set of implicit assumptions the *liberal transnational approach to NGOs*.

There are several fundamental problems with this approach, indeed some of the early proponents of the emancipatory potential of civil society have now rowed back on their more optimistic statements (Bebbington, Hickey, & Mitlin, 2008). Much NGO scholarship in recent years has focused on dismantling the assumptions of the liberal transnational approach. For the sake of convenience, we term this large category of diverse scholars as 'critics' of the liberal transnational approach. This book provides ballast to criticisms of the liberal transnational approach, but our findings also have implications for the critics. Both sets of scholars have overlooked the relevance of listening practices and linguistic issues in conceiving of the way that NGOs operate and their political and societal impacts. In many respects, our findings provide new and valuable dimensions to the contributions of the critics.

Below, we outline three common criticisms of the liberal transnational approach, and then suggest ways in which our research amplifies these criticisms and opens up new avenues of inquiry in ways that critics have not hitherto considered.

Complacency About the Emancipatory Potential of NGOs

The liberal transnational approach has been criticised for taking NGOs' claims about their emancipatory mission at face value, and not subjecting them to sufficient critical scrutiny (Amoore & Langley, 2004). Lewis partly ascribes this to 'normative bias' and idealism about the potential of NGOs to contribute to social transformation (Lewis, 2005, p. 200). Critics argue for more attention to be given to the way that NGOs *reinforce* existing power structures, rather than destabilise or challenge them. These critics tend to focus their analysis at either the international or community level.

Critics who focus on the international level discuss how Northern donors co-opt NGOs to serve their political and economic agendas (see e.g., Banks, Edwards, & Hulme, 2015; Choudry & Kapoor, 2013; Hearn, 2007). NGOs have been accused of reproducing liberal hegemony by promoting Northern norms within Southern contexts. Language issues in NGO work are rarely discussed in the literature, apart from in terms of anglophone political discourse. Development NGOs have been accused of reinforcing Northern ideology by promoting the normative framework encapsulated by buzzwords such as 'good governance' and 'human rights' (Cornwall & Eade, 2010). It is argued that buzzwords are used to legitimise liberal hegemony by constructing problems and deficiencies in the host societies that can be 'corrected' with the assistance of external (Northern) actors. Less frequently, buzzwords are used to rationalise donor withdrawal. For example, it has been argued that aid initiatives to boost 'resilience' do not reflect a genuine desire on the parts of Northern governments to help poor people cope with the manifold challenges of their existence. Rather, it is a strategy of donors to legitimise their abdication of responsibility in crisis situations (Joseph, 2013). Critics argue that by taking money from donors who are keen to promote these discourses, NGOs are co-opted into reproducing the political and economic conditions that keep the poor in their disempowered and impoverished conditions (Merz, 2012; Wright, 2012).

Our exposure of the centrality of buzzwords in NGO projects gives credence to criticisms about the dominance of Northern conceptions of development. The persistent failure of some NGOs and donors to listen to communities by engaging with local languages reflects poorly on organisations that claim to pursue an emancipatory mission. It suggests a chronic lack of interest and respect for the lifeworlds of those that they proclaim to help. Externally funded NGO projects typically centre on concepts that are linguistically and culturally foreign to the territory where they are implemented. Buzzwords reflect Northern (particularly anglophone) histories, interests and norms. The prevalence of English in international development delimits the conceptual framework of development and delineates the realm of the possible. The current aid system grants little capacity for speakers of marginalised languages to advocate for alternative understandings of 'the good life' in their own tongue. We argue that the Listening Zones between communities and powerful development actors are structured by systemic exclusions in this regard. We hope that the research will encourage NGO scholars to reflect further on how liberal hegemony is partly sustained through language use—both the anglocentricity of development discourse, and the unquestioned cultural value attached to particular dominant languages in the field, English in Malawi, Spanish in Peru and Russian in Kyrgyzstan.

As noted above, there are critics of the liberal transnational approach to NGOs that highlight the failure of these organisations to deliver their emancipatory mission at the community level. For example, NGOs have long been criticised for conducting discriminatory and/or naïve participatory exercises that amplify the voices of those in the community who already enjoy a privileged status, such as men and the educated. NGOs have been accused of presenting the outcomes of participation to the donor as authentic voices of the community, when rather they conceal power relations *within* the community, and *between* the community and NGO (see e.g., Cooke & Kothari, 2001; Guijt & Shah, 1998; White, 1996). Our research contributes to this literature by illuminating the role of language in the reproduction of local-level power dynamics. We demonstrate that the language practices of NGOs can reinforce linguistic power structures, by erecting barriers to participation from certain linguistic and cultural groups. This manifests in two ways. Firstly, language practices may reinforce exclusion *within* the organisation. For example, our Peru case study revealed that NGO participants felt that the linguistic capital of English afforded greater opportunities in terms of job promotion, which parallels findings in different contexts (Roth, 2019). These findings suggest that Southern staff in INGOs with limited fluency in English may experience linguistic discrimination in the workplace, which could intersect with other categories of marginalisation such as ethnicity. Secondly, language practices may also deepen the exclusion of marginalised groups from NGO participatory processes at the grassroots. Numerous participants in this research have insisted that English buzzwords have no direct equivalent in local languages and have limited resonance with local people. Our case studies revealed that those in the community who are not familiar with the language or dialect that fieldworkers use cannot fully participate in consultative exercises such as needs assessment or end of project evaluations. If NGOs do not incorporate relevant linguistic groups in listening exercises, the discourse of participation will become a 'tyranny' that reinforces, rather than challenges existing inequalities (Cooke & Kothari, 2001).

Our project paves the way for future research based upon direct observation of NGO participatory processes at community level, interpreted through the conceptual lens of the Listening Zone. The purpose of this research would be to test the claims of our interviewees that many NGOs do not accommodate the inclusion of marginalised languages and dialects in their listening practices. It would be necessary to be sensitive to the intersectional nature of discrimination in such an endeavour. For example, it is typical that marginalised languages are spoken by groups that experience ethnic discrimination in their locality and wider society. This can present complex challenges to their ability 'to be heard' in participatory activities by NGOs and the rest of the community.

Implicit Assumptions About the Representative Function of NGOs and Their Accountability to Communities

Critics argue that the liberal transnational approach implicitly presumes that NGOs represent the opinions and interests of the excluded and marginalised. It has been presumed that they are responsive (and therefore somewhat accountable) to the people that they proclaim to represent. In early literature, NGOs were portrayed as organisations that were people-centred and that spoke for the poorest (Drabek, 1987). In the words of one of our DFID participants, this supposed ability to connect with the grassroots is the 'major selling point' of NGOs.

Nonetheless, critics argue that funding and bureaucratic imperatives have distanced NGOs from those that they claim to represent. They see donors as paying lip service towards valuing the role of NGOs as representatives of the local community, whereas in reality NGOs are used as tools to implement policies that are in the donors' interest (Arts & Elbers, 2011; Bebbington et al., 2008; Edwards & Hulme, 1996; Hearn, 2007). NGOs are under pressure to align with donors' preferences in order to secure grants in a highly competitive funding environment. They have therefore been accused of exhibiting competitive profit-seeking behaviours that produce dysfunctional outcomes (Bob, 2005; Cooley & Ron, 2002). Activists and scholars have criticised NGOs for becoming highly professionalised, more like development consultants than the voluntarist associations that they once were (Choudry & Kapoor, 2013). Donors have increasingly pressured NGOs to demonstrate value for money, which means that organisations have become incentivised to chase targets, produce quantifiable measurements of project success and become further removed from their proclaimed role as representatives of the poor. It is argued that these developments have had negative implications for the accountability practices of NGOs. For example, Burger and Owens (2010) report that NGOs are likely to misrepresent the extent of community consultation in project design and evaluations because of the pressure they are under to maintain good reputations with donors.

Our research reveals that similar donor–NGO relationship dynamics explain the underfunding of language in development work. Several of our INGO and SNGO participants suggested that language needs tend to be underfunded because they are not properly budgeted for in project proposals—sometimes for fear that donors will not welcome high operating costs. Competition for grants is very intense, and donors tend to prioritise applications that offer the most value for money. Our interviews with DFID officials suggested that donors will generally presume that NGOs have sufficient language capacity to conduct a project. They may not necessarily notice or ask questions if interpretation and translation needs are not specifically costed in the budget. NGOs are therefore incentivised to omit or minimise the inclusion of language costs in their proposals in an attempt to appear more cost-effective than their rivals. Our participants suggest that the underfunding of language needs undercuts the ability of NGOs to listen to communities and understand their experiences and opinions. This bolsters the claims of critics that the financial dependence of NGOs on their donors weakens their ability to represent the poor.

Our research adds a new dimension to the critical literature on the representative potential of NGOs by posing a fundamental question: Do fieldworkers actually have the language capacity to converse with their partners and intended beneficiaries? If not, then surely their claims to listen to and speak for the poorest are severely compromised before one even considers questions of funding and management. The ability to communicate in a mutually intelligible language (either directly or through an interpreter) is a crucial prerequisite for NGOs to build meaningful relationships with communities. It is necessary for NGOs to establish the needs and desires of those that they claim to represent and ensure that their activities are in line with those preferences. Currently, many NGOs lack the linguistic capacity to ensure that their 'constituencies' endorse their work. These organisations leave themselves open to the accusation of being self-appointed and illegitimate representatives. Their inability or unwillingness to enhance their listening practices undermines their claims to be representatives of the poor. Practical considerations of language and listening have generally not been included in the literature on NGO legitimacy (Atack, 1999; Collingwood & Logister, 2005). We hope to inspire those interested in abstract questions of NGO representation and legitimacy to attend to concrete problems arising from linguistic practices.

Our research also opens up a new front in accountability research. Despite the extensive literature on accountability issues in both IR and Development Studies (see e.g., Gugerty & Prakash, 2010; Jordan & van Tuijl, 2006), there is barely any focus on the role of language in enabling NGOs to be accountable to communities. As one of our Malawian SNGO participants stated: "how can you be accountable when you cannot even speak the language?" Listening is an essential component of accountability, and the shared language is necessary to enable communities to be heard in exercises involving needs assessment, project design and monitoring and evaluation. Beneficiary feedback mechanisms do not always have to be based on spoken or written language (for example, some basic feedback exercises ask participants to signal their approval or dissatisfaction by selecting a picture of a happy or a sad face). However, the richest forms of feedback that enable participants to fully express their ideas and opinions will be based on language. We argue that speaking local languages and demonstrating cultural awareness is essential for NGOs to foster relations of mutual respect with communities. Notions of 'respect' are often featured in discussions about the values that should underpin NGO accountability, albeit in a rather nebulous way. Future research on accountability from a linguistic perspective could investigate the extent to which NGOs can enhance local perceptions of their 'respect' for communities in development projects by ensuring that their fieldworkers communicate in the vernacular. It would be interesting to examine how this might compare with local perceptions associated with projects that rely on a local interpreter, and/or projects that use interpreters external to the community.

The Decontextualisation of NGOs

The liberal transnational approach has been criticised for failing to acknowledge the profound differences between NGOs in terms of mission, history, size, operation and relationship with government and the people that they claim to represent. In Keck and Sikkink's classic formulation, NGOs in transnational networks are constituted by "shared values and a common discourse" (1998, p. 2). But IR scholars DeMars and Dijkzeul (2015) argue that Keck and Sikkink are guilty of 'theoretically homogenising' NGOs. For DeMars and Dijkzeul, to explain NGOs as constituted by transnational norms "is to portray NGO organizations and activists as wholly cosmopolitan creatures… but rooted in and shaped by no particular country or place" (2019, p. 77). The liberal transnational approach implicitly presents NGOs as detached from their geographic and political context when there is evidence that national origins exert a profound influence on the way that NGOs act (Stroup, 2012). Decontextualised accounts of NGOs also occlude the power hierarchy *within* and *between* organisations. There are several single case studies and ethnographic studies of NGOs that have exposed the operation and effects of internal power structures (Hilhorst, 2003; Hopgood, 2006; Wong, 2012). Critics highlight the importance of being attentive to the hierarchies and power struggles between peer organisations and partners (DeMars & Dijkzeul, 2015; Stroup & Wong, 2017).

Our research provides validity to the thrust of these criticisms from a linguistic perspective. Our findings raise questions about the extent to which 'shared values and a common discourse' exist between partner organisations that have a relationship structured by linguistic exclusions. The case study chapters indicate that colleagues in multilingual organisations and partnerships experience frequent difficulties in listening and communicating with one another. The liberal approach has wholly overlooked the 'friction' (Tsing, 2005) of language differences that shapes relationships between actors, which is ironic considering that transnational networks are conventionally understood to be partially constituted by dense exchanges of information and communication.

This study underlines the futility of generalising across the highly diverse NGO sector, and the value of analysis that is heavily contextualised by prevailing conditions at the local/national level. The project encompassed a broad range of organisations, from large INGOs that have operations that span the globe to small organisations based in local communities. These organisations have markedly different approaches to relationships with 'beneficiary' communities, from Christian Aid that largely accesses the voices of the poor through intermediary organisations, to Tearfund that works directly with local partners. The organisations that we have surveyed also have markedly different understandings of the role of language in building relationships with local communities. Tearfund's conception of using interpretation and translation to empower local communities, for example, contrasts with the approach of most large organisations that 'outsource' translation to professionals or local volunteers. Furthermore, our findings suggest that the attitude of the donor towards languages can be an important part of providing an enabling environment for the development of local civil society organisations. For example, the SNGO participants in the Peru case study (Chapter 8) spoke favourably about the willingness of donors with offices in-country to allow the submission of funding proposals in Spanish. The research further underlines the value of understanding NGOs within their national contexts, and particularly their (usually neglected) linguistic contexts.

We are distinguished from much of the liberal transnational and critical literature by selecting the status of English as a key variable for our choice of country case studies. Use of this variable enabled us to explore the extent to which competence in Anglocentric development discourse shapes power hierarchies *within* organisations. Studies of the internal dynamics of NGOs have generally not examined how 'linguistic capital' accentuates power differentials, with the notable exception of Roth (2019). Our interview participants have claimed that English language competence is an essential requirement to progress in the organisation. English is associated with power, privilege and opportunity. This was echoed by Roth's (2019) findings, which suggest that systematic language discrimination may intersect with other features of disadvantage, such as ethnicity. Ironically, although bi/multilingual NGO staff perform essential functions in making sure that the organisation runs effectively (e.g., translating project proposals, feedback from the community, etc.), our interview participants reported that they did not tend to be rewarded for their efforts. Instead, the 'burden of bilingualism' (see Chapter 5) means that employees are expected to assume responsibilities beyond their normal job description. The values that are assigned to certain language and translation skills seemingly play a significant part in the reproduction of hierarchies in NGOs.

We were also able to provide some novel insights into the power hierarchies *between* organisations through the lens of language. Our research aligns with the critical development literature on the power dynamics between INGOs and SNGOs (Lister, 2000). There are instances in our case study chapters where partnership is portrayed by participants as constructed on hierarchical and paternalistic lines. This has long been a criticism of INGOs (Baaz, 2005), although again, the contribution of language to power inequalities in partnerships has not been fully explored. Language exacerbates the asymmetry in power because, as several of our interview participants claimed, it is an essential resource with which to secure donor funds. The key to success in funding proposals is the ability to speak the preferred jargon of the donor, and to fulfil paper-based reporting requirements that rely on competence in project/NGO management (Bornstein, Chapman, & Wallace, 2006). Organisations with these skills are associated with higher status and greater credibility than those without. Southern partners that have success stories to share, which might increase their chances of receiving funding in the future if they were to meet the ear of an interested donor, are not able to garner wide publicity if they are not able to express themselves in English or another widely spoken international language. We argue that future research should pay more attention to how language shapes inequalities and hierarchies across the development NGO sector.

Listening Studies

This volume began with a review of current research in Listening Studies, noting the tendency for listening to be theorised in the context of interpersonal relations, human resource management and therapeutic practice, with relatively little interrogation of the wider fields of institutional, governmental and political communication. Listening research, as Purdy suggested (2000), had its roots in the post-enlightenment individualist 'psychology project', viewing listening as an individual rather than a community process. More recently however, listening scholars have begun to look at the critical role of space in framing listening (*International Journal of Listening*, Special Issue, 2019). Arnett (2019) argues, for example, that dialogic listening must involve being attentive to place and space and developing an active awareness of the biases we bring to the encounters. Our Listening Zones research provides supporting evidence that the physical and imaginative spaces of listening are key in creating listening experiences, and that listening by institutions like INGOs and donors must be read contrapuntally with the spaces of their origins. The project implicitly calls for listening research to engage more overtly with the historical, social and political problematics that create the Listening Zones, particularly in the case of those groups and organisations who claim that listening to others is a vital part of their rationale and mission.

The conceptual framework of the Listening Zones took as its first principle the multilingualism of the spaces of encounter, the fact of what Dreher terms, 'cosmopolitan listening' (2009, p. 448) as a given in transnational settings. Our conclusions point to the relevance of language as a social category in its own right, to be seen alongside gender, class and age as creating exclusions and marginalities, and supporting existing power hierarchies. Further listening research might helpfully engage with the implications of these conclusions in other examples of politico–social meetings beyond the more traditional research sites of international classrooms and intercultural pedagogy. Whilst the Listening Zones research has investigated the role of language mediators—translators and interpreters—and the perception of institutions and communities of the translation process, much more work remains to be done on the influence of linguistic mediation on transnational listening itself. What is the effect of listening through others, listening indirectly, and how might we begin to investigate such 'vicarious listening' within a transnational context?

Intercultural Studies

Intercultural Studies, particularly through the work of Pratt (2008), and Apter (2006), have provided our initial notion of 'Zone', which has framed the research, encouraging the project to adopt multilingualism as a starting point, to prioritise the actual workings of communicative and auditory relationships on the ground, to focus on the co-creation of meetings and to assume that these are spaces of potential hybridity and learning. As we embarked on the research, the UK Arts and Humanities Research Council had just completed an important set of related projects on Diaspora, Migration and Identities (AHRC, 2015) which emphasised the importance it attached to transnational and transdisciplinary research. The Council's subsequent major research theme, 'Translating Cultures', initiated well over 100 projects that sought to examine transnational and globalised connections between and across languages and cultures, within a context in which political upheaval, the mass movements of people, and digital transformations were seen to be reconfiguring societies in the twenty-first century. The broad range of research stimulated by this initiative has placed 'translation' at the centre of these changes, and opened up the meanings of the term 'translation' to embrace the "transmission, interpretation, transformation and sharing of languages, values, beliefs, histories and narratives" (Translating Cultures 2019, p. 4). The three large flagship grant awards for example investigated identity and diaspora, creativity and multilingual research and 'translanguaging' (using a mix of language resources and bodily communication to make oneself understood) in diverse wards of British cities. It would be fair to say, however, that within the enormous richness of the work generated by the theme, translation and interpretation (in the more restricted interlingual sense of the words) have been less evident, albeit with very notable exceptions such as grants to investigate the mediation of indigenous rights in Peru, the Translation of the deaf self and the highly innovative Translator in Residence programme at the British Library.

Our research has demonstrated the importance of examining the role of interlingual translation itself, as opposed to the metaphorical use of the term, in order to gain an understanding of power relationships in transnational contexts. Interlingual translation, we have concluded, by its presence, its absence or the particular characteristics of its appearance (unidirectional/bidirectional) creates conditions of cultural transfer on the ground, supports existing power hierarchies and marginalises groups and communities. Interlingual translation in this sense is not primarily a matter of communication or the passing of messages, but rather a constitutive element of international politico–social relations. With the recent very considerable public investment in Global Challenges research, the importance of emphasising the interlingual meaning of translation becomes ever more urgent. Research cooperation of this sort, which seeks to foster equality and sustainability across countries, institutions and disciplines, must of necessity engage with the presence and associated costs of interlingual translation, as well as the conceptual, political and ethical risks inherent in its occlusion.

Cultural studies have had a long-standing engagement with 'voice', and the intercultural impetus provided by the 'Translating Cultures' theme has built on this work in areas like protest and dissent (Baker, 2016), ethnographic linguistics (Blackledge & Crease, 2019) and participatory video (Cooke, Dennison, & Gould, 2019). What has arguably been less explored, however, is the practice of listening in transnational relations, the positionalities of the actors involved, the contours and definition of what might be effective listening and the possible links between listening and empowerment. The Listening Zones project, prioritising listening as opposed to voice, has turned the spotlight on the responsibilities of those with notionally greater power, and the ways in which listening itself supports or subverts existing hierarchies. Our conclusions call for those institutions that claim to be listening to others to become more listening-aware, and to demonstrate how they prepare themselves in practice to listen in worlds that have never been monolingual (Gramling, 2016).

Translation Studies

Research in Translation and Interpreting Studies (T&IS) has become increasingly interested in the role of translation and translators in society, as evidenced through its 'sociological turn' during the 2000s (Fukari & Wolf, 2007). Scholars have investigated translation in a variety of contexts, such as war and conflict (Baker, 2006; Baker & Kelly, 2013; Footitt & Kelly, 2012; Salama-Carr, 2007), translation and interpreting in hospitals, courts and asylum seeking settings (Angelelli, 2004; Inghilleri, 2005; Tipton & Valero-Garcés, 2017), in political institutions and activist communities (Baigorri-Jalón, 2004; Boéri & Maier, 2010; Koskinen, 2008; Schäffner, Tcaciuc & Tesseur, 2014), as well as online through volunteer networks and crowdsourcing (Baker & Piróth, 2019; McDonough Dolmaya, 2012; Pérez-González & Susam-Saraeva, 2012; Rogl, 2017). The enhanced sociological focus has placed aspects such as the translator's agency, power and ethics at the centre of translation and interpreting research. Although all of these issues are pertinent in the context of development programmes, translation and interpreting in development settings had, until recently, received relatively little attention in T&IS. The seminal work of Marais (2014), bringing together Translation Theory and Development Studies, has been the start of a series of publications, mostly small-scale case studies, which have aimed to address this gap (Chibamba, 2018; Marais, 2018; Marais & Delgado Luchner, 2018; Todorova, 2018). The Listening Zones research constitutes one of the first major projects that has addressed questions on translation, interpreting and development. Its research findings provide a number of insights which are relevant, in the first instance, for research that engages with contexts of development as well as those of humanitarian crisis, community translation and interpreting, and activist and volunteer translation and interpreting and by extension for debates in the disciplines of T&IS more widely. The findings are summarised below as situated in three areas.

Translation in Development and Crisis Settings

Our research has predominantly focused on translation as constituted in international UK-based development programmes, delivered by international NGOs. Because these organisations also deliver emergency aid in humanitarian crisis, our research also contributes some insight to contexts of language mediation in crisis settings (Federici, 2016; Federici & O'Brien, 2020). As described in Chapter 5, translation and interpreting needs in both contexts tend to have a low profile in the aid sector, despite the transnational character of INGO work. Research conducted on the topic of language mediation in crisis settings has demonstrated that translation and interpreting is often not systematically included in emergency response policies, which leads to gaps in practice and ultimately has a negative effect on service delivery (Cadwell, Federici, Gerber, Marlowe, & O'Brien, 2018; Cadwell, Federici, Gerber, & O'Brien, 2019). Arguments can be made about the important role of translation in humanitarian settings now being better recognised (see Chapter 5), yet our findings point to the low status of language and translation in development, with international donors continuing to expect INGOs to have the language capacity necessary to deal with linguistic needs in development programmes. From the perspective of INGOs, our findings demonstrated that language needs tended to be overlooked in project planning, delivering and evaluation. Much translation and interpreting work was done informally and ad hoc by NGO workers, who argued for the importance of translation and interpreting in trust building and in establishing long-term working relationships, in which demonstrating respect was crucial. Taking the body of research on crisis translation and development programmes together, what emerges is a picture in which translation and interpreting have been systematically overlooked in institutional policies, but tend to be recognised by individual aid workers, particularly in the light of trust building (see e.g., Cadwell, 2015).

The research has provided important evidence of the need—and appetite of individual aid workers—to include language and translation needs in institutional policies and frameworks and to formalise the link between language needs and achieving two-way communication for greater accountability, in accordance with aims expressed in international frameworks such as the SDGs or the Grand Bargain (Cadwell et al., 2019). For T&IS specifically, the research has provided evidence of the many informal translation and interpreting practices, which have traditionally not been the focus of these disciplines. The findings thus point to the need for T&IS to engage more deeply with these disparate contexts in order to, firstly, extend existing interpretations of what constitutes translation and interpreting, and secondly, to be able to make a meaningful contribution to other disciplines in which translation and interpreting practices have remained overlooked, as discussed further below.

Understandings of Professional Translation and Interpreting Practice

Debates about professionalism in T&IS are often linked to those of ethical and professional obligations towards clients and the quality and provision of translation and interpreting services. Particularly in the context of community interpreting (in courts, hospitals, asylum seeker settings, etc.), where the availability of professionally trained interpreters tends to be limited, meaning so-called 'non-professionals' may be called on to provide these services, the problematics of professionalism have been much debated (Antonini, Cirillo, Rossato, & Torresi, 2017). Equally, the very definitions of 'volunteer', 'pro bono', 'citizen' or 'community' translator, and 'professional' versus 'non-professional' translation and interpreting continue to be areas of contention. However, a major shortcoming of this body of research is that it has predominantly focused on Northern contexts. Translation and Interpreting Studies have been described as being rooted in the North, and various scholars have called for the 'Eurocentric' bias of these disciplines to be redressed by including a plurality of views and voices in scholarly debates (Bassnett & Johnston, 2019; Flynn & van Doorslaer, 2011).

Although the Listening Zones project has been conducted by Northern scholars, and thus cannot fully respond to these calls, the research has engaged with translation as taking place in contexts that have previously been under researched in T&IS, namely those of development, in countries such as Malawi, Peru and Kyrgyzstan. The research findings from these contexts have implications for current understandings of professionalism in T&IS. As described in Chapter 5, notions of professionalism in the Northern context tend to include such characteristics as having been enrolled in a professional training programme, having the skills to use translation technology tools and having knowledge of and adhering to the codes of conduct of professional translation or interpreting bodies, such as the AIIC (Association internationale des interprètes de conférence) or the UK's Institute of Translation and Interpreting. However, our research findings challenge this conceptualisation of professionalism. Research participants argued that critical skills and knowledge included an in-depth knowledge of development practice and its related discourse, familiarity with the local culture and language and the ability to establish trust between communities and NGO workers. These findings emphasise the need for T&IS to include these characteristics of translation and interpreting in Southern and/or informal contexts more overtly into existing definitions, along much the same lines as previously argued by African-based scholars such as Marais (2014) and Chibamba (2018). Moreover, as briefly addressed in Chapter 5, the research findings also challenge the established binary categories, common in the Global North, of translation (as written language mediation) and interpreting (as oral mediation). The findings point to the need for a more in-depth engagement from T&IS scholars with contexts outside the North, in a dialogue of exchange and co-creation with scholars based in the South, following recommendations of scholars such as Phipps (2019) on decolonising multilingualism, or, in this case, of decolonising translation.

Raising the Profile of Translation in Other Disciplines

From its inception, the basic assumption underlying the disciplines of T&IS was that translation was an important process that should be taken into account in efforts to understand processes of transmission of ideas, texts and cultural practices (Bassnett & Johnston, 2019). The invisibility of translation and the translator is an issue that has been debated in the discipline for years (most notably through the work of Venuti, 1995). Translation scholars have argued that research in discourse analysis and sociolinguistics tends to overlook the role of translation in the processes of meaning-making (Schäffner, 2004; Tesseur, 2017). Others have noted that whilst the concept of translation itself is at times used in other disciplines, 'translation' tends to be used in its metaphorical sense and generally little or no reference is made to T&IS research (Alfer, 2017; Zwischenberger, 2017). Aiming to address these issues, scholars have called for T&IS to systematically engage in transdisciplinary dialogue and collaboration, in order to bring concrete insights from T&IS to the conceptualisation of translation in other disciplines (Alfer, 2017; Bachmann-Medick, 2009; Gambier & van Doorslaer, 2016; Zwischenberger, 2017).

Our research has engaged in such interdisciplinary dialogue by bringing together a team of researchers working in different disciplines, and by presenting and publishing our research in different disciplinary venues, including panels at the BISA conference (British International Studies Association) and the IATIS conference (International Association for Translation and Intercultural Studies), and publishing in journals including *Development in Practice, Disaster Prevention and Management,*

Journal for Translation Studies in Africa, Journal of Multilingual and Multicultural Development, Journal of War & Culture Studies, Journal of Sociolinguistics, Language and Intercultural Communication, Translation Spaces and *The Translator*. Overall, these presentations and publications have aimed to remedy traditional perceptions of translation as a neutral, transparent activity by drawing attention to the many ways in which translation is closely linked to power relationships, access to information and funding, and cultural hegemony. For example, the research has demonstrated that choices about the use or non-use of translation automatically entail consequences for inclusion or exclusion, it has discussed the problematics of translating development-related concepts as grounded in specific histories and cultural contexts, and has analysed the role of the translator/interpreter as one that can have a considerable effect on the outcomes of development projects. Furthermore, the conceptualisation of the Listening Zones has helped to uncover the many informal translation processes that take place in the in-between spaces of development programmes and has demonstrated that several NGO staff engage in informal translation to enhance mutual understanding, as described in Chapter 4. The findings thus demonstrate that it is important for disciplines such as Development Studies to include the study of translation practices in their research: it can enhance understandings of the power relationships, agency and ethics that influence development programmes in their attempts to engage in equitable dialogue and ensure inclusion. The Listening Zones research and its findings thus provide an example of the type of collaborative interdisciplinary research called for by scholars such as Alfer (2017), Zwischenberger (2017) and Gambier and van Doorslaer (2016), and will hopefully serve as the first step in a continuing dialogue between scholars from T&IS and those from Development Studies and IR about the role of translation in international development.

Researching Multilingually

The Listening Zones conceptual framework we have employed in this research uses 'Zones' as a critical tool to enable the relationality of encounters to be set within clearly delimited geographies which are not framed by the nation state or by ethnicities. The concept, as applied to International Development, assumes from the outset that spaces of development are multivocal and multilingual. It prioritises the actual workings of communicative relationships rather than broad classifications of identity like nation state, ethnicity, or North/South. It positions the co-creation of the listening space itself as the focus of study, rather than representing listening as an incidental stage within a teleological development cycle, and it assumes that these are spaces of potential hybridity and learning, that the 'global' and the 'local' are not necessarily located in separate silos. Our investigations have led us to argue for the place of temporality in constructing the Listening Zones, i.e., the role of institutional history in the contemporary positioning of key actors, and for the importance of spatiality: the physical and imaginative distances between key actors. In the Listening Zones of Development, we have found that language, rather than simply being synonymous with communication, is actually a social category in its own right, a component in creating, reinforcing or subverting the hierarchies of power. To this extent, engaging with the multilingualism of development has taken us beyond apparently 'softer' issues of relationality and trust to address the politics of power, inclusion and marginality.

As researchers observing and interpreting listening, we were also constituting the practice. Language, we therefore argued, had to be a key part of our self-reflection in a multilingual research site. Unfortunately, issues of doing research multilingually do not tend to be overtly discussed at anglophone universities in training courses, publications or funding applications (Andrews, Attia, Fay, & Holmes, 2013; Danero Iglesias & Gibb, 2016). For obvious reasons, it was particularly pertinent to the project that we reflected on the implications of the language in which we conversed with our participants (see Chapter 5).

In the first instance, choosing a language for data collection implies including certain participants and excluding others. Who we listened to as researchers in our country case studies was to a considerable degree determined by our language choices. In many ways, our choice of language could be said to mirror some of the praxis of development practitioners, and the hierarchies that are thereby created. Thus, Crack interviewed her informants in English, and in so doing was implicitly reflecting some of the traditional power relationships of development work that we have encountered in this project. Grassroots organisations that did not have English language capacity could not be listened to directly. Footitt interviewed in Spanish, which is not her first language, in an effort to come alongside her informants. But there were clear limitations to this self-integration tactic. Inevitably, as a non-native speaker, she continued to be perceived as a foreign intervener, albeit one seeking to reach out to her colleagues. However, when talking with first language Quechua speakers, she implicitly presumed her informants would use the ex-colonial language (Spanish) as their vehicular language, thereby replicating Crack's situation in Malawi. In Kyrgyzstan, Tesseur employed an intermediary, an interpreter, for conversations with both Russian and Kyrgyz speakers, and in so doing experienced at first hand the role and complexity of brokerage in development practice. This decision brought with it a whole set of complex power dynamics, which most likely affected all stages of the research, i.e., from participant selection, the interpreted event itself, to feeding back to participants and sharing findings. Although researchers such as Borchgrevink (2003), Edwards and Temple (2008), Turner (2010), Caretta (2015) and Bowlby, Evans, Kébé, Ribbens McCarthy, and Wouango (2017) have provided some guidance on the ethics and power dimensions of working with interpreters or multilingual research assistants, there are no clear-cut solutions to redress power imbalances and some degree of bias seems unavoidable. For the Kyrgyz case study, such bias may include, for example, the selection of research participants—given that some of these contacts came through the interpreter's professional network—and the responses of participants, which depended on the way in which the interpreter may have translated questions and answers.

A second major concern in researching multilingually is the process of linguistic translation itself when communicating with participants. One issue, for example, was how to agree on translations of key concepts in the research. In Kyrgyzstan, lengthy discussions were held between the researcher, interpreter and some of the participants on how best to translate the concept of 'listening' itself, which was not associated with the same frameworks of accountability, for example, as was the case in English (see Chapter 4). Furthermore, the ongoing need for translation in order to continue communication and maintain any kind of dialogue with research participants after the research had taken place, to share the research results, and to receive feedback, was also a challenging process. For example, we translated a draft of our final report for NGOs and donors into Spanish and Russian and asked for feedback from participants. For Russian, comments were brief, tended to be uncritical and mostly served as 'thank you' notes. Since feedback was elicited over e-mail with the help of a translator and without face-to-face contact, it was very difficult to understand the true success of this attempt to include participants longer term in the research process. Secondly, Kyrgyz participants were excluded from this discussion. Our research findings became directly applicable to our own work: translators who can translate between English and Kyrgyz are rare. Thus, the Kyrgyz translation was what translation scholars would call an 'indirect' translation (Ringmar, 2012): it was produced from the Russian translation, unavoidably with a delay in time, and Kyrgyz participants were, therefore, not able to provide feedback directly before the final report was published.

These examples illustrate the challenges involved in attempting to conduct research multilingually. It is our hope that our self-reflection and self-criticism on our linguistic actions will contribute to our study's credibility and validity. Many of the linguistic issues we encountered are similar to those that INGOs themselves face when working transnationally. We hope that our findings will provide an opportunity for practitioners to reflect on practice and on their conventional ways of listening and engaging with languages. In this spirit, we have produced a report available in five different languages (INTRAC, 2018), written blogs and news articles (Crack, 2018; Crack, Footitt, & Tesseur, 2018; Crack & Tesseur, 2018), and have fed back verbally to practitioners in workshops, webinars and return field trips. The next chapter (Chapter 10), which focuses on policy recommendations for practitioners, directly draws on the suggestions of our research participants. We have tried to frame these from the perspective of the disempowered and less privileged, suggesting how the most powerful participants in our study (donors, NGO managers, INGOs) can adapt their policy and practices in a way that elevates the position of those who are less powerful in development (SNGOs, local workers, communities).

References

Arts, B., & Elbers, W. (2011). Keeping body and soul together: Southern NGOs' strategic responses to donor constraints. *International Review of Administrative Sciences, 77*(4), 713–732.

Ahmed, S., & Potter, D. M. (2006). *NGOs in international politics*. Bloomfield, CT: Kumarian Press.

AHRC. (2015). *Diaspora, migration and identities* (Final Report). Retrieved from: http://web.archive.org/web/20150907235258/http://www.diaspora.ac.uk/assets/PI-nal_report_Diasporas_Migration_Identities.pdf.

Alfer, A. (2017). Entering the Translab: Translation as collaboration, collaboration as translation, and the third space of "translaboration". *Translation and Translanguaging in Multilingual Contexts, 3*(3), 275–290.
Andrews, J., Attia, M., Fay, R., & Holmes, P. (2013). Researching multilingually: New theoretical and methodological directions. *International Journal of Applied Linguistics, 23*(3), 285–299.
Angelelli, C. (2004). *Medical interpreting and cross-cultural communication*. Cambridge: Cambridge University Press.
Antonini, R., Cirillo, L., Rossato, L., & Torresi, I. (Eds.). (2017). *Non-professional interpreting and translation: State of the art and future of an emerging field of research*. Amsterdam and Philadelphia: John Benjamins.
Amoore, L., & Langley, P. (2004). Ambiguities of global civil society. *Review of International Studies, 30*(1), 89–110.
Apter, E. (2006). *The translation zone: A new comparative literature*. Princeton: Princeton University Press.
Arnett, R. (2019). Response: Dialogic listening as attentiveness to place and space'. *International Journal of Listening, 33*(3), 181–187.
Atack, I. (1999). Four criteria of development NGO legitimacy. *World Development, 27*(5), 855–864.
Baaz, M. E. (2005). *The paternalism of partnership: A postcolonial reading of identity in development aid*. London: Zed Books.
Bachmann-Medick, D. (2009). Introduction: The translational turn. *Translation Studies, 2*(1), 2–16.
Baigorri-Jalón, J. (2004). *Interpreters at the United Nations: A history*. Salamanca: Ediciones Universidad de Salamanca.
Baker, M. (2006). *Translation and conflict: A narrative account*. London and New York: Routledge.
Baker, M. (2016). *Translating dissent: Voices from and with the Egyptian revolution*. Abingdon: Counter Press.
Baker, C., & Kelly, M. (2013). *Interpreting the peace: Peace operations, conflict and language in Bosnia-Herzegovina*. Basingstoke: Palgrave Macmillan.
Baker, M., & Piróth, A. (2019). *The ethics of volunteerism in translation: Translators without borders and the platform economy*. Retrieved from: http://www.pirothattila.com/Piroth-Baker_The_Ethics_of_Volunteerism_in_Translation.pdf.
Banks, N., Edwards, M., & Hulme, D. (2015). NGOs, states, and donors revisited: Still too close for comfort? *World Development, 66*, 707–718.
Bassnett, S., & Johnston, D. (2019). The outward turn in translation studies. *Translator, 25*(3), 181–188.
Bebbington, A. J., Hickey, S., & Mitlin, D. C. (Eds.). (2008). *Can NGOs make a difference? The challenge of development alternatives*. London: Zed Books.

Betsill, M. M., & Corell, E. (Eds.). (2008). *NGO diplomacy: The influence of nongovernmental organizations in international environmental negotiations*. Cambridge: MIT Press.

Blackledge, A., & Crease, A. (2019). *Voices of a city market: An ethnography*. Bristol: Multilingual Matters.

Bob, C. (2005). *The marketing of rebellion: Insurgents, media, and international activism*. Cambridge: Cambridge University Press.

Boéri, J., & Maier, C. (Eds.). (2010). *Translation/interpreting and social activism/Compromiso Social y Traducción/Interpretación*. Granada: ECOS.

Borchgrevink, A. (2003). Silencing language: Of anthropologists and interpreters. *Ethnography, 4*(1), 95–121.

Bornstein, L., Chapman, J., & Wallace, T. (2006). *The aid chain: Coercion and commitment in development NGOs*. Rugby: Intermediate Technology Development Group.

Bowlby, S., Evans, R., Kébé, F., Ribbens McCarthy, J., & Wouango, J. (2017). Interpreting 'grief' in Senegal: Language, emotions and cross-cultural translation in a francophone African context. *Mortality, 22*(2), 118–135.

Brass, J. N., Longhofer, W., Robinson, R. S., & Schnable, A. (2018). NGOs and international development: A review of thirty-five years of scholarship. *World Development, 112*, 136–149.

Burger, R., & Owens, T. (2010). Promoting transparency in the NGO sector: Examining the availability and reliability of self-reported data. *World Development, 38*(9), 1263–1277.

Cadwell, P. (2015). *Translation and trust: A case study of how translation was experienced by foreign nationals resident in Japan for the 2011 great east Japan earthquake* (Unpublished PhD thesis). Dublin City University, Dublin.

Cadwell, P., Federici, F., Gerber, B., Marlowe, J., & O'Brien, S. (2018). Language translation during disaster: A comparative analysis of five national approaches. *International Journal of Disaster Risk Reduction, 31*, 627–636.

Cadwell, P., Federici, F., Gerber, B., & O'Brien, S. (2019). *The international humanitarian sector and language translation in crisis situations*. London: INTERACT.

Caretta, M. A. (2015). Situated knowledge in cross-cultural, cross-language research: A collaborative reflexive analysis of researcher, assistant and participant subjectivities. *Qualitative Research, 15*(4), 489–505.

Chibamba, M. (2018). Translation and communication for development: The case of a health campaign in Zambia. *Translator, 24*(4), 301–317.

Choudry, A., & Kapoor, D. (2013). *NGOization: Complicity, contradictions and prospects*. London: Zed Books.

Collingwood, V., & Logister, L. (2005). State of the art: Addressing the INGO 'legitimacy deficit'. *Political Studies Review, 3*(2), 175–192.

Cooke, B., & Kothari, U. (Eds.). (2001). *Participation: The new tyranny?*. London: Zed Books.

Cooke, P., Dennison, S., & Gould, W. (2019). The Voicing Hidden Histories project: Participatory video in development, soft power and film language. *Media Practice and Education, 19*(3), 270–282.

Cooley, A., & Ron, J. (2002). The NGO scramble: Organizational insecurity and the political economy of transnational action. *International Security, 27*(1), 5–39.

Cornwall, A., & Eade, D. (2010). *Deconstructing development discourse: Buzzwords and fuzzwords*. Oxford: Practical Publishing.

Crack, A. M., & Tesseur, T. (2018, August 28) Do languages have a low priority in development work? *CHS Alliance*. Retrieved from: https://www.chsalliance.org/get-support/article/do-languages-have-a-low-priority-in-development-work/.

Crack, A. M. (2018, August 20). Translating principles into practice. *Accountable Now*. Retrieved from: https://accountablenow.org/translating-principles-into-practice/.

Crack, A. M., Footitt, H. A., & Tesseur, W. (2018, August 8). Many NGO workers don't speak the local language—New research. *The Conversation*. Retrieved from: https://theconversation.com/many-ngo-workers-on-the-ground-dont-speak-the-local-language-new-research-100845.

Danero Iglesias, J., & Gibb, R. (2016). Breaking the silence (again): On language learning and levels of fluency in ethnographic research. *The Sociological Review, 65*(1), 134–149.

Davies, T. (Ed.). (2019). *Routledge handbook of NGOs and international relations*. London: Routledge.

DeMars, W. E., & Dijkzeul, D. (Eds.). (2015). *The NGO challenge for international relations theory*. London: Routledge.

DeMars, W. E., & Dijkzeul, D. (2019). Constituting NGOs. In T. Davies (Ed.), *Routledge handbook of NGOs and international relations* (pp. 75–89). London: Routledge.

Drabek, A. G. (1987). Development alternatives: The challenge for NGOs—An overview of the issues. *World Development, 15*, ix–xv.

Dreher, T. (2009). Listening across difference: Media and multiculturalism beyond the politics of voice. *Continuum: Journal of Media and Cultural Studies, 23*(4), 445–458.

Edwards, M., & Hulme, D. (Eds.). (1996). *Beyond the magic bullet: NGO performance and accountability in the post-cold war world*. North Hartford: Kumarian Press.

Edwards, M., & Hulme, D. (Eds.). (2013). *NGOs, states and donors: Too close for comfort?*. London: Macmillan Press.

Edwards, R., & Temple, B. (2008). Interpreters/translators and cross-language research: Reflexivity and border crossings. *International Journal of Qualitative Methods, 1*(2), 1–12.

Federici, F. M. (Ed.). (2016). *Mediating emergencies and conflicts: Frontline translating and interpreting*. London: Palgrave Macmillan.

Federici, F. M., & O'Brien, S. (Eds.). (2020). *Translation in cascading crises*. Abingdon and New York: Routledge.

Flynn, P., & van Doorslaer, L. (Eds.). (2011). Eurocentrism in translation studies. *Special Issue of Translation and Interpreting Studies, 6*(2).

Footitt, H., & Kelly, M. (2012). *Languages at war: Policies and practices of language contacts in conflict*. Basingstoke: Palgrave Macmillan.

Fukari, A., & Wolf, M. (Eds.). (2007). *Constructing a sociology of translation*. Amsterdam: John Benjamins.

Gambier, Y., & van Doorslaer, L. (Eds.). (2016). *Border crossings: Translation Studies and other disciplines*. Amsterdam and Philadelphia: John Benjamins.

Götz, N. (2008). Reframing NGOs: The identity of an international relations non-starter. *European Journal of International Relations, 14*(2), 231–258.

Gramling, D. (2016). *The invention of monolingualism*. London: Bloomsbury.

Gugerty, M. K., & Prakash, A. (Eds.). (2010). *Voluntary regulation of NGOs and nonprofits: An accountability club framework*. Cambridge: Cambridge University Press.

Guijt, I., & Shah, M. K. (1998). *The myth of community: Gender issues in participatory development*. Oxford: Practical Action Publishing.

Hearn, J. (2007). African NGOs: The new compradors? *Development and Change, 38*(6), 1095–1110.

Hilhorst, D. J. M. (2003). *The real world of NGOs: Discourses, diversity and development*. London: Zed Books.

Hopgood, S. (2006). *Keepers of the flame: Understanding Amnesty International*. Ithaca: Cornell University Press.

Inghilleri, M. (2005). Mediating zones of uncertainty: Interpreter agency, the interpreting habitus and political asylum adjudication. *The Translator, 11*(1), 69–85.

International Journal of Listening. (2019). Themed issue on ethics, listening and space, *33*(3).

INTRAC. (2018). *The listening zones of NGOs: Languages and cultural knowledge in development programmes* (Final Report). Retrieved from: https://www.reading.ac.uk/web/files/modern-languages-and-european-studies/Listening_zones_report_-EN.pdf.

Jordan, L., & van Tuijl, P. (Eds.). (2006). *NGO accountability: Politics, principles and innovations*. London: Earthscan.

Joseph, J. (2013). Resilience as embedded neoliberalism: A governmentality approach. *Resilience, 1*(1), 38–52.

Kaldor, M. (2003). *Global civil society: An answer to war*. Cambridge: Polity.
Keane, J. (2003). *Global civil society?*. Cambridge: Cambridge University Press.
Keck, M. E., & Sikkink, K. (1998). *Activists beyond borders: Advocacy networks in international politics*. Ithaca: Cornell University Press.
Korten, D. C. (1987). Third generation NGO strategies: A key to people-centered development. *World Development, 15*, 145–159.
Koskinen, K. (2008). *Translating institutions: An ethnographic study of EU translation*. Manchester: St. Jerome.
Lewis, D. (2005). Individuals, organizations and public action: Trajectories of the 'non-governmental' in development studies. In U. Kothari (Ed.), *A radical history of development studies: Individuals, institutions and ideologies* (pp. 200–221). Croydon: CPI Group.
Lewis, D., & Kanji, N. (2009). *Non-governmental organizations and development*. London: Routledge.
Lister, S. (2000). Power in partnership? An analysis of an NGO's relationships with its partners. *Journal of International Development, 12*(2), 227–239.
Marais, K. (2014). *Translation theory and development studies: A complexity theory approach*. New York and Abingdon: Routledge.
Marais, K. (2018). Introduction: Translation and development. *The Translator, 24*(4), 295–300.
Marais, K., & Delgado Luchner, C. (2018). Motivating the translation-development nexus: Exploring cases from the African Continent. *The Translator, 24*(4), 380–394.
Martens, K. (2002). Mission impossible? Defining nongovernmental organizations. *Voluntas: International Journal of Voluntary and Nonprofit Organizations, 13*(3), 271–285.
Matthews, J. T. (1997). Power shift: The rise of global civil society. *Foreign Affairs, 76*(1), 50–66.
McDonough Dolmaya, J. (2012). Analyzing the crowdsourcing model and its impact on public perceptions of translation. *The Translator, 18*(2), 167–191.
Merz, S. (2012). 'Missionaries of the new era': Neoliberalism and NGOs in Palestine. *Race & Class, 54*(1), 50–66.
Pérez-González, L., & Susam-Saraeva, Ş. (2012). Non-professionals translating and interpreting: Participatory and engaged perspectives. *The Translator, 18*(2), 149–165.
Phipps, A. (2019). *Decolonising multilingualism: Struggles to decreate*. Bristol: Multilingual Matters.
Pratt, M. L. (2008). *Imperial eyes: Travel writing and transculturation*. Abingdon: Routledge.
Price, R. (2003). Transnational civil society and advocacy in world politics. *World Politics, 55*(4), 579–606.

Purdy, M. (2000). Listening, culture and structures of consciousness: Ways of studying listening. *International Journal of Listening, 14*(1), 47–68.
Ringmar, M. (2012). Relay translation. In L. Doorslaer & Y. Gambier (Eds.), *Handbook of translation studies* (Vol. 3, pp. 141–144). Amsterdam and Philadelphia: John Benjamins.
Rogl, R. (2017). Language-related disaster relief in Haiti: Volunteer translator networks and language technologies in disaster aid. In I. Torresi, L. Cirillo, L. Rossato & R. Antonini, R. (Eds.). *Non-professional interpreting and translation: State of the art and future of an emerging field of research* (pp. 231–255). Amsterdam and Philadelphia: John Benjamins.
Roth, S. (2019). Linguistic capital and inequality in aid relations. *Sociological Research Online, 24*(1), 38–54.
Salama-Carr, M. (Ed.). (2007). *Translating and interpreting conflict.* Amsterdam and New York: Rodopi.
Schäffner, C. (2004). Political discourse analysis from the point of view of translation studies. *Journal of Language and Politics, 3*(1), 117–150.
Schäffner, C., Tcaciuc, L. S., & Tesseur, W. (2014). Translation practices in political institutions: A comparison of national, supranational, and non-governmental organisations. *Perspectives, 22*(4), 493–510.
Scholte, J. A. (2004). Civil society and democratically accountable global governance. *Government and Opposition, 39*(2), 211–233.
Steffek, J., & Hahn, K. (Eds.). (2010). *Evaluating transnational NGOs: Legitimacy, accountability, representation.* London: Springer.
Stroup, S. S. (2012). *Borders among activists: International NGOs in the United States, Britain, and France.* Ithaca: Cornell University Press.
Stroup, S. S., & Wong, W. H. (2017). *The authority trap: Strategic choices of international NGOs.* Ithaca: Cornell University Press.
Tesseur, W. (2017). Incorporating translation into sociolinguistic research: Translation policy in an international non-governmental organisation. *Journal of Sociolinguistics, 21*(5), 629–649.
Tipton, R., & Valero-Garcés, C. (Eds.). (2017). *Ideology, ethics and policy development in public service interpreting and translation.* Bristol: Multilingual Matters.
Todorova, M. (2018). Civil society in translation: Innovations to political discourse in Southeast Europe. *The Translator, 24*(4), 353–366.
Translating Cultures. (2019). *Final report.* Liverpool: University of Liverpool & AHRC.
Tsing, A. (2005). *Friction: An ethnography of global connection.* Princeton: Princeton University Press.
Turner, S. (2010). Research note: The silenced assistant. Reflections of invisible interpreters and research assistants. *Asia Pacific Viewpoint, 51*(2), 206–219.

Venuti, L. (1995). *The translator's invisibility: A history of translation*. London and New York: Routledge.

White, S. C. (1996). Depoliticising development: The uses and abuses of participation. *Development in Practice, 6*(1), 6–15.

Wong, W. H. (2012). *Internal affairs: How the structure of NGOs transforms human rights*. Ithaca: Cornell University Press.

Wright, G. W. (2012). NGOs and Northern hegemony: Causes for concern and ideas for change. *Development in Practice, 22*(1), 123–134.

Yanacopoulos, H. (2015). *NGO advocacy, engagement and activism*. Basingstoke: Palgrave.

Zwischenberger, C. (2017). Translation as a metaphoric traveller across disciplines. *Translation and Translanguaging in Multilingual Contexts, 3*(3), 388–406.

CHAPTER 10

Recommendations for Practitioners and Next Steps: The Conversation Goes On

Introduction

The research on which this volume is based was originally stimulated by conversations with practitioners during a workshop held in January 2014 on the theme, 'Do NGOs need a languages policy?' NGO staff argued at this meeting that whilst they could see that languages might play a central role in the exercise of power, and in decisions on what 'counted' as voices to be heard, there was relatively little awareness within the sector as a whole of the ways in which unequal power relations in development might be magnified through languages (Workshop Report, 2014). At the end of the discussion, practitioners called for some evidence-based research which would raise awareness of these issues and contribute to vital policy change.

Whilst the research was taking place, NGO colleagues contributed as part of an Advisory Group and in well-attended open workshops. They also commented on ongoing papers from the project, so that the recommendations in the final report, *Respecting communities in International Development: languages and cultural understanding* (Footitt, Crack, & Tesseur, 2018) were directed, as they requested, at raising awareness of languages and stimulating changes in policies and practice. This chapter will outline these recommendations for donors and for INGOs. As writers of this book, we see discussions around the role of languages and cultural understanding in development as part of an important ongoing conversation in the sector, and the chapter will briefly outline what immediate

H. Footitt et al., *Development NGOs and Languages*,
https://doi.org/10.1007/978-3-030-51776-2_10

responses there have been to the recommendations since the publication of the report in June 2018, and what directions conversations might conceivably take in the future.

Donors

Recommendations

Recommendations for donors call on them to reflect on their current practices at each stage of the development cycle—when issuing a call for applications, when selecting projects and monitoring and evaluating them, and in initiatives to build local capacity and sustainability.

When issuing a Call for Applications donors could:

- ensure that the style of language used and the format of the application form is simple and straightforward
- let applicants apply in their first language or in a lingua franca in which they have capacity
- translate the Call for Applications and the accompanying instructions into local languages and provide glossaries on key terminology
- reimburse translation costs of successful applicants
- explicitly state that applicants should indicate how they plan to ensure communication with local communities
- invite applicants to include interpreting and translation costs in their budget
- explicitly note inadequacies in communicating with communities and respecting them culturally in feedback on failed applications.

When selecting projects and during monitoring and evaluation (M&E) donors could:

- ask organisations to demonstrate their 'language and cultural policies' and value those NGOs that can articulate these policies
- provide resources to pilot communication materials in advance, using the appropriate local language or dialect
- ensure that M&E frameworks encourage NGOs to reflect on how language issues affect project outcomes

- encourage INGOs to translate successful project proposals into local languages, so that SNGOs and communities can have an in-depth understanding of what is planned
- provide opportunities to implementing organisations to give feedback in their first language about whether projects are having the desired effect.

To support local capacity building and sustainability donors could:

- make available resources for SNGOs without English language capacity to translate information on their organisation into English so that they can share their knowledge and work
- consider funding civil society support groups to set up English language courses for SNGOs.

Immediate Responses

Among donors, DFID responded formally to these recommendations after a House of Lords written question posed by Baroness Coussins (2018):

> To ask Her Majesty's Government what assessment they have made of the report by the Arts and Humanities Research Council, 'Respecting communities in International Development: language and cultural understanding', published in June, in particular its finding that the lack of attention to language by the Department for International Development and others can frustrate the success and sustainability of development programmes.

The then Minister of State, Lord Bates, replied (Bates, 2018):

> We recognise the value of language capability for the delivery of our core mission and programmes. In particular, it enables us to understand contextual issues and needs, and helps us to communicate, engage stakeholders, develop positive relationships, and influence across our delivery chain. To ensure that we have deep capability in terms of local context, culture and languages, we employ Staff Appointed in Country (SAIC) as a core part of our operating model. Of the 1345 DFID staff employed in our overseas offices, 61 percent are SAIC. Our SAIC work in a range of advisory, needs assessment, programme design and management, and evaluation roles. SAIC are recruited with a high level of English capability. For DFID's UK

> staff deploying to locations overseas where English is not an official operating language, we seek to recruit people with the specified level of local language required for those roles. Where this is not possible, we provide language tuition to develop people to the required proficiency level. This tuition is delivered in a variety of ways dependent on the needs of the individual and the team they will be joining, e.g., via group tuition and some is immersive 1:1 tuition undertaken overseas. Through our procurement and funding processes we also verify that our delivery partners have the capability to understand and operate in the relevant country context. We are reviewing our current approach to language capability and considering how language skills feature through DFID's resourcing and employee lifecycles. We will consider the findings of the report as part of our review.

In addition, an issue of DFID's monthly in-house programme management newsletter drew the attention of staff to the recommendations and to the importance of some of the issues raised.

Next Steps

Whilst general awareness of the crucial role that languages and cultural understanding play in development may have been raised, the response to date, in the case of DFID, has largely centred on internal staffing issues, rather than on the project cycle itself, and on ways in which languages can be formally embedded within the processes of posting calls, selecting projects, monitoring and evaluating programmes and supporting local capacity building. A comparison with the historic treatment of 'gender' by institutional and government donors may be instructive here. As in the early days of discussions about gender in development, there now seems to be some awareness of the importance of languages, but the issues related to this still seem to be largely located outside the priority concerns of the Ministry. Unlike gender, languages have yet to be 'mainstreamed', prioritised, and fully integrated within donor framings of project activity. It should be said that this conversation on donor responsibility has thus far been limited to DFID, to whom the recommendations were chiefly addressed, rather than extending out to other large institutional or private donors potentially working within different parameters.

INGOs

Recommendations for INGOs focus on three areas: firstly, the need for INGOs to overtly recognise and support the existing multilingualism of their own organisations and hence to address current language-derived inequalities that may exist; secondly, as in the case of donors, the importance of embedding languages within the project cycle, from planning through to implementation, and monitoring and evaluation in order to establish effective listening relationships with local communities and thirdly, the imperative for INGOs to understand the role of languages within their efforts to develop and sustain local capacities.

Recommendations

To recognise the importance of languages within their own organisations INGOs could:

- ensure that the multilingualism of the organisation is seen by staff to be institutionally valued, and integral to an understanding of cultural contexts. One way of achieving this is to actively encourage the acquisition of additional language skills within the organisation
- recognise the 'burden of bilingualism' carried by some staff in the INGOs, i.e., the informal work of language mediation undertaken by bilingual/multilingual personnel in addition to their normal work and outside agreed job descriptions
- address some of the discomfort felt by staff working for the INGO about their level of English, especially the written language, and their perception that because of this the institutional playing field is not level
- ensure translators and translation coordinators in the organisation are given visibility on staff web pages to raise awareness of translation services.

When planning projects INGOs could:

- think about language at the design phase of a project, and listen to the words that the community itself uses in the needs assessment stage

- provide language support during early discussions with communities, helping to facilitate a dialogue, and create relationships of trust
- include a budget line for translation and interpreting.

When starting a project and during monitoring and evaluation INGOs could:

- translate successful project applications into local languages so that partners and communities can have an in-depth understanding of what is planned in order to give them access to the information and knowledge they need to increase involvement and local ownership
- feed back regularly to the community to check that the project is meeting original expectations, and make necessary amendments
- work with local interpreters wherever possible and seek to establish a register of translators and interpreters who have worked in and have an understanding of development
- translate reports into local languages and feed back to partners in their first languages.

To support SNGOs and communities in developing local capacity INGOs could:

- work together with SNGOs to produce glossaries of key terms in languages of the communities that can be a common resource
- share learning on the place of languages in communication strategies with other NGOs in pre-existing NGO networks
- consider providing skills training in a language that is accessible to SNGOs
- consider providing access to English language training.

Immediate Responses

Anecdotal evidence on early responses to the report suggests some slight differences between the reactions of large INGOs based in the UK, and smaller SNGOs in the case study countries. Key advocates in the former appear to have used the research within their organisations to raise awareness of the role of languages, writing internal blog posts and pointing to the relationship between languages and institutional commitments to localisation and the Core Humanitarian Standards. The research has also stimulated some measure of cross-institutional networking and sharing of good practice between the (often internally isolated) translators in INGOs. However, within those INGOs that have no central languages/translation policy, it has clearly been difficult to effect much immediate change, with colleagues describing any future implementation of the recommendations as being subject to 'slow recognition', 'ripple effects' and 'change of mind set'. In comparison, responses from SNGOs in Peru and Malawi point to more concrete attempts to address some of the recommendations—for instance, establishing a language policy which affects recruitment and staff development, and using the report to leverage financial resources in order to translate material into local languages. In some cases, colleagues suggest that the report has acted as a 'wake-up call' and has begun to stimulate greater demand from the community itself for material in the vernacular.

Next Steps

Although this evidence is partial, the apparent difference between the reactions of INGOs in the UK, and those of some SNGOs echoes research findings in this volume related to the salience of location (whether personnel are based in the UK or within the countries) in conditioning attitudes to languages. At the beginning of the conversation in 2014, practitioners alluded to the central role of languages in the exercise of power relations. A potentially important avenue to pursue now is for organisations to conceive of languages outside the anodyne heading of 'communication', and to instead position them as active creators of the exclusion and marginalisation that they themselves seek to address. In these terms, INGOs can tackle the challenges posed by the 'foreignness' of development as an integral part of their broader ongoing reflections on decolonising the development project. A recurring theme in our recommendations is the potential to effect change by networking between INGOs, between SNGOs and INGOs, and between SNGOs. The enormous experience of UK INGOs in influential networks like BOND, and within their own global alliances, provides a strong basis for the sector to move forward together in the cost-effective production of glossaries, and in the sharing of good practice on the ground as suggested, for example, in the project Report (Footitt et al., 2018, pp. 28–31).

Recommendations for Higher Education
Helping the next generation of practitioners to engage with the importance of languages and cultural understanding also implies seeking to give a greater emphasis to these issues in undergraduate and postgraduate university courses in development:

During curriculum review HE could:

- address the importance of languages and cultural knowledge in delivering projects that are respectful to communities, drawing on the database of cases presented by this project
- investigate the possibilities of setting up support networks of student volunteers who would work with an SNGO for a short time to assist in their language/translation needs.

Seeing language as a social category in its own right and understanding its implications in constructing hierarchies of power encourages a reassessment of ongoing inequalities, helping us to see the relationality of development projects—“eat their bread and drink their tea” (KYR 8, INGO Worker, Bishkek). It may also serve to widen our own languages by inflecting the discourses of development with the multilingualism of the world. After all, as Wittgenstein argued, “the limits of my language means the limits of my world” (1974, p. 68).

References

Bates, M. W. (2018, October 30). Development aid: Written question—HL10805. *Parliament Business*. Retrieved from: https://www.parliament.uk/business/publications/written-questions-answers-statements/written-question/Lords/2018-10-18/HL10805/?fbclid=IwAR1usL91QQORfhFsxf-FrrC5Nc1oH4l9vpjv4q-qjRnlFPfDWwa-yHLbBa4B.

Coussins, E. (2018, October 30). Development aid: Written question—HL10805. *Parliament Business*. Retrieved from: https://www.parliament.uk/business/publications/written-questions-answers-statements/written-question/Lords/2018-10-18/HL10805/?fbclid=IwAR1usL91QQORfhFsxf-FrrC5Nc1oH4l9vpjv4q-qjRnlFPfDWwa-yHLbBa4B.

Footitt, H., Crack, A., & Tesseur, W. (2018). *Respecting communities in international development: Languages and cultural understanding*. Retrieved from: www.Reading.ac.uk/listening-zones-ngos/.

Wittgenstein, L. (1974). *Tractatus Logico-Philosophicus* (B. McGuinness & D. Pears, Trans.). London: Routledge.

Workshop Report (2014, January 20). *Do NGOs need a languages policy?* (Workshop Report, University of Reading). Retrieved from: https://www.intrac.org/wpcms/wp-content/uploads/2016/09/DO-NGOs-Need-a-Languages-Policy_Workshop-Report.pdf.

Index

H. Footitt et al., *Development NGOs and Languages*,
https://doi.org/10.1007/978-3-030-51776-2

The manufacturer's authorised representative in the EU is Springer Nature Customer Service Centre GmbH, Europaplatz 3, 69115 Heidelberg, Germany. If you have any concerns regarding our products, please contact ProductSafety@springernature.com

Printed and bound by CPI Group (UK) Ltd, Croydon, CR0 4YY
22/09/2026
02221064-0003